Transcendence and Beyond

THE INDIANA SERIES IN THE PHILOSOPHY OF RELIGION
MEROLD WESTPHAL, GENERAL EDITOR

Transcendence and Beyond

A Postmodern Inquiry

Edited by John D. Caputo and Michael J. Scanlon

INDIANA UNIVERSITY PRESS
BLOOMINGTON AND INDIANAPOLIS

This book is a publication of

Indiana University Press
601 North Morton Street
Bloomington, IN 47404-3797 USA

http://iupress.indiana.edu

Telephone orders   800-842-6796
Fax orders   812-855-7931
Orders by e-mail   iuporder@indiana.edu

The paper used in this publication meets the minimum require-
ments of American National Standard for Information Sciences—
Permanence of Paper for Printed Library Materials, ANSI
Z39.48-1984.

MANUFACTURED IN THE UNITED STATES OF AMERICA

Library of Congress Cataloging-in-Publication Data

Transcendence and beyond : a postmodern inquiry / edited by John D. Caputo and
Michael J. Scanlon.
    p. cm. — (The Indiana series in the philosophy of religion)
    Includes bibliographical references and index.
    ISBN 978-0-253-34874-6 (cloth : alk. paper) — ISBN 978-0-253-21903-9 (pbk. : alk.
paper) 1. Transcendence (Philosophy)—Congresses. 2. Transcendence of God—
Congresses. 3. Philosophy and religion—Congresses. 4. Religion—Philosophy—
Congresses. I. Caputo, John D. II. Scanlon, Michael J.
    BD632.T73 2007
    212'.7—dc22
                                2006039418

1 2 3 4 5   12 11 10 09 08 07

To **Jacques Derrida**, 1930–2004. *In memoriam, in gratitude.*

We're smiling at you, too.

Contents

Contents

ACKNOWLEDGMENTS

The editors wish to acknowledge the support of Villanova University in making possible the conference "Religion and Postmodernism 4: Transcendence and Beyond," on 18–20 September 2003, upon which this volume is based. We thank in particular Rev. Edmond Dobbin, O.S.A., President of the University, for his continuing support and encouragement; Dr. John Johannes, Vice-President for Academic Affairs; Dr. Helen Lafferty, University Vice-President; and Rev. Kail Ellis, O.S.A., Dean of the College of Arts and Sciences, without whose generous financial assistance we would not have been able to organize this meeting.

We also thank Terry Sousa, who met with her usual aplomb the work of organizing the meeting rooms, receptions and meals for everyone; and Anna (Misticoni) Monserrate, the secretary to the David R. Cook Chair of Philosophy and the Josephine C. Connelly Chair of Theology, whose efficient mastery of the matter of running a conference made everything easy for us.

Our gratitude also to Terry Di Martino and Villanova students Mariola Lezcano, Lisa Panik, and Kristen Ryback.

Transcendence and Beyond

Introduction

Do We Need to Transcend Transcendence?

John D. Caputo and Michael J. Scanlon

To Jacques Derrida

The idea behind the Religion and Postmodernism conference series, of which the present volume is the latest installment, has been to bring central ideas from the classical tradition into dialogue with the idea of postmodernity. A first conference on the gift was followed by one on forgiveness and a third on St. Augustine's *Confessions*.[1] We were blessed in these first three conferences to undertake these explorations in dialogue with Jacques Derrida, whose good humor and modesty touched everyone who was able to attend them. Derrida's work on these most classical of topics in the last fifteen years of his life has provided a profound impetus to all of us who have been driven to reflect upon and revisit our religious traditions under the impact of his powerful provocation. He charged the air of our conferences and captured the hearts of the many hundreds of attendees over the years with his sparkling wit and intelligence. Derrida himself, of course, was something of a reluctant bride in this marriage. He quite disliked the idea of "post-modernity" inasmuch as he refused to dissociate himself from the deeper ideals of the modern age and the Enlightenment, especially the ethical and political ideal of emancipation, much preferring to speak of a "new Enlightenment," one that was more enlightened about Enlightenment and more critical of the pretension to pure critique. He was also never very comfortable with the idea of religion. So getting him to a conference on religion and postmodernism was a tribute to his enormous graciousness, if not to our resourcefulness.

His death on 8 October 2004 deeply saddened everyone at Villanova, for he was a great friend to this institution, even as it saddened the hundreds of people who have attended these conferences over the years and were touched by the magnetism of his person, as well as the many thousands of his friends and readers around the globe. So it is with much pride, no little gratitude and a deep sense of mourning—about which Jacques often wrote so movingly—that we dedicate this volume to Jacques ("Jackie") Derrida, whose spirit will always animate these conferences. It was not only a pleasure to know him—it was a grace.

Beyond the Beyond

In the present volume we have taken up the question of "transcendence and beyond." In putting it this way we were, in the spirit of Derrida, setting the dynamics of this word loose upon the word itself: For if to transcend is already to pass beyond, we are trying to press forward beyond the beyond. Our most straightforward intention was to see whether and how this classical idea of transcendence plays out in a postmodern context—what it would mean, how it would need to be rethought, and whether we need in fact to get beyond its classical beyond to a more postmodern beyond. There is (no surprise!) a planned ambiguity in our "beyond." Do we need a transcendence that is ever-more beyond, a still-more transcendent transcendence—*plus de transcendance*? Or should we give up on that as an impossible attempt to make water wet, as Catherine Keller puts it so wittily, and take "beyond" transcendence to mean that we should put transcendence, like Satan, behind us—no more transcendence —*plus de transcendance*? Is it the case that, when seen in a postmodern light, transcendence must be itself transcended? If so, is this because the classical concept—if not the word "transcendence"—does not go far enough, and we must go farther? Or because it goes too far and must be rehabilitated for a more worldly life, where it must be refitted for a more material, gendered and planetary existence? After all, for all its authority and prestige, the word "transcendent" is a relative term: It depends on what is being transcended, and there is a long list of candidates—the subject, the self, the sensible world, beings, even Being itself—and so there is nothing to stop us from wondering whether transcendence itself is to be added to the list as still one more thing to be transcended.

Jean-Luc Marion and Gianni Vattimo are paradigmatic representatives of these two tendencies, of what we might call a certain "hypertranscendence," an even more transcendent transcendence; and "post-transcendence," where classical transcendence is left behind as so much metaphysics.

The first tendency is very much alive in the postmodern context where it tends to travel under the name of the *tout autre*, the "wholly other," which is most closely associated with Levinas, who provides a salient example of a hyperbolic transcendence. For Levinas, the classical idea of transcendence is clearly not enough for it represents a movement that for him is trapped *within* being, and hence within a sphere of "ontological" immanence, even if and especially when it asserts an ontology of supersensible being. The trap that transcendence springs for Levinas is to confine all travel within the borders of being—either in the classical movement from a lower mode of being to a higher one; from finite (sensible) being to infinite (supersensible) being; or, as in Heidegger, in a movement from beings to Being itself. So for Levinas what is truly called for is "escape" from this trap,[2] that is, a movement beyond beings and Being, *epekeinas tes ousias*, whose term is not transcendent being but being transcended; not a higher being but otherwise than being, which is what Levinas called "transascendence" in *Totality and Infinity*. This same dynamic or hyperbolic that unfolds in a deeply Jewish context in Levinas, is repeated and reorganized today in a Christian context in the work of Jean-Luc Marion, who takes the word "being" as an "idol"—a trap or screen or mirror in which we envisage ourselves, not God—and who has sought accordingly and in manifold ways to think God "without being." In both Levinas and Marion, the classical idea of transcendence proves to be not enough—it remains caught up in an ontological idolatry—and must give way to a certain ultratranscendence or more radical or hyperbolic transcendence beyond being.

The other tendency is to treat this transcendence to excess as itself excessive, and to rechannel the dynamics of the beyond into putting classical transcendence behind us. Then, both traditional transcendence and postmodern hypertranscendence are regarded as a kind of mythologization or alienation— taking what is our own and turning it into an alien force or power—that we need to get beyond in order to learn how to dwell rightly upon the earth. That move is captured paradigmatically in Vattimo's idea of the Incarnation as a divine *kenōsis* in which God abandons his eternity and pitches his tent among us even as we set about learning to savor the dwelling of God in flesh and time. That bit of "radical theology," as Vattimo himself knows, goes back to Hegel, is found again variously in the "death of God" theologies of the 1960s, flows freely in the philosophical theology of the "process" thinkers, flourishes today in various versions of ecofeminist thought, and is also found in what we nowadays call "secular theology," which is probably the best description of Vattimo's own work. Such a view is more comfortable with Tillich and a correlational theology, even as it is unnerved by Barth and by all revisitations in the night by the *tout autre*. Here the classical idea of transcendence is transcended by allowing God to quit God's traditional transcendence and to empty Godself without remainder into the world, into the spirit of love and the affirmation of the body. That trend is picked up in various studies in this volume—Vattimo, Caputo, Schrag, Keller and McFague give it more religious formulations, while David Wood thinks it puts its best foot forward as discalced atheism. Scandalized by Marion's concept of ultratranscendence—which Wood regards as an appalling and tragic misconception of human possibilities—the world is quite enough for Wood, and any meaningful sense of transcendence must be accomplished within the horizon of the world and achieve, let us say, a mundane transcendence.

But this topic may be viewed through several prisms. We recognized, for example, that the classical idea of transcendence is not without a gender and a sexuality, and that the issue we raise in this collection is deeply fraught with implications for feminist theory. It is a classically patriarchal model, representing a top-down, hierarchical, even imperial way to conceive the relationship of the divine to the human, and which has served, by unhappy extension, as a model of the relation of the masculine to the feminine and of the human to the nonhuman. So at the same time that it is a feminist issue, transcendence also poses an ecological issue. These two conceptions are not arbitrarily pasted together on the same page in order to advertise two of our favorite political causes. They are internally linked by means of the idea of hierarchical and sovereign power, and they represent parallel or twin forms of transcendence—that of "man" over women and of "man" over nature—each constructed on the model of God's transcendence over the world. Levinas is symptomatic in this regard. While we hear a great deal from Levinas about the absolute respect we owe the other, about the "transascendence" of the wholly other, we find his remarks about the feminine troublesome and are deeply worried when he tells us that the natural world lacks this depth. So it was of the utmost importance to invite serious reflections upon the idea of transcendence from leading theologians like Catherine Keller and Sallie McFague, bold and innovative constructive theologians who have exposed theology today to its repression of women and of nature. Is there any way at all for "transcendence" to contribute to feminist thought? Or to ecology? Is it not possible to describe the majesty of the natural world in the terms of another notion of transcendence? What are the resources of a peculiarly feminine imaginary to re-think transcendence?

It should come as no surprise that a good deal of the discussion about transcendence comes to a head in and converges on the question of creation—of an omnipotent creator god who produces the world with a single word and produces it from nothing. That is surely the greatest exercise of divine heavy-lifting in the history of western theology. So the task we set ourselves of re-thinking the notion of transcendence also forces us to revisit the idea of creation, and we were fortunate to have two studies that addressed that question, by Catherine Keller and James Mackey, from related but different standpoints. They both describe the immanent life, movement and vitality of the natural world in connection with a divine productivity, Mackey moving creatively within the orthodox idea of *creatio ex nihilo*, while Keller makes a target out of this orthodox conception. How are we to bring divine productivity into balance, without negating the dynamism of nature? How pay our respects to nature's own momentum without absorbing divine creativity into the world?

As in the past, we also thought it necessary to test the presuppositions of postmodernism by hearing from thinkers who were not favorably disposed to the idea, who looked upon it with some suspicion (as did Derrida himself). So, we were fortunate to have Elisabeth Schüssler Fiorenza, who thinks in terms inspired by the Frankfurt school of critical theory, and who raised important questions about the political import of postmodern rhetoric. What is the political payoff of talking in terms of the wholly other, or of the ultratranscendence of Jean-Luc Marion? James Mackey also raised important questions about the limits of postmodern reflection and postmodern theories of signs.

The idea was to get a multiplicity of voices into our discussion—people who are religious and people who are not, people who are favorably disposed to postmodernism and people are not—and to see if we could, as Derrida would have said, produce an event, or better, let an event happen.

Keynote Essays

Jean-Luc Marion's masterful contribution to this collection, "The Impossible for Man—God," belongs to the growing discussion of the question of "the impossible" in postmodern literature. Marion's idea of the "saturated phenomenon" is here orchestrated in terms of the idea of the impossibility of impossibility for God. If, for God, nothing is impossible, the very idea of the impossible is impossible. God does not violate this principle; rather, this principle does not reach as far as God. As God is more than being, God exceeds logical and ontological principles, whereas "modernity" is marked precisely by submitting God to such principles.[3] The "hypergivenness" of God overflows or saturates the screens or horizons erected by human thought (such as the "principle of non-contradiction"). God transcends the classical logico-metaphysical conceptions of the possible and the impossible, which confine God within the horizon of being and human conceivability—that is, of the "idol." But Marion is in search of a transcendence that is unconditional, without or beyond being and its principles—the beyond of the "icon"—not one that is subject to the conditions of being and essence, of intuition, concept and principle. For if God is God, then it is impossible for God to be given in any intuition or phenomenal experience, to be contained by any concept or governed by any principle. But it is this very impossibility—this infinity and incomprehensibility—that makes God "possible" as God. God alone lets Godself be defined by indefinable impossibility, for God begins where human possibility ends. What is impossible for us is precisely God's characteristic possibility, for with God nothing is impossible.

We unleash the iconic power of the concept of impossibility only when we realize that this is a conditional concept—we need this concept and we understand things on its horizon—while confessing the impossibility of impossibility for God. Impossibility is not on God's horizon; it never enters God's mind. To erect a "principle of non-contradiction" which God does not violate, to which God submits, is unworthy of God. To think a more *radical impossibility*, something that would be completely unconditioned, is to think an impossibility that transcends all impossibility, not just a non-contradiction concocted in our minds. God's impossibility—the impossibility of impossibility—simply saturates and annuls the logico-metaphysical impossible, simply affirms itself *à partir de soi*. We ourselves have some access to such a thing through the experience of our birth, which is the miracle, the impossible, of answering a call that we never heard, as Levinas would put it.

Impossibility is furthermore liable to degenerate into an idol if, as happens in metaphysical theology, God is defined as omnipotent, which emphasizes that God can do anything God pleases so long as it does not violate the principle of non-contradiction. Marion searches for a more radical idea framed by love and fidelity, displacing the abstract and arbitrary power to do anything, indiscriminately, as if God were a fearsome tyrant. The Annunciation—where the angel Gabriel assures Mary that with God nothing is impossible—is not a tribute to God's omnipotence, but a manifestation of God's commitment and God's fidelity. "Let this be done according to God's word," for God will be true to his word. When human beings speak, they may or may not follow through—but not so God. God will keep God's promises. God is not someone powerful enough to do anything God wants, but someone who wants only by loving. The issue is not that God can do what God wants, but what God wants to do. The most radical possibility of all is forgiveness, which belongs to God alone—for we human beings are not able to forgive, and it is not our place to forgive. What is radically impossible for us is the highest and most radical possibility for God, with whom nothing is impossible.

It would be difficult to find a view more perfectly and symmetrically opposed to Marion's than **Gianni Vattimo**'s "Nihilism as Postmodern Christianity."[4] By "nihilism," Vattimo is not suggesting an "anything-goes relativism." Rather, reading Nietzsche through Heidegger, he means a weakening or withering-away: (1) of the strong theoretical structures of metaphysical thinking, strong notions of the really real, objective being or objective reality; (2) of strong notions of epistemological correspondence in favor of truth as the issue of hermeneutical conversation; (3) of strong notions of moral absolutes in favor a principle of charity and sensitivity to situations; and (4) of strong or authoritarian principles in politics in favor of emancipatory and democratic processes. What Vattimo describes as "weak thought," Anglo-Americans call "nonfoundationalism" and most Continentalists (including Vattimo), following Gadamer, would call "hermeneutics." Indeed, when Quine denies that there are any uninterpreted facts of the matter—which is one more dogma of (modern) empiricism—he is not far from Vattimo. Nor are Vattimo's views far from the brand of pragmatic nonfoundationalism espoused by Rorty, with whom he has collaborated in recent years. Vattimo does not denounce the word "postmodern," which describes for him this late moment at the end of modernity, when the grip of strong metaphysical claims has been sundered and we learn to make our way by means of revisable interpretations.

In his recent works, Vattimo speaks of his "recovery" of Christianity.[5] His views on weak thinking translate quite felicitously into a weak theology—for atheism, also, is strong thinking. He seeks a Christianity after metaphysical theology—a postmodern Christianity that belongs to "secular theology" and comes in the wake of the "death of God theology." The death of foundationalist metaphysics spells the death not only of the classically transcendent God, but also of a metaphysical atheism, thereby opening the door to a recovery of the nonmetaphysical God. While this opening is deployed in Heidegger in the name of the God of the poets, it applies to the God of the Scriptures, who is no less nonmetaphysical. If nihilism spells the *death* of the two-worlds Christianity of the Christian-Platonic tradition, it also implies the *birth* or rebirth of the sacred, now conceived as the advent of the Kingdom of God on earth (a new idea of immanence). The key to this rebirth is a symbolic rendering of the Incarnation as the "weakening of God" on high into a more immanent dweller here below—a God come down from the heavens in an act of *kenōsis* to pitch his tent among us in a kingdom of brotherhood and charity here on earth.

All this implies a theology of secularity for Vattimo. The so-called "secular order" ought now to be reconceived positively—not in opposition to the religious, but as the place where the biblical message is concretely deployed. Max Weber is taken as saying that capitalism is applied Protestantism, Christianity concretely at work in the world. Secularization is the realization of the sacred; not its abandonment, and not a completely autonomous order opposed to the religious, as it is theorized in Hans Blumenberg and in Enlightenment thinking generally. Sacred history and secular history converge, for secularization is the latest stage of sacred history. Divinity is not transcendent ("wholly other") but incarnate; and the Incarnation, the event "inaugurating the dissolution of divine transcendence,"[6] is a cipher for religion's immanent secular life.

Re-imagining Traditional Transcendence

The main body of essays is divided into two groups. The authors in the first group take as their aim a rethinking, reenvisioning, revisiting or reconceptualizing of the classical concept of transcendence so as to bring it into contact with contemporary discourse. The second group seeks to actually relocate transcendence on the plane of immanence, to use Deleuze's expression, in the course of which they also tend to emphasize the primacy of love. As Merold Westphal points out very astutely in the concluding roundtable, this emphasis poses an interesting dilemma. Although advocates of strong and uncompromising ideas of transcendence, like Marion and Barth, emphasize that God is love, many of the authors in this second group of essays worry whether love can flourish in the rare atmosphere of such an uncompromising idea of transcendence.

We begin with **Richard Kearney**'s "Re-imagining God," because his essay bears the most interesting relation to Marion. Like Marion, Kearney too wants to re-think God by rethinking and delimiting a merely logico-metaphysical conception of the possible and the impossible—but with rather more emphasis on the possible than the impossible. This is also the basis for a difference of opinion between Kearney and Derrida, as Kearney points out in the round-table. The differences are subtle but vast. However different Marion and Derrida may be, Kearney distrusts their common emphasis—which is for him an overemphasis—on the impossible over the possible. If Marion, Derrida and Kearney alike all affirm "the possibility of the impossible," Kearney can live with this expression only by approaching it through a valorizing and redescribing of the "possible" itself, not the impossible. The accent falls on the possible for Kearney for two reasons: (1) unlike Marion, Kearney is more interested in staking out the hermeneutical horizons of human experience than in trying to reach God's point of view by abolishing the human point of view; (2) Kearney worries that Derrida's and Marion's emphases leaves us disabled rather enabled, which is why his focus is on the possible (and why his study is also deeply sympathetic to much of what is going on in the second group of essays).

"God, if God exists, exists not just for God but for us." One of the most telling ways in which the infinite comes to be experienced and imagined by finite minds is as *possibility*—that is, as *the ability to be*—even, and especially, when such possibility seems impossible to us. Kearney fills out his poetic conjecture by means of three concentric circles—*scriptural, testimonial* and *literary.* Kearney cites several scriptural passages to illustrate that nothing is impossible with God. He refers to Christ's renunciation of absolute power in his *kenōsis,* from the beginning to the end of his life. He translates the theophanic utterance to Moses not as, "I am who am," but as "I am who may be"—if we answer his call. The testimonial genre explores a poetics of the Kingdom by religious writers down through the ages. These writers reverse the traditional priority of actuality over possibility and point to a new category of possibility—divine possibility—beyond the traditional opposition between the possible and the impossible. Their poetics extends the range of reference to take in soundings of *posse* which transcend the confessional limits of theism and atheism, enjoying as they do a special liberty of imagination—a "poetic license" to entertain unlimited variations of experience. Kearney seeks to reinterpret the possible as eschatological *posse*—beyond, otherwise than, or more than the impossible—close to Kierkegaard's "passion for the possible" as portal to faith. He ends with a final eschatological image from the poetics of the Kingdom—the God who knocks on our doors ceaselessly until there is no door unopened.

Michael J. Scanlon takes his point of departure from the Christian understanding of God in its official formulation in the doctrine of the Trinity, which is a distillation of the New Testament's story of God's creative and redemptive presence in and for the world through Jesus Christ and in the divine Spirit. As doctrine, it is a more or less conceptual clarification of the denser, symbolic language of the scripture which presents an "economic Trinity"—a portrayal of God as dynamically self-involved in the world. In time, the Church Fathers moved from this portrayal of God acting triunely in the world to affirm that the God who *acts* triunely does so because this God *is* eternally triune; a movement from the "economic" to the "immanent Trinity," here "immanent in God." Thus we have the long tradition of speaking of God as three persons (from the Latin, *persona*) or three hypostases (from the Greek, *hupostases*). God is the One whom Jesus called Father, his eternal Word, Wisdom or Son, and their eternal Spirit. In derivation, the terms Word, Wisdom and Spirit are symbols of divine *immanence* in the world and are found in the Old Testament. The inspiration for this essay comes from Karl Rahner's famous Trinitarian Rule: The economic Trinity *is* the immanent Trinity, and vice versa. Rahner never adequately developed the implications of the "vice versa" in terms of a divine "becoming," but some recent theologians have addressed this issue. It is possible, for instance, to interpret triune eternity eschatologically (of the *fullness* of time) rather than protologically (from *before* all time), as is traditional. Scanlon's essay presents such an attempt. The Trinity is then understood as God, the Father, Jesus, and the Spirit in the Church for the world. Transcendence and immanence, as forcefully clarified in James Mackey's talk, are not an either/or—they mutually imply one another.

The next two essays take a more critical distance from postmodern categories. As Catherine Keller will in her essay, **James P. Mackey** turns to the idea of creation. Mackey aims to bring a critical account of the Christian doctrine of divine creation together with an equally critical account of some reliable elements of the best of postmodern thought to see if prospects of collaboration emerge. He critiques common usages of the term "transcendence" as "the sin of onto-philosophy." Since the prime heuristic faculty of the human mind is the imagination, Mackey strongly affirms that the story of creation in Genesis is myth with the most positive meaning—stories that operate at the broadest, that is, metaphysical dimension. The highly abstract doctrine of *creatio ex nihilo* yields little positive about the world's beginning. We are reminded that just as the imaginative may produce the imaginary for the unwary, so also the characteristic temptation of abstract analysis is the reifying of its abstractions, producing onto-theology or onto-philosophy.

Instead of the usual understanding of God's creative work as a one-off act of divine omnipotence (God shouting the world into existence!), the author shows from the Hebrew text that the key image for divine creation is that of shaping, framing, forming, and not of irresistible force or power. The patient labor of the creator acts from within creation by activating all of the finite forms in collaboration to bring all of reality, including the creator, to its absolute form and final state. The old dualism of God "squatting" outside the world, acting from a so-called "transcendence" beyond the world is gone. Contemporary evolutionary theory fits quite nicely in our story of continuous creation wherein the creator engages the co-responsibility of all creatures for the future of all. The creator is immanent in space-time as he/she continually transcends each stage in the evolution of the universe.

Elisabeth Schüssler Fiorenza's "G*d—The Many-Named: Without Place and Proper Name" concludes this section of the volume. Schüssler Fiorenza voices a healthy suspicion of the rhetoric of postmodernism, even as James Mackey expressed his doubts about its semiology. The goal of this essay is to engender a critical reflection on the sociopolitical location, rhetorical situation, and political-religious function of the very abstract, postmodern, philosophical or theological discourses about the transcendent, the other, or the divine. The author uses a dictionary definition of transcendence: "existence above and apart from the material world" or "otherworldliness," "beyond the limits of human experience" and "beyond all categories." As a feminist theologian she will employ the four strategies of traditional G*d-talk to facilitate our speaking of the divine in a feminist key as she addresses the following issues:

- *The rhetorical problem.* When G*d is located in human subjectivity, the construction of G*d in language and metaphor becomes central. Resorting to the language of metaphor and symbol, the quest for God is changed from a metaphysical one to a rhetorical one which asks for both the proper name/representation of G*d, and the sociopolitical rules and contextualizations that have constructed G*d-talk.
- *The rhetorics of thea/o*-legein. The task of speaking about G*d is best positioned in the sphere of ethics and communicative praxis.
- *Feminist thealogical interventions in malestream discourses about G*d.* The feminist discussion of G*d-language has two focal points: One is the question of how to speak about the Divine in an andro-kyriocentric system that uses masculine terms such as "man" and "he" in both a gender-specific and a gender-inclusive way. The other way of feminist thea/o-logical inquiry is the rediscovery of the Goddess.
- *Traditional rhetorical strategies for speaking about G*d in a feminist key.* Only a theological strategy that approaches classic disclosures about G*d with a method of deconstruction and proliferation is able to develop a liberating way for engaging and transforming G*d-language.

Relocating Transcendence on the Plane of Immanence

The authors of the second group of essays move in an importantly different direction. They attempt to reenvision transcendence by relocating it in the world, as a certain mode of "being-in-the-world," and frequently come back to the idea of love. They argue in various ways for transcendence *in* the world, for the transcendence *of* the world, for relocating transcendence on the plane of immanence.

Catherine Keller's exercise in constructive theology opens this section. Drawing upon Genesis, process theology, ecological thought, chaos theory and feminist theory in order to radically rethink the orthodox tradition, her account of creation differs markedly from Mackey's and her account of the Trinity differs markedly from reigning orthodox ideas. Playing on the "rumors" (received ways of thinking about) of transcendence and immanence, Keller moves beyond the old "unbecoming," "breakaway" transcendence and re-deposit us "amidst the creaturely politics and sexes of the earth." Juxtaposing the radically "separative" transcendence of both Levinas *and* Simone de Beau-voir with the radical immanence of Gilles Deleuze, she takes the uprightness of Levinasian "wholly other" as the very paradigm of such separating transcen-dence, where the feminine is reduced to immanence—that is, to providing *l'infini*, the infinite and transcendent one, with a happy home and good soup. This was rightly criticized by Simone de Beauvoir, but with an equal-rights, me-too argument that wanted to secure such masculine transcendence for women as well. If then everyone is a man, in transcendent "separation from nurture and nature," no real alternative is being proposed. But if, following Irigaray (the next wave of feminism), we think of the infinite not as infinite distance but as the ever-unfinished; and of the transcendent not as exodus/ escape but as endless movement, as what is continually unfolding in the im-manent; then transcendence would not be a separating, but simply a differing.

The classical ideas of transcendence and immanence are the artifacts of classical politics (imperialism, patriarchy) and theology (divine sovereignty of the creator). *Creatio ex nihilo*—an idea supported by no biblical text—is a "scornful" logic that denounces matter, *mater*, matrix, the feminine *tᵉhôm* and the Platonic *khōra*. By annihilating the elements—the *tᵉhôm* and the *tōhû wā bōhû*—it turns Elohim into a controlling he-man-God. For Deleuze, the plane of immanence is already infinite, with the infinity of an overflowing, omni-dimensional "chaosmos" (a Joycean neologism in *Finnegan's Wake*). It moves —that is, "immanates"—infinitely, without being bound in. Deleuze comes closer to the Genesis story than Levinas. In Whitehead, the world transcends the old (separating) transcendence, but in order to make way for a transcen-dence that immanates by moving, and an immanence that transcends by immanating. Transcendence is endless self-transcendence, process or life un-folding in the world which is ever-unfinished (infinite). Keller concludes with a postmodern (and panentheistic) Trinity of three divine capacities, to which she adds an ethics as a way of living in a space of the endless mutations of immanating-transcending creatures.

The next four essays continue the task Keller set for herself, of reinscribing transcendence on the plane of immanence, making sustained attempts to rethink or reconfigure the idea of transcendence as a mundane event, an opening created in space and time, body and world.

In "Intimations of Transcendence: Praise and Compassion," **Sallie Mc-Fague** contends that the two most distinctive activities of religious people are gratitude toward God and compassion toward others, with thanksgiving being the most prevalent religious emotion. In this essay she plays with the model of the world as God's body, as a way of filling out how praise and compassion might be intimations of transcendence for Christians. This model rejects otherworldliness, as transcendence becomes radical immanence in line with Christian incarnationalism. The essay attends focally to two issues—the status of metaphor as a way to speak of transcendence, and the ways in which praise and compassion are intimations of transcendence. Unlike analogy and symbol, which make much bolder assertions, metaphor is a heuristic fiction that feeds the imagination with its assertorial lightness—its "is," undercut immediately with its "is not." Indeed, all theology should be content with metaphor — it is always just metaphor. While deconstruction has a predilection for the prophetic, the austere Protestant emphasis on the discontinuity between God and the world, the fertile Catholic sacramental imagination with its emphasis on the continuity between God and the world delights in metaphorical excess. Praise erupts naturally with the sensitivity that we live our ordinary lives within the divine milieu, while we respond to the needs of this suffering body of the world in current crisis and to the bodily needs of our suffering companions. The dualism of deism and theism disappears as we locate ourselves in the realm of panentheism and perhaps pantheism. We are that part of the body of God that has become conscious of its proper role—to work with the incarnate God for the wellbeing of the earth. And for us well-off human beings, the cost of doing this work will be enormous.

David Wood undertakes a "deconstructive genealogy" of transcendence, one which has a lot in common with what Bultmann called "demythologizing," by arguing: (1) that the idea of transcendence is a notion that is tied up with a spatial metaphor that is hard to shake; and (2) that this idea always turns out to signify a way human beings have of responding to an experience of limit, and is one that, if understood literally, betrays the experience by cloaking it in a mythological apparel. Wood insists that we distinguish epistemological transcendence, the transcendence *of* the "external" world (where "consciousness" is an inner chamber), from metaphysical transcendence, being transcendent *to* the world, outside space and time. Heidegger has shown in *Being and Time* that epistemological transcendence is based upon a bad analysis of our experience of the world; there is no outside because there is no inside either. So, too, a God outside space and time is an artefact derived by imagining a super-being located somewhere in a world outside this world. The multiple senses of transcendence are simply ways of playing out what Heidegger calls being-in-the-world. We are constituted by our limits and life is largely a matter of renegotiating these limits. All genuinely useful notions of transcendence are accommodated by the central Heideggerian figure of Dasein's transcendence (Dasein *is* transcendence) to the world (not *of* the world), to the horizon of the world within which inner-worldly entities present themselves. Such transcendence is a function of Dasein's projection upon—or transcendence-toward—death as our ultimate limit, our ultimate "beyond." Wood finds genuine senses of transcendence in our experience of the natural, the animal, the erotic, the ethical and of language. We could call this "God," but there is no need to do so and, furthermore, to do so is to risk being tripped up by a spatial metaphor.

Wood's essay resonates with **John D. Caputo**'s essay on Derrida, where it is agued that the principal sense transcendence would have for Derrida is a temporal one. There is, in Derrida, a discourse on the "beyond"—"all the movements in *hyper, ultra, au-delà, beyond, über*"—which in his work characteristically takes the form of a certain "messianic" beyond. The passion of the "beyond" takes shapes as a passion for "going where you cannot go," a passion for the impossible—so Caputo, like Kearney, is part of this conversation on the impossible with Marion and Derrida—which is also, Caputo adds, the passion for existence. But for Derrida, this hyperbolic passion for the place (the beyond) does not buy into what Catherine Keller calls the "rumor" of another world, but instead has a completely temporal meaning—for there is no other place to go. The passion for the impossible is for something that breaks up and breaks into the present, for the "event" of a radical and constitutive unforeseeability, a radically unprogrammable future. That wounding, destabilizing, circum-cutting, eye-opening yet blinding exposure to the unforeseeable event, takes place in virtue of what Derrida calls the "to-come" (*à venir*), which is the principal focus of Caputo's analysis. The "event" (*événement*, from *venir*) is a function of the to-come; it occurs by reason of the very idea of the to-come. Hence in Derrida the legitimate force of the word "transcendence" is to be found in the affirmation of the coming of the event. This is not to be thought of, Caputo argues, as a work of (Kantian) *idealization* of a definite but distant form, but rather as a work of infinite qualitative *intensification* of an immediate and pressing demand (passion). Transcendence, if there is such a thing in Derrida, is a function of the *à venir*—an infinite qualitative temporal intensification, an infinite self-transformation of our temporal lives, a passion for the impossible. Caputo tracks the dynamics of the beyond in Derrida by taking as his point of departure what Derrida calls the "democracy to come."

Calvin O. Schrag also finds the gift of transcendence in the given world by way of his idea of transcendence as "transversality." Classical ideas of transcendence are vertical, turning on spatial metaphors (recall David Wood's argument) of what is *up* or *above*—the coming of the *tout autre* "from on high," in Levinas—and this in contrast to a horizontal, Deleuzean plane. The intermediate position, transcendence in immanence, is found in Whitehead and Hartshorne, for whom the absolute unfolds in space and time. Schrag proposes we split the difference between vertical and horizontal and think about transcendence as transversality, which is "diagonal." That is also a spatial metaphor: The idea is not to get rid of metaphors, but to find the most felicitous ones which carry the least metaphysical freight; those least likely to implicate us in a dualistic metaphysics of a supersensible world above, a temporal one here below. In a transversal, coherence is achieved not by imposing a higher (vertical) principle from above upon the elements below, but by the internal links that spring up *among, across* and *amidst* (*trans-*) the elements themselves. Elements link up, reach across, weave themselves into non-totalizing wholes; protected from sheer dispersal, mere juxtaposition (horizontality). The transcendence of God is not that of a vertical highest being (traditional theism), nor of a horizontal Being itself (Tillich), but transversal "works of love" (Kierkegaard). The name of God is the name of the love that traverses the elements—of a verb—of something to do.

How to move beyond the beyond of classical metaphysics? Does the classical beyond go far enough? Is classical transcendence still stifled by being, so that it is not beyond enough? Or is the classical beyond itself stifled by a figure of speech—trapped by a spatial metaphor that, presupposing space, needs to be radically rethought by a new appreciation of space and time? Do we need to re-think transcendence in terms of a more radical way to transcend space and time? Or do we need to re-think space and time in such a way as to appreciate their intrinsic transcendence? It is the complexity of this cluster of questions that the essays that follow will help us appreciate.

NOTES

1. *God, the Gift and Postmodernism,* ed. John D. Caputo and Michael J. Scanlon (Bloomington: Indiana University Press, 1999); *Questioning God,* ed. John D. Caputo, Mark Dooley and Michael J. Scanlon (Bloomington: Indiana University Press, 2001); *Augustine and Postmodernism: Confessions and Circumfession,* ed. John D. Caputo and Michael J. Scanlon (Bloomington: Indiana University Press, 2005).

2. See Emmanuel Levinas, *On Escape,* introduced and annotated by Jacques Rolland, trans. Bettina Bergo (Stanford: Stanford University Press, 2003).

3. Heidegger first made this argument in connection with the principle of sufficient reason; see Martin Heidegger, *The Principle of Reason,* trans. Reginald Lilly (Bloomington: Indiana University Press, 1991).

4. The essay by Vattimo we present here was written especially for this volume. The paper presented in Vattimo's absence at the conference was a different one; it was entitled "The Age of Interpretation," and was subsequently published in Richard Rorty and Gianni Vattimo, *The Future of Religion,* ed. Santiago Zabala (New York: Columbia University Press, 2005), pp. 43–54. Our thanks to Merold Westphal, who graciously agreed to read and comment on "The Age of Interpretation" at the conference.

5. For a nice overview of Vattimo's religious standpoint, see Gianni Vattimo, *After Christianity,* trans. Luca D'Isanto (New York: Columbia University Press, 2002).

6. Ibid., p. 27.

PART 1. KEYNOTES OF TRANSCENDENCE

The Impossible for Man—God

Jean-Luc Marion

1. What Transcendence Does Not Transcend

Transcendence—the concept will not take us very far, nor truly "beyond." Not, at least, if we take it in the two ways admitted by philosophy.

First, according to phenomenology, transcendence is defined with respect to consciousness, precisely as what surpasses the immanence of consciousness to itself. In particular, we speak of transcendence with regard to what intentional consciousness targets, when consciousness makes itself the "consciousness of something," namely of something other than itself—"that universal ground-property of consciousness, which is to be the consciousness *of* something, to carry within as *cogitatio* its own *cogitatum*."[1] What does consciousness reach by aiming for it? It reaches of course a meaning, which appears in the end as a phenomenon in its own right when consciousness is *adequately* filled by intuition. In this case, intentional consciousness transcends itself to grasp the phenomenon of a thing, since indeed "the thing names itself as simply transcendent."[2] The thing transcends consciousness in that it stands outside of consciousness, even though it never stands without it. Far as tran-

Translation by A. Davenport

scendence of this kind may lead, consciousness never overcomes itself, on this model, except for what remains, more often than not, an object. Taken in this first way (Husserl), transcendence never goes beyond the entitative object. Transcendence therefore remains immanent to the horizon of being. And if we radicalize this first level of transcendence by directing it, not only to the entitative object, but, by reducing being in its totality, to Being itself (Heidegger), then by definition transcendence will never reach beyond Being. On the contrary, erected henceforth as the "transcendent pure and simple,"[3] Being will by right be the term of every intentional aiming and every advance of every possible transcendence.

The transcendence of Being does not disclose transcendence, but instead closes and limits it. The paradox involved does not single out phenomenology. Phenomenology, in all likelihood, may have inherited it from the very first explicit formulations of the concept of *metaphysica*, such as those found, for example, in Duns Scotus. Scotus affirms that the first division of being divides being into finite and infinite, thereby ruling on the distinction between God and creature. It follows immediately from this ruling that whatever complies with *"enti ut indifferens ad finitum et infinitum"*—which is to say *ens*—transcends the difference and is therefore *"transcendens et est extra omne genus."*[4] Transcendentals, of course (as opposed to predication by categories), do not speak of God as belonging to a genus, which God transcends, yet all of them, starting with the chief among them, namely being (or rather entity, *ens*), transcend the difference between finite and infinite: *"sunt talia quae conveniunt enti ut est indifferens ad finitum et infinitum."*[5] Consequently, the transcendence of transcendentals—much as these transcendentals determine God as the infinite being, and therefore determine God in his transcendence—still boils down to being and locks itself inside being: *"de ratione transcendentis est non habere praedicatum supraveniens, nisi ens."*[6] In other words, not only does being as a transcendental still contain God's transcendence within its own boundaries, it is actually called upon to define it—in both senses of the term: It establishes God's transcendence, but at the price of giving it definition. One might, of course, wish to radicalize divine transcendence by increasing its density to the point of *"ipsum esse"* (following St. Thomas) instead of deploying it within the confines of the concept of entity (following Duns Scotus, and later Suárez). One might—and, I suppose, one should. Such a move, however, does not change the fundamental situation with regard to transcendence, since *ipsum esse* cannot itself be conceived, at least from our standpoint (*quoad nos*), except as the real composition of essence and *esse*. This composition defines all that is created positively and, by contrast, defines the divine exception —God, or what is in such a way that in him alone the essence coincides with the act of being—to the point that *esse* absorbs essence and, so to speak, dispenses God of the need to have an essence at all: *"Deus igitur non habet essentiam, quae non sit suum esse."*[7] The fact that God's transcendence no longer stakes itself within a concept of entity (which always turns out to be univocal since it is the first transcendental, if not a *supertranscendentalis*),[8] does not suffice to set it free, since it remains coiled within the chasm of essence and *esse* and therefore definitively within the horizon of being.

Thus the two chief meanings of transcendence in philosophy, different as they are, share a common feature: Neither transcends the horizon of entity, much less the horizon of being. Transcendence, in philosophy, even and especially the transcendence that we would like to assign to God as his proper mark, is defined as what does not rise beyond being—into which it runs, instead, head on, as the ultimate transcendental.

2. A Question Outside of Being

This ultimate transcendence, however, must be transcended if God is whom we have in mind, supposing at least that we have not buried the question beforehand in onto-theology, but are prepared to let it exercise its privilege— namely, its freedom with regard to being.

Of course, we may tailor the question of God to fit common usage and frame it on the model of questions concerning the things of the world— according to their being. We typically feel that we do justice to what we call "God" when we reduce the question of God to an inquiry into God's existence. Hence the widespread formula: "I believe in God if he exists; but if he does not exist, I reserve the right not to believe in him." Yet it should be immediately apparent that transposing *this* particular question to the realm of existence, innocent and rational as the move may seem, fails to hold up to analysis. The reasons are many. First, our mode of reasoning may turn out, in the privacy of our decisions, to be the inverse of what it presents itself to be, so that the true form of our argument actually is: "Since I don't believe in God anyway, I will conduct myself as though he did not exist." Or, conversely: "Since I have decided to believe in God regardless, I will conduct myself as though he existed." Adhering to one or the other position no longer *results* from the reasons invoked but precedes them and makes instrumental use of them: When it comes to God, the relationship between belief and existence is likely to invert itself. It follows from this that being, insofar as it claims the title of horizon or transcendental, offers no privileged access to the question of God and provides no grounds for a decision procedure. Rather it disconnects God and being absolutely. Hence a new alternative emerges, paradoxical perhaps, but perfectly rational. In *this* particular case, it might well be that God (to my knowledge) exists without my believing in him or, conversely, that God (to my knowledge) does not exist, without this preventing me from believing in him. There is nothing absurd about this way of framing the problem: For indeed, if God by definition surpasses the regime of common experience and the condi- tions it sets on what is possible in a worldly sense (and God would not, other- wise, deserve the title "God" since he would be a worldly phenomenon among others), in what way would his existence (which is to say his being inscribed among phenomena existing in the world) serve as the criterion for my belief or rejection? Moreover, identifying the question of God with my belief is by no means self-evident. To do so is characteristic of a very peculiar theoretical stance, which assumes that the question of God requires that a preliminary question first be answered regarding his existence, and therefore that a proof of his existence be supplied. The underlying assumption is nothing less than the perfect hegemony, without exception, of the horizon of being, such as metaphysics understands it, based on the principle (which does not take over before Suárez) that "*absolute Deus cadit sub objectum hujus scientiae [meta-physica . . .] quia haec scientia est perfectissima sapientia naturalis; ergo considerat de rebus et causis primis et universalissimis, et de primis principiis generalissimis, quae Deum ipsum comprehendunt.*"[9] We need only articulate this principle to see the opposite hypothesis spring forth: Natural science can only include natural entities among its general causes and universal principles, taken according to their conditions of intelligibility to finite intellects. Far from metaphysics being able, however *transcendentalis* (or rather precisely because metaphysics is transcendental according to transcendental *ens*), to define conditions of intelligibility and possibility for "God" by means of a glaringly unquestioned univocity, God can only be instaurated as God on the basis of his pre-ontological condition and pre-transcendental freedom. As long as the "*Differenz zwischen Sein und Seiendem erscheint dann [. . .] als die Transzendenz, d. h. als das Meta-Physische,*"[10] transcendence remains metaphysical, even when it overcomes metaphysics. Transcendence that is taken according to *these* meanings does not open up transcendence but instead slams it shut. Before the world comes into being, and thus before being unfolds its horizon, God poses the question of God—a question that no one is free to avoid since God defines himself, prior to any proof of existence, as "the one whom everyone knows, by name."[11] It follows that the end of metaphysics and even the repetition of *Seinsfrage*, far from ruling out or relativizing the question of God, bring instead and by means of contrast its irreducible character to light: Do we have access to a transcendence without condition or measure?

But then the difficulty deepens and mutates. If, on the one hand, the horizon of being does not allow us to stage what is properly at stake in the knowledge we have of God's name; if, on the other hand, nothing appears within this horizon that is not a certificate-bearing entity: Must we not conclude that there is no possible phenomenalization of God and, moreover, that this very impossibility defines God? Are we not, in the era of nihilism, led by our inner fidelity and devotion to thought to admit God in philosophy strictly as what is empirically impossible and lies outside phenomenalization as a matter of principle?

3. The Impossible Phenomenon

We must ask, first: What do possible and impossible mean here? The terms refer to experience, namely to what experience allows and excludes—therefore to what *may* or *may not* appear and let itself be seen, the phenomenon. How, in turn, is a phenomenon defined? It seems reasonable here to privilege the answers, for the most part convergent, that Kant and Husserl have given us, since these two thinkers have almost single-handedly established the only positive concept that we have of the phenomenon. A phenomenon is defined through the adequacy of an intuition (which gives and fulfills) to a concept or meaning (which is empty and to be filled and validated). Based on this premiss, a thing can appear to me in two ways: Either I determine what I have received in intuition by identifying it with some concept that I impose on it, so that it is no longer an unintelligible event of consciousness (or a case of intuition) but precisely such and such an object or describable entity; or the concept that I might have actively formed (through spontaneous understanding or through conscious intentionality) on my own initiative ends up finding empirical validation in some intuition, which comes subsequently to fill it and to qualify it as such-and-such an object or entity. It matters little which one of the two serves as the starting point for achieving adequacy, since in all cases the phenomenon only appears by internally conjugating intuition and concept.

What about God? It seems immediately clear that I have neither an intuition nor a concept at my disposal in this case. I have no intuition at my disposal, at least if by intuition I mean what is susceptible to be experienced within the parameters of space and time. For by "God" I mean above all and by definition the Eternal—or at least what no more begins to endure than it finishes enduring, since it never begins at all. I mean, also as a matter of definition, what is nonspatial—what is located nowhere, occupies no extension, admits of no limit (what has its center everywhere and its circumference nowhere), escapes all measure (the immense, the incommensurable), and therefore is not divisible or susceptible of being multiplied. This twofold impossibility of entering intuition rests neither on any doctrinal preference nor on any arbitrary negativity, but results from the unavoidable requirements of the simple possibility of something like God. The most speculative theology agrees with the most unilateral atheism to postulate that, in God's case, all formal conditions of intuition must be transgressed: If intuition implies space and time, then there can never be any intuition of God because of the even more radical requirement that there *must* not be any intuition, if God is ever to be considered.

Atheism is not alone in denying even the slightest intuition in God's case, since Revelation also insists that "No one has seen God" (John 1:18). A distinctive mark of God is thus the impossibility of receiving an intuition of him. But there is more (or maybe less). If peradventure I suppose myself to have received an intuition exceptional enough to be assigned to something like God, I would have to have at my disposal a concept that allows me to identify this intuition or, what amounts to the same, a concept that this intuition would validate and which in return would confer on it a form and meaning. But I cannot—again by definition—legitimately assign any concept to God, since every concept, by implying delimitation and comprehension, would contradict God's sole possible definition, namely that God transcends all delimitation and therefore all definitions supplied by my finite mind. Incomprehensibility, which in every other case attests either to the weakness of my knowledge or to the insufficiency of what is to be known, ranks, here and here only, as an epistemic requirement imposed by that which must be thought—the infinite, the unconditioned, and therefore the inconceivable. *"Ipsa incomprehensibilitas in ratione infiniti continetur."*[12]

While none of the concepts that I use to designate God have the power, by definition, to reach God, all of them nonetheless remain to some extent relevant, insofar as they can be turned from illegitimate affirmations into legitimate negations. Indeed if my eventual concepts designating God say nothing about God, they say something about *me* insofar as I am confronted by the incomprehensible: They say what it is that I am able to consider, at least at a given moment, as an acceptable representation of God; they articulate, therefore, the conception that I make for myself of the divine—a conception that imposes itself on me as the best since it defines precisely what is maximal or optimal for me. In short, the concepts that I assign to God, like so many invisible mirrors, send me back the image that I make up for myself of divine perfection, which are thus images of myself. My concepts of God turn out in the end to be idols—idols of myself.[13]

The radical failure of conceptualization with respect to God gives rise to a double consequence. First, the "death of God," resting as it does necessarily on the premiss of a particular concept of "God" (moral God, final cause, *causa sui*, etc.), only disqualifies each time what actually corresponds to the concept, leaving all other concepts (an open-ended series, but each new concept is as inadequate as the first) still to be revised and critiqued. In other words, every specific form of conceptual atheism remains regional and provisional, while any claim to a universal and final atheism betrays ipso facto its failure to reach the conceptual level in the first place, and therefore falls into ideology and violence. In short, the "death of God" gives immediate rise to the "death of the death of God." Secondly, the same difficulty applies, symmetrically, to every form of theism. Whenever theism tries to reach conceptual formulations that are definitive and dogmatic, it condemns itself to idolatry no less than does atheism. The two differ from one another only as a positive idolatry differs from a negative idolatry. Whether or not we decide in favor of God's existence seems at first blush to make a meaningful difference, but the difference turns out, in truth, to be indifferent, as soon as we recognize that in both cases the conclusion is reached only on the basis of defining or conceptualizing God's presumed "essence." Both conclusions thus ratify the same dogmatic idolatry. Both cases also assume that "being" or "existing" signify something that is knowable to us even when applied to "God"—which is not self-evident in the least and betrays a second idolatry, namely the chief idolatry, which is the idolatry of Being itself. The impossibility of assigning a concept to God thus stems from God's very definition, namely that he admits of no concept. Such a conclusion, once again, is not unique to atheism or characteristic of a particular philosophy: Revelation is the first to prohibit the conceptualization of that which "bears the name which is above every name" (Philippians 2:9), which is to say "the love which surpasses all knowledge" (Ephesians 3:19). God therefore is distinguished as well by the impossibility of being conceptualized.

4. The Impossible Experience

Confronted with this double impossibility, we have no choice but to proceed from the common determination of phenomenality to the conclusion that the phenomenon of God is impossible. As we saw, speculative theology admits this result in metaphysics to the same extent as does atheism. Speculative theology, however, which conducts its thought within faith and in view of belief, diverges radically from atheism when it comes to interpreting this phenomenal impossibility. For speculative theology the very impossibility of a phenomenon of God belongs to a real and indubitable experience of God. Indeed if God cannot *not* be thought as beyond phenomenal conditions—unintuitable and inconceivable—this impossibility results directly from his infinity, taken as the hallmark of his incomprehensibility. What belongs properly to God (for philosophy, this is the infinite) characterizes him as what by definition surpasses the finite. Now for us, phenomenal conditions remain at all times finite (the sensory nature of intuition implies its finitude and our concepts belong to our finite understanding), to the point that it has been possible to conclude that Being deploys itself as finite.[14] Consequently, God's infinity can only contradict our finite knowledge of the phenomenon. Translated into epistemological terms, this takes the following form: If incomprehensibility attests to the impossibility of phenomenalizing the infinite, it nonetheless postulates, on a negative mode, a positive experience of the infinite. In other words, the epistemic impossibility of the phenomenon of God (namely his incomprehensibility) is itself experienced as a counter-experience of God.

This inversion—the impossible phenomenon as the paradoxical possibility of a counter-experience—may be contested and has in fact been contested often enough. One can argue for example that incomprehensibility no more offers a formal account of God than does infinity, since it offers nothing to the understanding except the general impossibility of experience as such. The fact that I am unable in this case to comprehend anything is not enough to infer, on the sly, the unverifiable but actual presence of anything whatsoever. On the contrary, and in a more trivial way, the fact that I understand nothing confirms straightaway the ontic inconsistency of an object of any kind. The failure of the *ratio cognoscendi* simply reproduces the failure of the *ratio essendi*. I fail to understand anything because there is, precisely, nothing there generally (*überhaupt*) to understand or even to be conceived. Experience as such becomes impossible. Nor is there any question of a noumenon, since some apparition might well appear (an idol, an illusion) without anything appearing in and of itself.[15]

In short, if we reject the ontological argument because it rests on the simple possibility of passing from concept to existence, must we not a fortiori exclude passing from impossibility (non-concept, non-intuition) to existence?

We will have to conclude, regarding God, that all we ever find is a triple impossibility—impossibility with regard to intuition; impossibility with regard to concept; and impossibility, therefore, with regard to experiencing the slightest phenomenon.

5. The Imprescriptible

There remains nonetheless something that cannot be prescribed[16]—something that remains forever an open question, which cannot be classified away as settled, which asks for its case to be pleaded without cease—the *causa Dei*, as a matter of fact. The question of God has the characteristic feature of always making a comeback, of being incessantly reborn from all attempts to put it to death, in theory as well as in fact. We must recognize as a rational datum that the question of God remains entirely pertinent even if God's existence as such is problematic, or downright impossible to establish. Even on the supposition that a transcendental illusion is involved or that the question is ill-framed, we must still confront it, and confront it all the more. The very fact that the illusion of God survives the phenomenal impossibility of God and any experience of him, is what constitutes the question. The question is simply a rational fact, since no rational mind, especially not the most reticent, can pretend not to understand the question of God, even and especially if the inherent impossibility of the question is clearly grasped.[17] The paradox is this: How are we to understand the sense of what we cannot but affirm to be impossible? In other words, we may well proscribe the knowledge of God (of his essence, of his existence, of his phenomenon) but not the question as such of God, which always remains to be inexhaustibly deconstructed every time it makes itself be heard, which is to say at all times. This question alone seems to enjoy the exorbitant but irreducible privilege of having the ability (and therefore the duty) to pose itself to us in spite of (or because of) our impossibility of answering. The question of God survives the impossibility of God. Reason itself requires therefore that we give a rational account of this paradox: We must either explain it, or give up and give in to it.[18]

It goes without saying that having recourse at this point to some psychological explanation or presumed "religious need" would be of no avail. The problem is not to guess how the imprescriptibility of the question is experienced, but to explain how the impossible endures as a possibility—in other words, to conceive how the thought of the impossible remains, in the end, possible. The whole difficulty lies in the status of this possible impossibility. The question at stake thus concerns the limits of modality and, therefore, the limits of our rationality.

How can we conceptualize what escapes us? The aporia comes no doubt from the fact that we seek an answer outside of the question itself. Let us stick to our starting point—to the fact, namely, that God's impossibility in no way annuls the possibility of the question of God. How are we rightly to conceive of this paradox? Precisely by recognizing God's privilege—*God, and God alone, lets himself be defined by impossibility as such.* Indeed we enter the realm where it becomes possible to raise the question of God, and therefore of the incomprehensible, as soon as we confront the impossible—and only then. God begins where the possible *for us* ends, where what human reason comprehends as *possible for it* comes to a halt, at the precise limit where our thought can no longer advance, or see, or speak—where the inaccessible domain of the impossible bursts open. What is impossible to human reason does not place the question of God under interdict, but rather indicates the threshold beyond which the question can be posed and actually be about God—transcending, by the same token, what does not concern him in the least. In God's case, and in God's case alone, impossibility does not abolish the question but actually makes it possible.

Now regarding this conclusion, we note a unique convergence: At least three points of view, which otherwise largely stand opposed to one another, explicitly endorse this trial-by-impossibility method of determining the question of God.

1. Metaphysics, to the extent that it constructs the "God of the philosophers and scientists," construes God as the omnipotent case, the case in which power is possessed over all things, including over what remains impossible for us. Pagan philosophy concurs: *"Nihil est, inquiunt, quod deus efficere non possit"* (Cicero).[19] Medieval thought agrees: *"Deus dicitur omnipotens, quia potest omnia possibilia absolute, quod est alter modus dicendi possibile"* (Thomas Aquinas).[20] And both extend into modern metaphysics: *"infixa quaedam est meae menti vetus opinio, Deum esse qui potest omnia"* (Descartes).[21] This determination has such deep roots that not even efforts to marginalize the question of God fail to endorse and privilege divine omnipotence. Thus Locke: "This eternal source, then, of all being, must also be the source and origin of all power; and so *this eternal Being must be also the most powerful.*"[22]

2. Unexpectedly, moreover, attempts to "destroy" metaphysics have kept intact the determination of God as "the one for whom the extraordinary does not exist" (Kierkegaard).[23] Phenomenology (Husserl, Levinas, Henry, etc.) and also the philosophy of history (Bloch, Rosenzweig, etc.)—both of which approach the question of God from the standpoint of possibility and of the future—have abundantly confirmed this choice.[24] Not even the rift cut into

philosophy by the "end of metaphysics" seems to jeopardize the paradox that God comes to thought only as the possibility of impossibility. Instead, the paradox is radicalized.

3. This first level of agreement, surprising in itself, provokes nothing short of astonishment once we recognize a second double-convergence, this time between these two philosophical eras on the one hand, and Revelation on the other (Jewish and therefore Christian). For indeed here as well—or rather here especially—the impossible defines man's limit with respect to God. Man has his domain and rules his world as far as the possible extends; but as soon as the impossible emerges, there God's proper realm emerges, where holiness reigns (really *his* unique holiness), transcending whatever is possible *for us*. The impossible gives man the only indisputable sign by means of which God allows himself to be recognized: "Nothing is impossible on God's part" (Genesis 18:14). The distance imposes itself so radically that even Christ before the Cross invokes it in the form: "Father, all things are possible to thee" (Mark 14:36). The impossibility for us of seeing the phenomenon of God, and of experiencing it, is precisely and specifically radicalized by the recognition that God alone has power over all that is possible and therefore also over the impossible. His impossibility for us is part and parcel of his own proper possibility: He appears as the "only sovereign (*monos dunastēs*) [. . .] who alone is immortal and dwells in inaccessible light, whom no man has ever seen or can see" (1 Timothy 6:15–16).

Three standpoints, which otherwise diverge—namely metaphysics, philosophy that overcomes metaphysics, and Revelation—thus agree at least on this one point: The impossible, as the concept above all concepts, designates what we know only by name—God.[25] Impossibility, no doubt, defines the proper place of the question of God only with variations and at the price of equivocity (which will have to be assessed), yet always according to the same principle: The threshold between possibility and impossibility *for us* is strictly what unfolds impossibility as what is possible *for God*. It comes down to thinking what Nicolas of Cusa formulated in a simple and powerful paradox: "*Unde cum Deo nihil sit impossibile, oportet per ea quae in hoc mundo sunt impossibilia nos ad ipsum respicere, apud quem impossibilitas est necessitas.*"[26] To put it another way: Since possibility for us exclusively defines the world and since God's eventual region begins with impossibility (for us and according to the world), then to proceed toward God means to advance to the outer marches of the world, to step beyond the borders of the possible and tread at the edge of impossibility. The only possible pathway to God emerges in, and goes through, the impossible.

In order to embark on it, we must return to the texts that impose this paradox and attempt to think conceptually about three verses of the synoptic gospels. Two of these coincide: "With men, this is impossible, but with God all things are possible" (Matthew 19:26), and "With men it is impossible, but not with God; for all things are possible with God" (Mark 10:27). What is involved is not a simple contrast between certain impossibilities which are supposed to be found on man's side, and other possibilities, found in turn on God's side. Indeed the same exact things change from being impossible with men to being possible with God: "*Ta adunata para anthrōpois dunata para tō Theō estin—*What is impossible with men is possible with God" (Luke 18:27). What we must probe is how the impossible is converted into the possible when we pass from man to God.

6. God's Operational Name

Before continuing further, let us pause to consider for a moment the still very abstract determination of God that we have reached: God manifests himself in such a way that nothing is impossible with him.

The first implication concerns the inversion of the possible and the impossible, or more exactly the conversion of the impossible *for us* into the possible *for God*. The only region that we have a right to assign to God starts precisely when we run into an impossibility, when we factually stumble against what is impossible for us. Let us be precise: The impossible delineates only the region of finitude—namely ours—and indicates this region alone. The experience of the impossible therefore unlocks as of yet no access to God's own proper region, so long as we have not crossed the threshold. And how could we cross it, confined as we are within finitude? Indeed we cannot do so effectively speaking (we will never accomplish the impossible, nor is this asked of us), yet we cross it by mentally considering what remains incomprehensible for us, namely by conceiving that what is irreducibly impossible for us *can* or *could* become possible in its own right if we were to pass over to God's standpoint. We must mentally conceptualize what remains incomprehensible for us— namely conceptualize that God starts where the impossible translates into the possible, precisely where the impossible appears as though it were possible. Conversely, if any impossibility were to remain irreducibly impossible (for our logic or in our experience), we must not, on this ground, impose closure to the question of God but instead conclude only that we have not yet reached God's own proper region but dwell, still, inside our own. As long indeed as we are dealing with what is impossible, we are dealing only with ourselves, not yet with God. In principle, God cannot come up against the impossible, since, if an impossible remained impossible for him (if it remained possible than anything were impossible to him), *he would not be God*—but some "god" afflicted with impossibility, like us, human beings—for whom alone the impossible remains possible. Contrary to us, God defines himself as that to which (or rather as he for whom) there is no possibility of impossibility.

This leads to a second consequence: If no impossibility operates or has sway *over* God, then nothing can ever make God *himself* impossible. It turns out, as a matter of principle, *that it is impossible for God to be impossible.* We have now reached the point where the objection according to which the impossibility of God is proved on the grounds of intuition, meaning, and therefore phenomenality, collapses. Even once it is granted, the impossibility of experiencing the phenomenon of God obviously concerns us only and our standpoint, where alone the impossible can (and must) impose itself. The impossibility of God has meaning only for us, who alone are capable of experiencing the impossible (in particular the impossibility for us of acceding to the impossible). It has no meaning *for God.* Such an impossibility specifically does not concern *him,* for whom the impossible is by definition impossible. The impossibility of God turns out to be possible only for us, not for God. If we seriously consider that God lets himself be thought only in the form of the impossibility *for him* of impossibility, then it turns out that it is impossible for God not to turn out to be at least always possible and thinkable—if nothing else as the impossible. Nor can anyone object that, in this case, the impossibility of impossibility for God remains inaccessible to us and teaches nothing about him, since we conceive the hiatus, irreducible as it is, by understanding why and how God remains impossible *for us*—which is to say, specifically, *for us but not for him.* We thus conceive God insofar as he is not confused with us and insofar as the difference is forever drawn. Which is what had to be demonstrated.

Finally, it follows that the so-called "ontological" argument becomes subject to revision, which radically transforms it. The argument, in metaphysics and according to Kant's formulation, consists in deducing God's existence from the concept of God's essence and other pure concepts (without recourse to experience).[27] The chief difficulty, contrary to what is stubbornly claimed and repeated, does not lie in the illegitimacy of passing from a concept to existence as a position external to the concept.[28] It lies instead, far more radically, in assuming that a concept adequately defines the divine essence in the first place. The argument inevitably results in forging an idol of "God" (sec. 3, above). How is this aporia overcome? By renouncing all presumed concepts of God and rigorously sticking to his incomprehensibility. Yet how are we to conceive this incomprehensibility in such a way as still to be able to think at all? By conceiving it not only as the impossibility of every concept, but also as the concept of impossibility—impossibility, namely, as the distinctive hallmark of God's difference with regard to man. Concerning God, indeed, we cannot without contradiction assume any concept other than the concept of impossibility to mark his specific difference—God, or what is impossible *for us.* From the moment that we substitute, for a comprehensible concept, the incomprehensible concept of the impossible, the whole argument is turned upside down: It no longer proves God's existence, but the impossibility of his impossibility, and therefore his possibility. God turns out to be the one whose possibility remains forever possible, precisely because it turns out that nothing remains impossible for him, especially not himself. The necessity of God's possibility flows from the impossibility of his impossibility.

Such a reversal of the argument into a proof of the unconditional possibility of God based on his concept (as impossible), strange as it may seem, has already received a formulation—by Nicholas of Cusa. Let our starting point be the thematization according to which St. Thomas Aquinas framed the difference between God and what is created: In the created case, essence always remains really distinct from *esse*, just as potency differs from act; on the contrary, in God, essence is not only always identified in act with *esse* but (at least according to certain passages) disappears into *esse* to the point that in God the whole essence, which is to say the whole power and potency, is accomplished in act, as *actus essendi*. Nicholas of Cusa affirms this distinction, but reverses the way in which it is applied: A created entity can only actualize its potency, which, in itself limited, is all the more exhausted qua potency that it is stabilized in act, which is also limited; consequently no created entity accedes to the level of infinite possibility, since both its essence and its act instaurate its finitude. God, on the contrary, actually is all that he is potentially, according to a double infinity of act *and of possibility: "Ita ut solus Deus id sit quod esse potest, nequaquam autem quaecumque creatura, cum potentia et actus non sint idem, nisi in principio."*[29] God and creature are opposed less by act (relative to essence) than by the privilege in God of possibility, of the possibility of actualizing infinite possibility—in other words, by *possest*. Thus, whereas *"nulla creatura est possest,"* God transcends creation first and above all by a definitive, irreducible and eternal possibility, in short by an uncreated possibility— *"increata possibilitas est ipsum possest."*[30] God's omnipotence, which is to say his denomination based on the impossibility for him of impossibility, results in a possibility that is eternal and infinite, originary and ultimate. God's omnipotence means here less an unlimited efficient power than the perfect actuality of possibility as such:

> Esto enim quod aliqua dictio significet simplicissimo significatu quantum hoc complexum; posse est, scilicet quod ipsum posse sit. Et quia, quod est, actu est, ideo posse esse est tantum quantum posse esse actu. Puta vocetur possest [. . .] est dei satis propinquum nomen secundum humanum de eo conceptum. Est enim nomen omnium et singulorum nominum, atque nullius pariter. Ideo dum Deus sui vellet notitiam primo revelare dicebat: 'Ergo sum Deus omnipotens,' id est 'Sum actus omnis potentiae.'[31]

God lets himself be named according to the actuality of the possibility of power, not according to the simple assumption of power in act, even infinite. In God, possibility trumps active efficiency because God's highest efficiency consists in surpassing impossibility (for us) by making it possible— which he does by virtue of the necessity in him of the impossibility of impossibility.

Jean-Luc Marion

7. From the Impossible as Self-contradictory to the Impossible as Advent

It remains for us to understand the two terms that are inverted in God's case—the possible and the impossible. We will mark the inversion henceforth by writing "the [im-]possible." Metaphysics indeed has its own way, too, of understanding the relation and mutual interplay of these terms.

If as a matter of fact the "highest principle with which we usually start a transcendental philosophy is the standard division into possible and impossible,"[32] God will still be defined in terms of his relationship to the impossible, precisely under the figure of omnipotence. Through a strange reflexivity, this very omnipotence can only deploy itself by letting itself always be bound by the limits of impossibility, not by transgressing them. God can certainly make (effectuate) all things, but on the express condition that things be inscribed within the domain of the possible and not turn out to be contradictory:

> Deus dicitur omnipotens, quia potest omnia possibilia absolute, quod est alter modus dicendi possibile. Dicitur autem aliquid possibile vel impossibile absolute ex habitudine terminorum [praedicatum repugnat subjecto . . .] Quaecumque igitur contradictionem non implicant, sub illis possibilibus continentur, respectu quorum Deus dicitur omnipotens.[33]

The position will quickly show itself to be untenable, for obvious reasons. Namely: (1) In the end it reduces God to the role of an efficient laborer, working on behalf of some possibility, essence or formula "to which, so to speak, God submits himself." The order of Reason imposes itself on God as it does on creatures, law of "all intelligences and of God himself."[34] The road is open to determining God within the limits of ordinary reason, pure and simple. But there is more: (2) If the possible, which limits divine omnipotence, is defined as what is not self-contradictory—adopting Wolff's definition, that "*Possibile est quod nullam contradictionem involvit seu quod non est impossibile*"[35]—then the non-contradictory as such remains to be defined. How does a concept contradict itself? According, obviously, to the norms, rules and axioms of conceptualization. One cannot speak of absolute contradiction, but only always of *contradictio in conceptu*.[36] Now what concept other than one of our own representation can be at stake here? "*Nihil negativum*, irrepresentabile, *impossibile, repugnans (absurdum), contradictionem involvans, implicans, contradictorium*"; therefore "*Non nihil est aliquid*: repraesentabile, *quidquid non involvit contradictionem, quidquid non est A et non-A, est possibile*."[37] The representable and the non-representable come into play only within *our* conceptualization; therefore within our finite conception; therefore within our finitude. There is no contradiction other than what is conceivable, and nothing is conceivable that is not within our own conceptualization—and therefore *quoad nos*, for us, for our finite mind. If the point is to assign a contradiction (and therefore an impossibility) to God, we must come up with an absolute contradiction, contradictory for an *infinite* understanding. The demand obviously makes no sense, since our understanding is by definition finite. We will never know the slightest thing about what is impossible or contradictory from the point of view of God's infinity. These will remain perfectly undecidable since we will never have access to the conditions of the question. The notion of contradiction as such supposes finitude: Therefore if God is God—which is to say infinite—no contradiction, by definition, can apply to him. With God, nothing is impossible—even, or rather especially, in the sense of a metaphysical impossibility, which does not even concern him.

What sort of impossible is transgressed by God—beyond the impossible that is limited to non-contradiction—remains, however, to be understood. Heidegger unquestionably deserves credit for having challenged the metaphysical distinction between possible and impossible by affirming that, "Higher than actuality stands possibility."[38] The mere inversion of the terms as such does not, however, suffice to redefine them—especially not to redefine possibility. In order for possibility to free itself it must, by definition, escape all condition of possibility that advenes to it externally. This is true to the point that radical possibility must, paradoxically but necessarily, eschew the slightest de*finition*, because any finitude limiting it would indeed contradict it. Radical possibility would, as such, transcend all limit and, being thus completely unconditioned, would give us access, finally, to the transcendence which we seek. Formally, such possibility would define itself as the transcendence of all impossibility—taking its point of departure not in some non-contradiction concocted within the limits of representation and positive conceptualization, but negatively, in transgressing these very limits, namely within what remains impossible for conceptualization and representation. Possibility taken in the radical sense would take its point of departure in the impossible, by transcending it, which is to say by annulling it through effectively bringing it about. Radical possibility would start with the impossible and, without passing through conceptualization of a non-contradictory possible for finite representation, would impose it within effectivity. *Radical possibility or effecting the impossible.* In contrast to possibility as de-*fined* by metaphysics, radical possibility would not transform possible things into effective things, but *impossible* things into effective things, directly. It would effectively bring about [im-]possibilities hitherto unthinkable.

How can this be, if I know of no such [im-]possible? But am I sure that I know of none? No doubt I know of no such [im-]possible as long as I define myself as *ego cogitans*, thinking according to my own representation and concept. By adopting this posture, indeed, I submit everything that can advene through the screen, so to speak, of my own conceptualization and finitude. Hence causality (whether it starts with me as causal agent or with some cause other than myself) never brings about anything, by definition, except what my concept has foreseen for it as possible, according to what is non-contradictory for my representation. I do not, however, define myself always, or even primarily, as *ego cogitans*, according to a conceptual representation. I emerge, or rather I *have* emerged into existence through a very different mode—on the mode of an event in which I myself advene to myself without having either predicted it, or understood it, or represented it, precisely because I was not yet there—nor was I, a fortiori, already thinking at the advent of the event. Before being, in short, I had to be born. Birth, or rather *my* birth, precedes any thought of my own. Consequently, it precedes all possibility as defined by concept and representation.[39] Even if, retroactively, I am quite able, based on someone else's testimony, to reconstitute what came before me and even reduce it to a representable possibility, even a predictable one, such an interpretation does not retroactively establish a non-contradictory possibility that positively precedes the event of my advent. Rather the interpretation starts with the fact itself, without cause or predictability, in order to assign to it, after the fact and always only very partially, a coherence and conceivability through which absurdity is avoided and plausibility insured. What is more, all forms of genealogy and romanticized memories only come after the fact; not only belatedly relative to the event, which advenes without waiting for them, but also arrested in their tracks, suddenly mute, before the obscure moment, the silent and inaccessible moment of birth, gestation and conception—period without speech, consciousness or memory. Birth, *my* birth—which delivers me, bears me into the world and makes me—happens without me. I will never be able to join up with it. Birth made me without me, without my consciousness, or my concept, all of which follow thereafter. Advent of the event because originary, brought about without me. Brought about—advened, rather—without me, my birth advenes from itself without cause, or presupposition, or concept—in short, without possibility. My birth advenes to me in the form of a directly effective impossibility.

Thus I am forced to admit that the case of my birth provides me with the experience of radical possibility—namely the one from which I come and which has effectively made me. Better, by becoming effective precisely as an impossibility, my birth has unlocked possibles for me which are defined, not by my concepts, but by my birth—and which therefore unlock as many concepts in its wake. The impossible, turned effective, imposes possibles and allows concepts of possibles to be produced, in reverse order than the order of non-contradictory possibility.

Still, based on the [im-]possible that is my birth, how is an [im-]possible for God to be imagined? Does the disproportion between the two domains (finite and infinite) not forbid transition and assimilation? It probably does, if we cling to the division that remains internal to the horizon of the concept of being. But not if we focus on the advent of the [im-]possible as such. Indeed what birth accomplishes for each living being, creation brings about from God's standpoint—as long of course as we understand creation here in the theological sense, not as a mere taking of efficient causality to the limit. The point is that *for us* creation thematizes and gathers together the totality of events that advene of themselves—without concepts, without predictions, and therefore without cause—radical possibles, in short, which we not only receive from within it but from which, first and foremost, we receive ourselves. Certainly, for *me*, creation starts always and only with my birth. Yet by the same token my birth exposes me to the whole of creation, giving me access to every [im-]possible in its primordial [im-]possibility. God, the master of the impossible, effectuates creation by making the [im-]possibility of each birth effective, starting with my own.

We thus have access to radical possibility through the [im-]possibility of our own birth. Through it, moreover, we have access as well (by way of an analogy that deserves further scrutiny on some other occasion) to the radical [im-]possibility accomplished by God in the event which, paradigmatically, advenes *for us* from himself, creation. God, who initially aimed at unconditioned transcendence (secs. 1–4, above), for whom nothing remained impossible (secs. 5–6, above), is from now on certified as the one who unlocks radical possibility. As the master of the possible—not as the one who effectually brings about possible things and predicts them, but as he who makes them spring forth from [im-]possibility and gives them to themselves.

8. What God Recognizes (to Himself) as His Own Proper [Im-]Possible and therefore as the Possible for Him

The whole question now bathes in a new light. We remain firmly grounded in God's operational name: With him nothing is impossible that remains impossible with human beings. Since, however, the [im-]possible in question belongs to radical possibility, unconditioned by any possibility of representation or concept (both of which are finite by definition), it can no longer be understood as the outcome of a simple efficient act. God's relationship to radical possibility, therefore, can no longer be thought in terms of omnipotent efficiency. Metaphysically speaking, omnipotence corresponds only to God's knowledge of eternal possibles. Omnipotence as related to possibility in a metaphysical sense is coextensive with the domain of the non-contradictory as represented in concept. It follows that abstract and therefore arbitrary omnipotence no more suits the transcendent God of radical possibility than the representation of eternal possibles defines his overture of possibles. The problem is thus to characterize God's posture with regard to the [im-]possible without *reducing* or *degrading* it to the level of omnipotence. In other words, we must conceive of how God chooses his [im-]possibles for himself. How does the master of the [im-]possible determine what remains impossible for human beings, but is possible for him?

We are all the more entitled to ask the question that it stems directly from biblical texts. Let us consider the difficult narrative of the Annunciation. To the angel who announces the possibility of motherhood to her, Mary responds first with a factual impossibility: "I know no man" (Luke 1:34). Against this factual impossibility, the angel then asserts the principle of radical possibility as a right, pertaining to [im-]possibles: *"ouk adunatēsei para tou Theou pan rhēma"*—literally, "For on God's part, no saying, no word, shall be impossible" (Luke 1:37).[40] When Mary then accepts the annunciation that is made to her, she emphasizes the "saying" of the angel ("Let it be to me according to your word"), which announced God's "saying, *rhēma*." Mary's decision and faith concerning the [im-]possible is therefore not addressed to God's omnipotence (which the text never literally invokes) but to God's "saying." In what therefore does she really have faith? She has faith in the "saying, *rhēma*" that God has said, and thus in the commitment he has made. She believes God's word. She takes God "at his word" because she knows that every one of his words commits him once and for all. The point is not to acknowledge simple omnipotence (which commits to nothing and permits, on the contrary, every lie) but to have faith in God's good faith. To have recourse to God's omnipotence is useless, since it still remains immanent to our own finite point of view (like the reverse face of possibility according to represented non-contradiction). Instead, the task is to transcend our own finite point of view in order to pass over to God's point of view—or at least to aim for it, to admit it as an intention. In contrast to us, where saying commits to nothing (we lie), on God's part, saying and carrying out what is said coincide absolutely. More than the power to do anything, God has the power to say anything—not in virtue of his omnipotence but in virtue of his fidelity. God can say whatever and all that he wants because what he says, he does. Thus *rhēma* here signifies indivisibly both word and fact.[41] In the face of the [im-]possible, fidelity in God transcends and replaces omnipotence. God is all-powerful because he always keeps his word, not the inverse. Two details of the text, moreover, confirm this. (1) Rather than a simple assertion, we find a double negation: Negation of the possible, and negation of this negation on the side of God.[42] This implies that nothing will come about that stands opposed to God's word. (2) The verb is conjugated in the future ("nothing shall be impossible" = *adunatēsei*), suggesting that, as soon as Mary gives her consent, God will act, keep his promise, make it his business and that we will see the effect.[43] The possible, or rather the carrying out of the impossible (in the world that human beings know, namely virginal birth) will open up a proper possible for God alone—the Incarnation, which launches Redemption. Not only is the possible not the same for us and for God, the [im-]possible is not either.

We see indeed that the case is not simply one of contradicting, by means of an abstract omnipotence, the laws of the world and of being (even though in fact this happens); but rather to bring into play, at this price, an array of possibilities that are until then unthinkable and unimaginable, possibilities such that only God could foresee them and want them. It is not enough to recognize omnipotence as one of God's proper names—*"Dominus quasi vir pugnator. Omnipotens nomen ejus"* (Exodus 15:4, Vulgate)—rather, we must conceive that God does not will enactments of outlandish and ridiculous monstrosities. In contrast to the sort of omnipotence that we human beings dream of today, the impossibility of the impossibility that God exercises does not bring about just anything—by his power he makes all that he wants, but he wants only by loving.

Recourse to divine omnipotence pure and simple, moreover, struck people from the very beginning as somewhat fragile, abstract, insufficient. Celsus already reproached Christians for "taking refuge in the absurd escape that 'nothing is impossible with God' when they had nothing to answer"—namely, concerning the resurrection of the flesh. Origen, in turn, found himself obliged to specify that "we know full well that we understand all of this [namely, Luke 1:37] to apply neither to what does not exist at all (*adianotōn*) nor to what cannot be thought (*adianotōn*)."[44] The answer is a cautious one, but once again insufficient, since what right do we have to oppose unthinkables and non-existent things to God if "with him nothing is impossible"? More essentially, the question no longer consists in fixing a limit beyond which divine omnipotence would be going too far in some abstract sense (relative to what limit?), but in determining what it is that God can indeed want *as his word*—a word which he commits himself to keep, allowing himself to be taken "at his word." Neither logic, nor contradiction, nor the principle of identity, nor efficacy, nor the principle of sufficient reason, retains the slightest relevancy here, namely when the task is to conceive that to which God's word commits itself and commits God. Obviously, if God is God, he can do whatever he wants—that is not the question. The question, rather, is what God is able to want and wants to be able to do. What does he want, without restriction, to be able to do? What corresponds to him and therefore comes from him. St. Augustine explicates this remarkably:

> Negari se ipsum non potest, falli non potest (2 Timothy 2:13). Quam multa non potest et omnipotens est: et ideo omnipotens est, quia ista non potest. Nam si mori posset, non esset omnipotens; si mentiri, si falli, si fallere, si inique agere, non esset omnipotens: quia si hoc in eo esset, non fuisset dignus qui esset omnipotens. Prorsus omnipotens Pater noster peccare non potest. Facit quidquid vult: ipsa est omnipotentia. Facit quidquid bene vult, quidquid juste vult: quidquid autem male fit, non vult.[45]

God does whatever he wants, but the main thing is that he wants only what it becomes him to want—which is to say only what comes from him and answers to his love. God makes what it becomes God to make. Such is the impossible for man—what becomes God.

9. The Radical Impossibility: Forgiveness

In order to determine what it becomes God to want, and then to be able to do—which is to say to determine what God alone is able to have the power to do, since he alone is able to want it—we must turn once again to biblical texts. In particular, we must consider the passages in which Christ himself presents what remains impossible for us but is possible for God. Let us consider, in particular: "With men this is impossible [namely, that a rich man enter God's kingdom], but with God all things are possible—*para anthrōpois touto adunaton estin, para de Theōi panta dunata*" (Matthew 19:26 = Mark 10:27 = Luke 18:27, cited in sec. 5, above).

What [im-]possible does Christ here bring to light as the criterion separating man from God? "It is easier for a camel to go through the eye of a needle than for a rich man to enter the kingdom of God" (Matthew 19:24). Physical, worldly impossibility serves here as a sign to expose a much loftier impossibility, but which cannot be directly seen by the human eye or in broad daylight. Why does this specific impossibility for men (and not for God) fail to appear to men (but only to Christ, and therefore to God)? Because as far as men are concerned—namely the spectators of the dialogue, as well as the rich young man—the youth in question has *already* entered God's kingdom, since he has *already* kept the commandments. "All these I have observed"—hence his astonishment that he should fall short. "What do I still lack?" (Matthew 19:20). What indeed does he lack? Strictly speaking, he lacks nothing—except, precisely, having nothing: Owning nothing and keeping nothing outside of Christ himself ("Come, follow me"); which means becoming one with God through Christ, becoming holy like him ("If you would be perfect . . ." Matthew 19:21); and thus fulfilling the highest commandment, "You shall therefore be holy, for I am holy" (Leviticus 11:45; 19:2), in the form in which Christ reiterates it, "You, therefore, must be perfect, as your heavenly father is perfect" (Matthew 5:48).[46] What is impossible for man ("the rich young man") is the lack of *lack* (the lack of poverty and therefore of identifying with Christ alone)—a lack which cannot appear in a world in which we see only what is ("riches"). The impossible thus remains inaccessible to anyone who lacks the power to lack and cannot even see what he nonetheless knows is beyond his power. Only Christ sees this, even though he points to it only indirectly. We grasp at least that what is impossible here *for man* but *from God's viewpoint*, consists in what men do not even consider—a genuine conversion to God—infinitely more difficult than worldly impossibilities are *for us*.[47]

We read about this reversal of the possible and the impossible for men and for Christ (and therefore from God's viewpoint), namely the very way in which the [im-]possible comes into play, in the story of the paralytic's cure (Matthew 9:1–8; Mark 2:1–12 = Luke 5:17–26). A paralyzed man is brought before Christ, but Christ, strangely enough, instead of curing the physical ailment (as everyone expected since he had tirelessly done so before), declares the man cured spiritually. "Your sins are forgiven" (Matthew 9:2). Christ thus accomplishes what is possible to God and supremely impossible to men. Some of the men, or at least some "among the scribes," understand it in precisely this way, but only to denounce it as "blasphemy" (Matthew 9:3)—namely as a claim by

Christ to have God's rank. Nor are they wrong in this regard: To claim to be able to do the impossible is, on the part of men, indeed to claim to be God. How is Christ able to sustain his claim before men? When he accomplishes a relative impossibility—the physical and worldly cure of physical paralysis, an impossibility which is both effective *for us* and visible *to us* in the world—he attests that nothing is impossible with him in our world; and therefore that he holds the rank of God, from which in turn it follows that nothing is impossible with him *even outside the world.* By asking the question "Which is easier, *eukopōteron?*" (Matthew 9:5), he forces men to decide about God in him. Since for men nothing seems more difficult in the world than to cure a physical paralysis, Christ by accomplishing this feat accomplishes the impossible, which is God's prerogative. The choice, then, is either to deny the evidence of the world, which indeed establishes that he comes from God and is God; or to admit the visible evidence that he is indeed God, and therefore admit also that he has power over the true [im-]possible—namely, to forgive sins. Christ thus makes manifest what is impossible *from God's viewpoint,* namely to heal the heart.

What is at stake in the question, "which is easier, *eukopōteron?*" now comes to light. What is harder, indeed what requires, *from God's own viewpoint,* his power and transcendence, does not stem form what appears *to us* to be most difficult (namely modifying the a priori conditions of phenomenal experience), but what seems *to him* to be least within our reach (even if we are not even able to see this level)—to convert our hearts to God. The [im-]possible *for God* lies within the stone-hard human heart. God's operational and untransferable name—his ultimate transcendence—is articulated in his power to convert the hardened hearts of men, to remit their sins, to forgive them. Only God has the power, precisely, to forgive, because only love is able to forgive and has the right to do so. Now "there is only one who is good" (Matthew 19:17), and "No one is good but God alone" (Mark 10:18). Man cannot forgive because he has neither the power to forgive (in his heart, he remains a murderer), nor the right to forgive (every sin is ultimately against God). Evil remains imprescriptible for man, who is powerless to forgive it and therefore must recognize himself to be its prisoner. In order to grasp this more clearly, let us consider an unexpected text: The brutally corrected, almost blasphemous, reformulation by V. Jankélévitch of Christ's words on the cross. "Thus *we* might well say, *reversing* the terms of the prayer addressed to God by Christ in the Gospel according to St. Luke: Lord, *do not forgive them,* for they know what they do."[48] Let us admit that the magnitude here of the evil—that of the Shoa, the genocide of the Jews by the Nazis—explains, even justifies, such a bold reversal. Let us note as well that the reversal amounts to restoring a metaphysical (Aristotelian) definition of moral responsibility—a responsibility which is full and inescapable when we know what we are doing.[49] But we will also, in the end, ratify the correction: Does it not simply recognize as evident that *we, human beings,* in fact, *are not able to forgive*—any more than we are able to convert, or free ourselves of our sins on our own? There is a sort of second-order piety in this quasi-blasphemy; namely, the piety of stating clearly and directly that it is impossible in principle for man to forgive or even to ask for forgiveness, and that on the contrary this is possible only with God, as the prerogative of his radical transcendence. Only God has the power to forgive sins—which is to say the sins that all of us (who alone sin) commit in the final analysis against God (even when we inflict them first on other human beings). The impossible for man has the name God, but God as such—as the one who alone forgives the trespasses made against him.

The radical and non-metaphysical transcendence for which we have been seeking thus reveals itself with great clarity in the impossible—but in the only [im-]possible worthy of God, which is charity. Only with love, and therefore with "God who is love" (1 John 4:8, 16), is nothing impossible. God's transcendence manifests itself in charity, and only thus does transcendence reveal itself to be worthy of God.

NOTES

1. Husserl, *Cartesianische Meditationen*, Hua I, p. 72.

2. Husserl: *"So heisst das Ding selbst und schlechthin transzendent"* (*Ideen I*, Hua III, p. 96).

3. Heidegger, *"Sein ist das transcendens schlechthin"* (*Sein und Zeit*, sec. 7, p. 38).

4. [Respectively: "being insofar as it is indifferent to finite and infinite," and "transcendent and is outside of every genus."—Tr.]

5. ["They are such that they transcend being insofar as being is indifferent to finite and infinite."—Tr.] Duns Scotus, *Ordinatio* I, d. 8, n. 113, in *Opera Omnia*, ed. C. Balic (Rome: Vatican Polyglot, 1956), vol. 4, p. 206.

6. ["The definition of transcendentals is that no predicate stands above them, except being."—Tr.] Ibid., p. 206.

7. ["God thus *does not* have an essence that is not his very being."—Tr.] Aquinas, *Summa contra Gentiles*, bk. 1, chap. 21. See J.-L. Marion, "Saint et onto-theologie," *Revue thomiste* 95/1 (1995); which appears in translation in *Mystics: Presence and Aporia*, ed. M. Kessler and C. Sheppard (Chicago and London: University of Chicago Press, 2003).

8. The formula is mentioned by Petrus Fonseca, *Institutionum Dialecticarum libri octo* (Lyon, 1611), bk. 1, chap. 28; and is cited and discussed by Jean-François Courtine in *Suarez et le système de la métaphysique* (Paris: Presses Universitaires, 1990), p. 267. On the doctrine of transcendentals, see Courtine, *Suarez et le système*, p. 355ff.; and Ludger Honnefelder, *Ens inquantum ens: Der Begriff des Seienden als solchen als Gegenstand der Metaphysik nach der Lehre von Johannes Duns Scotus*, Beiträge zur Geschichte der Philosophie und Theologie des Mittelalters, n.s. 16 (Münster: Aschendorff, 1979); as well as Theo Kobusch, "Das Seiende als transzendentaler oder supertranszendentaler Begriff," in *John Duns Scotus: Metaphysics and Ethics*, ed. L. Honnefelder, R. Wood and M. Dreyer (Leiden: Brill, 1996).

9. Francisco Suárez, *Disputationes metaphysicæ*, disp. 1, sec. 1, n. 19, in *Opera Omnia*, ed. C. Berton (Paris: Vivès, 1866), vol. 25, p. 8, my emphasis: ["God in an

absolute manner falls under the object of this science [[metaphysics . . .]] because this science is the most perfect *natural* wisdom; therefore it treats of all first and most universal things and causes, and of the most general first principles, which include God himself."—Tr.]. See my analysis in J.-L. Marion, *Sur la théologie blanche de Descartes: Analogie, création des vérités éternelles et fondement,* 2nd ed. (Paris: Presses Universitaires, 1991), p. 110ff.

10. Heidegger, "Zur Seinsfrage," *Wegmarken,* Gesamtausgabe, vol. 9 (Frankfurt: Klostermann, 1967), p. 395.

11. Jules Renard, *Journal 1887–1910,* ed. L. Guichard and L. Signaux (Paris: Pléiade, 1960), p. 227.

12. ["Incomprehensibility as such is contained in the definition of infinity."—Tr.] Descartes, *Vae Responsiones,* in *Oeuvres de Descartes,* ed. C. Adam and P. Tannery (Paris: Vrin, 1964–1976) (henceforth AT), vol. 7, pp. 368, 3–4.

13. Hobbes says it with great clarity:

> Whatsoever we imagine is *Finite.* Therefore there is no idea or conception of anything we call *Infinite.* No man can have in his mind an image of infinite magnitude; nor conceive infinite swiftness, infinite time, or infinite force, or infinite power. When we say any thing is infinite, we signify only, that we are not able to conceive the ends, and bounds of the thing named; having no conception of the thing, but of our own inability. And therefore the Name of God is used, not to make us conceive him; (for he is *Incomprehensible*; and his greatness, and power are unconceivable;) but that we may honour him. (*Leviathan,* bk. 1, chap. 3)

14. Heidegger has established not only the finitude of *Dasein:* "*Ursprünglicher als der mensch ist die Endlichkeit des Daseins in ihm*" (*Kant und das Problem der Metaphysik*).

15. See Jocelyn Benoist, in his critique of my first works: "Is it enough not to be in order to be a concept of God?" And: "It is hardly sufficient, either, to not be an object in order to be God" (*L'idée de la phénoménologie,* Paris: Beauchesne, 2001, pp. 86, 96). I am obviously arguing against my own thesis concerning the unavoidable necessity of the counter-experience as the only mode of experience appropriate to the phenomenality of saturated phenomena. See J.-L. Marion, *Etant donné: Essai d'une phénoménologie de la donation* (Paris: Presses Universitaires, 1997); in translation as *Being Given: Toward a Phenomenology of Givenness,* trans. Jeffrey L. Kosky (Stanford: Stanford University Press, 2002).

16. [In the legal sense of "rendered invalid by prescription."—Tr.]

17. Descartes: "*Qui autem negant se habere ideam Dei, sed vice illius efformant aliquod idolum etc., nomen negant et rem concedunt*" (*Secundae Responsiones,* AT 7, pp. 139, 5–7).

18. [The French here involves a play on words that cannot easily be rendered in English.—Tr.]

19. ["There is nothing, they say, that god cannot effectuate."—Tr.] Cicero, *De Divinatione,* bk. 2, sec. 41; in *De senectute; De amicitia; De divinatione,* ed. and trans. W. A. Falconer (Cambridge, Mass.:Harvard University Press, 1923), p. 468.

20. Aquinas, *Summa Theologica,* bk. 1, q. 25, a. 3, resp.: "God is called omnipotent because he can do all things that are possible absolutely, which is the second way of saying that a thing is possible."

21. Descartes, *Meditationes*, med. 1, in AT 7, pp. 21, 1–2: "Infixed, so to speak, in my mind is an old opinion, that there is a God who can do all things."

22. Hume, *An Essay concerning Human Understanding*, bk. 4, sec. 10; ed. P. H. Niddich (Oxford: Oxford University Press, 1975), p. 620. The emergence of modern "atheism" has naturally had to assume still a residual definition of the nonexisting or supposed nonexisting "God"; this was precisely the notion of "universal cause," as W. Schröder has established in *Ursprünge des Atheismus: Untersuchungen zur Metaphysik- und Religionskritik des 17. und 18. Jahrhunderts* (Stuttgart, 1998), p. 209ff. On the privilege of causality (as the most abstract and empty of determinations), see also J.-L. Marion, "The Idea of God," in *The Cambridge History of Seventeenth-Century Philosophy*, ed. M. Ayers and D. Garber (Cambridge: Cambridge University Press, 1998), vol. 1, pp. 265–304; this article is reproduced as chap. 10 of J.-L. Marion, *Questions cartésiennes II: L'ego et Dieu* (Paris: Presses Universitaires, 1996).

23. Kierkegaard, *Samlede Vaerker*, 2nd ed., ed. A. B. Drachmann, J. L. Heiberg and H. O.Lange (Copenhagen: Nordisk Forlag, 1920–1936), vol. 9, p. 81; the French translation appears as *Les Oeuvres de l'amour* in the *Oeuvres Complètes*, ed. P.-H. Tisseau and E.-M. Tisseau (Paris, 1980), vol. 14, p. 62. Cf. Augustine: "*omnipotens, qui facis mirabilia solus*" (*Confessions*, bk. 4, chap. 15, par. 24).

24. The clearest indication of this conclusion is found in the recent work of John D. Caputo, for example: "It can be said in defense of the Kingdom of God that it is not simply impossible, but rather, let us say, *the* impossible." This is from "The Poetic of the Impossible and the Kingdom of God," in *The Blackwell Companion to Postmodern Theology* (Oxford: Oxford University Press, 2001); which is reprinted in *Rethinking Philosophy of Religion: Approaches from Continental Philosophy*, ed. Philip Goodchild (New York: Fordham University Press, 2002). See also *A Passion for the Impossible: John D. Caputo in Focus*, ed. M. Dooley (New York: SUNY Press, 2003); and "Apostles of the Impossible: On God and the Gift in Derrida and Marion," in *God, the Gift, and Postmodernism*, ed. John D. Caputo and Michael J. Scanlon (Bloomington: Indiana University Press, 1999), which appeared also in *Philosophie* 78 (2003).

25. Cf. Georges Bataille, *Le petit*, in *Oeuvres complètes* (Paris: Gallimard, 1971), vol. 3, p. 47: "*A la place de Dieu . . . il n'y a que l'impossible et non Dieu.*" ["Instead of God . . . there is only the impossible and not God."—Tr.]

26. Nicholas of Cusa, *Trialogus de possest*, in *Werke*, ed. Paul Wilpert (Berlin, 1967), vol. 2, p. 66; or in the *Philosophisch-theologische Schriften*, ed. L. Gabriel, D. Dupré and W. Dupré (Vienna, 1966), vol. 2, p. 340: "Hence, as nothing is impossible with God, we must, by means of what is impossible in the world, raise ourselves to contemplate God, with whom impossibility is necessity."

27. Kant, *Critique of Pure Reason*, A590/B619, or A602/B630.

28. One could indeed argue that Descartes and Hegel answer Kant correctly: In the case of all other entities, we are right to distinguish concept and existence, but this "habit" no longer holds in God's case, who by definition constitutes an exception to the general rule governing common beingness. (For Descartes, cf. *Meditationes*, med. 5, in AT 7, pp. 66, 2–15; *Iae Responsiones*, in AT 7, pp. 116, 8–19; and *Principia philosophiæ* I, 16. For Hegel, cf. *Wissenschaft der Logik*, ed. G. Lasson, Hamburg: Meiner, 1934, vol. 1, p. 75.)

29. ["So that God alone is what he can be, which no creature can, since potency and act are not the same, except in the first principle."—Tr.] Nicholas of Cusa, *Tria-*

logus de possest, in Wilpert, p. 646; in Gabriel et al., p. 274. Also: *"Deus sit absoluta potentia et actus atque utriusque nexus et deo sit actu omne possibile esse."*

30. ["Uncreated possibility is his very *possest.*" In other words, God is necessarily possible.—Tr.] Nicholas of Cusa, *Trialogus de possest*, in Wilpert, p. 654; in Gabriel et al., pp. 300, 302.

31. Nicholas of Cusa, *Trialogus de possest*, in Wilpert, p. 649; in Gabriel et al., p. 284. See also: *"supra omne nomen quo id, quod potest esse, est nominabile, immo supra ipsum esse et non esse omni modo quo illa intelligi possunt"* (Wilpert, p. 653). Possibility here is exactly equivalent to indifference with regard to the difference between being and nonbeing.

32. Kant, *Critique of Pure Reason*, A290/B346.

33. Aquinas, *Summa Theologica*, bk. 1, q. 25, a. 3, resp.:

> God is called omnipotent because he can do all things that are possible absolutely; which is the second way of saying a thing is possible. For a thing is said to be possible or impossible according to the relation in which the very terms stand to one another [. . .] Therefore, everything that does not imply a contradiction is numbered among those possible things, in respect of which God is omnipotent.

(For Aquinas, see also the *Summa contra Gentiles*, bk. 1, chaps. 22, 25.) This limitation of divine omnipotence to what is logically possible remains Duns Scotus's position:

> Alio modo 'omnipotens' accipitur proprie theologice, prout omnipotens dicitur qui potest in omne effectum et quodcumque possibile (hoc est in quodcumque quod non est ex se necessarium nec includit contradictionem). (*Ordinatio* I, d. 42, n. 9, in *Opera Omnia*, ed. C. Balic, Rome: Vatican Polyglot, 1963, vol. 6, p. 343; and even by way of *potentia absoluta*: see *Ordinatio* I, d. 44, n. 7, p. 365ff.)

And even Ockham's position—see *Quodlibet* III, q. 3; VI, q. 6. On Ockham, see also Philotheus Boehner, *Collected Articles on Ockham*, ed. E. M. Buytaert (New York: Franciscan Institute, 1958), p. 151ff.; as well as the texts translated by Elizabeth Karger in her article "Causalité Divine et Tout-Puissance," in *La puissance et son ombre: de Pierre Lombard à Luther*, ed. O. Boulnois (Paris: Aubier, 1994), pp. 321–356.

34. Malebranche, *Traité de Morale*, bk. 2, pt. 9, chap. 12, in *Oeuvres complètes de Malebranche*, ed. A. Robinet (Paris: Vrin, 1958–1984), vol. 11 (ed. M. Adam, 1966), p. 226.

35. Christian Wolff, *Philosophia prima sive Ontologia* (Frankfurt and Leipzig, 1730), § 79.

36. Descartes, letter to Arnauld of 29 July 1648, in AT 5, pp. 223, 229; see my clarification in J.-L. Marion, *Sur la théologie blanche de Descartes: Analogie, création des vérités éternelles et fondement*, 2nd ed. (Paris: Presses Universitaires, 1991), pp. 296–303.

37. A. G. Baumgarten, *Metaphysica* (Halle, 1739), § 7; in the recent edition (Hildesheim and New York: Olms, 1982), see § 8.

38. Heidegger, *Sein und Zeit*, sect. 7, p. 38.

39. On birth, see some clarifications in J.-L. Marion, *De Surcroît: Etudes sur les phénomènes saturés* (Paris: Presses Universitaires, 2001); in translation as *In Excess: Studies in Saturated Phenomena*, trans. Robyn Horner and Vincent Berraud (New

Jean-Luc Marion

York: Fordham University Press, 2004), p. 49ff.; or see "La raison du don," in *Philosophie* 78 (2003): p. 17ff.

40. *"Para tou Theou,"* following the Nestle-Aland text, in the genitive not the dative: Not only "for him" but "from his standpoint, his side" (*Novum Testamentum Graece et Latine*, 25th ed., ed. E. Nestle and K. Aland, Stuttgart: Württembergische Bibelanstalt, 1967, ad loc.). See, at both extremes: Straek-Billerbeek, who translates *"von vor Gott her"* (*Kommentar zum Neueun Testament*, Munich, 1924, vol. 2, p. 100); and C. Tresmontant, who translates "coming on God's part" (*Evangile de Luc*, Paris, 1987, p. 10). [The Vulgate translates: *"quia non erit impossibile apud Deum omne verbum"*; and the Revised Standard Version gives: "For with God nothing will be impossible."—Tr.]

41. As at Luke 1:42 (cf. Acts 10:37); and see H. Schürmann's remarks in *Das Lukasevangelium* (Freiburg and Vienna: Herder, 1969), p. 57. In contrast, Thomas Aquinas suprisingly reduces the Lucan formula, *"non erit impossibile apud Deum omne verbum"* (Vulgate), to the possible as non-contradictory—*"id enim quod contradictionem implicat verbum esse non potest, quia nullus intellectus potest illud concipere"* (*Summa Theologica*, bk. 1, q. 25, a. 3, resp.)—and therefore lowers divine transcendence to the level of metaphysics as simple omnipotence. He therefore limits it as well by what is possible: *"sub omnipotentia Dei non cadit aliquid quod contradictionem implicat"* (bk. 1, q. 25, a. 4).

42. As also in Mark 14:36: "Abba, O Father, all things are possible with thee."

43. This point is emphasized by J. Reiling and J. L. Swellengrebel: "The future tense, however, is preferable because it shows that the reference is also to what will happen to Mary" (*A Translator's Handbook on the Gospel of Luke*, Leiden: Brill, 1971, p. 62ff.); and also by F. Bovon: *"die futurische Form steht im Rahmen einer Theologie der Hoffnung: Gott wird bald die mögliche Unmóglichkeit verwirklichen"* (*Das Evangelium nach Lukas*, Zurich: Neukirchener, 1989), p. 77ff.

44. Origen, *Contra Celsum*, bk. 5, chaps. 14, 23; in the *Sources Chrétiennes* edition as *Contre Celse*, ed. M. Borret (Paris: Cerf, 1967–1976), vol. 3, pp. 48, 70. A similar answer is given by Gregory of Nazianzius in sections 10 and 11 of his thirtieth theological discourse (*Sources Chrétiennes* no. 250, ed. P. Gallay, Paris: Cerf, 1978, p. 243ff).

45. Augustine, *De Symbolo*, I, 2, PL 40, col. 627. See further,

> sicut nec potestas ejus [sc. dei] minuitur, cum dicitur mori fallique non posse. Sic enim hoc non potest, ut potius, si posset, minoris esset utique potestatis. Recte quippe omnipotens dicitur, qui tamen mori et falli non potest. Dicitur enim omnipotens faciendo quod vult, non patiendo quod non vult; quod ei si accideret, nequaquam esset omnipotens. Unde propterea quaedam non potest, quia omnipotens est. (*De Civitate Dei*, bk. 5, ch. 10, sec. 1; trans. and ed. G. Bardy and G. Combès, Paris: Cerf, 1959, vol. 1, p. 684)

In the same vein, we may note Hugh of St. Victor's effort to redefine a possible of non-ontic order:

> Ergo summe potens est, quia potest omne quod possibile est, nec ideo minus potest, quia impossibilia non potest: impossibilia posse non esset posse, sed non posse. Itaque omnia potest Deus, quae posse potentia est; et ideo vere omnipotens

est, quia impotens esse non potest. (*De Sacramentis christianae fidei*, II, 2, PL 176, col. 216)

Or Aquinas's attempt:

peccare est deficere a prefecta actione; unde posse peccare est posse deficere in agendo, quod repugnat omnipotentiae; et propter hoc Deus non potest peccare, quia est omnipotens. (*Summa Theologica*, bk. 1, q. 25, a. 3)

In any event, we may well doubt whether even a critical redefinition of what in itself is possible would suffice to reach the [im-]possible on God's side.

46. I am following here Jean-Marie Lustiger's remarkable commentary in *La Promesse* (Paris: Parole et Silence, 2002), p. 24ff.

47. Similarly, for men it is more difficult that the heaven and earth pass away, whereas for God this remains "much easier (*eukopōteron*) than that a single dot of the law become void (Luke 16:17)—which is to say of that to which God has committed his Word—therefore concerning Christ and through him. In the law, God literally (practically to the dot) risks his word, and therefore his Word, Christ. He risks his head and his life—which he will in fact lose.

48. V. Jankélévitch, *L'imprescriptible: Pardonner? Dans l'honneur et la dignité*, 2nd ed. (Paris, 1966), p. 43; reprinted as *Pardonner?* (Paris: Le Pavillon, 1971); my italics.

49. Aristotle, *Nicomachean Ethics*, bk. 3, ch. 1, 1110a1ff.

two
Nihilism as
Postmodern Christianity

Gianni Vattimo

Let me begin by clarifying what I mean by nihilism in this essay. I take as a guiding concept the idea of nihilism found in Nietzsche, or, to be more precise, as it is taken up by Heidegger where he defines that process at the end of which there is nothing any longer to Being as such. However, it is not my intention to discuss the lesser or greater "correspondence" between these notions with nihilism as an object. It would go against the ensemble of theses I want to put forth here, as well as against the thought of Nietzsche and Heidegger. Nihilism is not a historical process that could be described objectively in a more or less adequate manner. For even if we take definitions like those found in Nietzsche, such as the devaluation of all supreme values or the history through which in the end, the true world has become a fable, it would be difficult to say whether we are dealing with descriptions that are objective, adequate, or correspondent. In the very use of the term "nihilism," we are already involved in a situation that in turn can only itself be defined as nihilistic. This is not because we are speaking of nihilism, but rather, as would be the case with terms like religiosity, modernity and Christianity, because none of these terms can reasonably evoke, refer to, or describe an "object" in relation to which one might demonstrate their descriptive adequacy. As we all well know, this too can be the beginning point from which we might understand the meaning of Heidegger's or Nietzsche's thought, and ultimately of all those philosophers who have taken seriously the historical experience of truth, ranging from Dilthey to Gadamer and Rorty. For these philosophers it is problematic, and ultimately impossible, to single out an array of objects of which one might speak in a different manner from that characterizing the discourse on entities such as nihilism, religion and Christianity. None of the "objects" which appear to us solid as such within a moderate vision of the difference between the natural and human sciences is ever, truly, an object. And this, ultimately, is already in fact nihilism. It is a "fact"—and the term here is not *Tatsache*, I believe, but rather Vico's *factum*—that we cannot discuss anything unless we have an interest in it, in other words, unless we are involved in the act of interpretation. I shall not elaborate here the reasons why we should not be satisfied with the distinction between natural sciences (which are those that would speak of "objects") and the human sciences (which are those that would speak of facts). It seems to me that as soon as we posit the idea of interpretation, nothing can escape its ambit. This is because clearly the very distinction between the two types of sciences and their respective realms should answer the question, whether it is itself a description or an interpretation. As Nietzsche writes, "There are no facts, only interpretations. And this too is an interpretation. So what?"

The experience we have when considering the implications of this statement is similar to the meaning of the postmodern religiosity that I want to address here. I am aware that the term "postmodern" is no longer as popular as it was two decades ago, when it was at the center of Lyotard's work. The fact that it has run its course, perhaps losing its legitimacy with respect to "the spirit of the times," might provide a valid objection to a rigorously modern perspective. Rimbaud's *"il faut être absolument moderne"* is precisely the precept that characterizes and delimits modernity. Accordingly, the truth is revealed through the progression of time, and whoever wants to be in the truth must conform to the trends of the time. This is not true, as we know, for those who argue that modernity is "over." Naturally even those who think postmodernity, retain the stigma of historicism—it is impossible to move with impunity through modernity, even when one believes one is overcoming it. Consider certain statements by Lyotard in which he expressed the *non plus ultra* of the dissolution of metanarratives. I quote from memory, but the statements can be found in the essay Lyotard wrote for the famous issue of *Critique* about the "Landing in America" of French thought: "Stalinism has undermined Marx, environmental disasters have undermined the optimism of positivism," and so on. What we have here are events that once narrated render impossible, or "deny," certain meta-narratives. Proclaiming the end of modernity is a historicist statement, too, which seems to imply an injunction "to conform" to a new situation. Nonetheless, there is a gap with respect to modernity, and it is very significant: No modern has ever argued that time itself demands a duty to conform. It was only because—during the Enlightenment, but also in Hegel— time proceeded in accordance with a line of affirmation of truth, a truth which Reason already grasped and anticipated, that one had to be modern (though for Hegel this was more problematic than for Enlightenment thinkers). Post-modernism has taken stock of the fact that time does not proceed along a progressive and unitary line. Thus, it is orphan of all rigorous and historical rationality, and it knows only that it must "make do with the tools on board." The dissolution of the modern metanarratives does not push the postmodern back toward absolute metaphysical beliefs—or at least this generally is not the case. Rather, the experience it has of the dissolution of metanarratives opens postmodernism to the understanding of myths, understood not as metaphysi-cal truths, but as myths that cannot be truly denied by any absolute, or meta-narrative, or reason.

Therefore, I would speak of a weak historicism, which knows that it has no other resources outside its (own) history—not History, naturally; but the (his)stories that feed its memory and from which its life as a speaking and conscious being depends.

As one can see from the citation from Lyotard, what "denies" Stalinism, Positivism, and metanarratives more generally are not further metanarratives, but rather events that belong to our collective history. It is not that theories are proven to be false; rather, in situations like those singled out by Lyotard, though I believe more deeply and more globally with the end of colonialism, we can no longer think "metaphysically"—in terms of foundation or progress. Weak historicism is at the same time a "chaotic" historicism, for in the post-colonial world it encounters multiple cultures, truths, and so on. The evidence that there are multiple interpretations makes an awareness of the hermeneutic character of all experience inevitable. Whoever harkens back to Heidegger's philosophy, as I do here, cannot put forth apodictic or logico-metaphysical proofs for his own arguments. He can only make an effort to "conform, or correspond, to the event." This means appealing to experience—understood not in abstract empiricist terms as the "data" of sensations, but as what appears to us "naturally" as the most reasonable (perhaps "obvious") interpretation of the situation in which we find ourselves. Now, the argument of those who speak of postmodernism is that this situation, which we all share insofar as we live in this historical world (in the geographic space of the West), can be characterized as the loss of a center, the devaluation of absolute values, the dissolution of Being as stability of principles both unquestioned and unques-tionable. This is because now more than at any time in the past, many cultures openly clash with one another in this world to defend their validity, mostly in definitive and human terms in their most essential meanings. However, the openness with which these horizons clash, and the awareness by now achieved (certainly in the postcolonial West) of the relationship (if not identity) between absolute principles and dominant power, renders the experience of plurality inevitable for thought. Accordingly, it is also impossible to maintain an absolute, "strong" concept of Being and of its putatively eternal structures. One thought that comes to mind whenever I ponder on the relation between these phenomena and religion—and more specifically my own, Roman Catholic religion—is the following: Whenever he meets the Dalai Lama or any other representative of a non-Christian religion, does the Pope really believe that the poor fellow is condemned to hell, since he has not converted to Roman Christianity? Does he preach to them on the necessity of embracing the Faith of Jesus, the Apostles, and their successors? None of us thinks so. But this means that we no longer live in a world united by "objective" Truths, and that even the Pope—implicitly, and especially without revealing it too clearly to the faithful—takes cognizance of the fact that we have entered postmodernity, where "it is no longer possible" to act as in the past even in matters of religion, as the Church itself would like to continue doing today (I am thinking of the continuous attempts to intervene in state laws, especially in Italy, on matters of Catholic morality, which only the Church identifies with "natural" morality).

What is the religious element in this "loss of center," in the devaluation of supreme values, and in the exhaustion of objectivity and absoluteness of first principles? At a very simple level, I believe we can say, from a Christian point of view, that Jesus Christ has freed us from the Truth. This liberation is also a liberation of religiosity more generally, which is the only way—I am not aware of others—in which religious experience can have meaning. If I name Jesus Christ, it is clear that I speak from the point of view of Christianity. But this is not a preference at the expense of other religions. Having freed us from "objective" Truth (that is to say, as Heidegger would say, from metaphysics) Jesus Christ has freed all religious experiences also—thereby reducing himself (reducing Christianity itself) and all these other religions to their basic essence. The Christian tradition knows well the idea that Charity matters above all else. Saint Augustine—so harsh and sometimes fanatical in other texts—is right when he writes: "*Ama et quod vis fac.*" Love and do what you want. And then: "Love God above all things and your neighbor as yourself"; and, "Whenever two or three of you gather in my name (in charity) I am present in your midst." In the postmodern condition of the end of metaphysics, it has become possible to experience concretely this reduction of the "religious" to its "essence." To be sure, I am well aware of the suspicion with which twentieth-century theology (i.e., Karl Barth) has viewed the notion of "religion," considering it too natural to have anything to do with God. Different but analogous reasons are behind René Girard's powerful critique of sacrificial religion, whose violence was revealed precisely by Jesus' preaching. These critical perspectives and the reasons that sustain them should prevent us from considering our religious experience as the ultimately authentic one, freed from all historical limitation —no longer *per speculum et in ænigmate*, but face-to-face. We may only hope

Gianni Vattimo

that the Babel of postmodernity, the end of metaphysics, the dissolution of Being, and nihilism are not just expressions of our historical limitations, but also of our specific calling. For hermeneutics, after all, historical limit and a specific calling toward an experience of "truth" are identical: There "is" no object which our historical perspective might prevent us from viewing in its entirety. Here a statement comes to mind from Dietrich Bonhoeffer, which after all inspires my entire argument: *"Einen Gott den es gibt, gibt es nicht."* "A God who is, is not."

This citation, perhaps, suffices to express the extent to which nihilism is decisive for any possible religious experience. Bonhoeffer was able to write this statement, and we can accept it, without thereby professing any form of atheism, precisely because we live in a postmodern condition—with all that is problematic in this "description" of our situation. (But isn't the "experience" to which empiricists and even positivists often appeal even more vague?).

I am not therefore arguing that postmodern nihilism opens the way to an authentic religiosity, finally uncovered in its true essence. Rather, my thesis is that nihilism is the (most likely, probable) form of religiosity of our epoch, to the extent that it can be called a postmodern one. True, if I speak of religiosity, then I should also specify what this term means.

Here we would need to open a long discussion that would have to recover Schleiermacher as well as the most radical enemy of liberal theology, Karl Barth, in a context that, I believe, does not betray one or the other. Religiosity can be defined only in Schleiermacher's terms, as the pure feeling of absolute dependence on an infinitude, which obviously does not allow itself to be defined in positive or metaphysical terms. Insofar as this feeling is "pure," perhaps—even beyond the intentions of these authors—it can contain all the "negativity" of twentieth-century dialectical philosophy, thus being not very far removed from Barth. Perhaps it can be found especially in Bonhoeffer's statement cited above. A "nihilistic" religiosity thus conceived is not an inert religiosity, or a lazy one that might be open to all compromise. As Nietzsche often said, nihilism actively works toward the destruction of those values that must be *um-wertet*. Nihilism's religious man works actively to destroy idols following Jesus' teaching, according to whom every time someone comes to tell us "here is the Messiah, or there He is," we must not believe him (Matthew 23:25–26). St. Paul's statement, *"per speculum et in ænigmate"* (1 Corinthians 13:12, Vulgate), should be understood more in a negative than in a positive sense. We do not see God so much in things, but rather we experience him in mirrors that always reveal enigmas which cannot be solved and which lead us astray. To be sure, this also makes problematic the "positive" aspects of Christianity—namely, its institutional expression in Churches, dogmas, authorities, and disciplines. But might not these very complexities—or even more, an active contestation of institutions, dogmas, and Churches—be what Christianity needs today?

48

PART 2. RE-IMAGINING TRADITIONAL TRANSCENDENCE

Re-imagining God

three

Richard Kearney

I come in the little things, saith the Lord
—Evelyn Underhill

God, if God exists, exists not just for God but for us. And the manner in which God comes to us, comes to mind, comes to be and to dwell as flesh amongst us, is deeply informed by the manner in which we think about God— in short, how we interpret, narrate and imagine God. This, I suggest, calls for a philosophical hermeneutics instructed by the various and essential ways in which God "appears" to us in and through "phenomena," and "signals" to us in and through "signs." It is my wager in this essay that one of the most telling ways in which the infinite comes to be experienced and imagined by finite minds is as *possibility*—that is, as *the ability to be*. Even, and especially, when such possibility seems impossible to us.

But let us be clear from the outset: I am not saying this is the only way, or even the most primordial way—just that it is a very telling way, and one which has been largely neglected in the history of western metaphysics and theology in favor of categories like substance, cause, actuality, omnipotence, absolute spirit, or sufficient reason. So I am not proposing *posse* as some newly dis-covered (or recovered) Master Word—some extraordinary Meta-Code which might unlock the ancient Secret of divine nature or naming. God forbid! Our proposal is far more modest than that—namely, a tentative exercise in poetic conjecture about a certain overlooked aspect of divinity, seeking guidance on the way from phenomenological description and hermeneutic interpretation.

I will proceed by means of three concentric circles—*scriptural, testimonial* and *literary*. Traversing this threefold "variation of imagination," I hope to identify some key characteristics of the God of the possible as it reveals itself to us poetically.

The Scriptural Circle

My efforts to rethink God as *posse* draw primarily from the biblical message that what is impossible for us is possible for God. This latter notion of messianic possibility is evident in many Scriptural passages. In Mark 10, for example, we are told that while entry to the Kingdom seems impossible for humans, all things are made possible by God. The exact text reads: "For humans it is impossible but not for God; because for God everything is possible (*panta gar dunata para tōi Theōi*)" (Mark 10:27). In similar vein, we are told in St. John's prologue that our ability to become sons of God in the Kingdom is something made possible by God: "Light shone in darkness and to all who received it was given the possibility (*dunamis*) to become sons of God." The term *dunamis* is crucial and can be translated either as power or possibility—a semantic ambivalence to which we shall return below. Further evocations of the possibilizing power (*dunamis pneumatos*) of the Spirit are evidenced in Paul's letters to the Corinthians and Romans; but perhaps most dramatically of all in the Annunciation scene where Mary is told by the angel that the *dunamis* of God will overshadow her, and that she will bear the son of God—"for nothing is impossible (*adunatēsei*) with God" (Luke 1:35–37).

In all these examples, divinity—as Father, Son, or Spirit—is described as a possibilizing of divine love and logos in the order of human history where it would otherwise have been impossible. In other words, the divine reveals itself here as the possibility of the Kingdom—or if you prefer to cite a *via negativa*, as the *impossibility of impossibility*.

A hermeneutical poetics of the kingdom looks to some of the recurring *figures*—metaphors, parables, images, symbols—deployed in the gospels to communicate the eschatological promise. The first thing one notes is that these figures almost invariably refer to a God of "small things"—to borrow from the wonderful title of Arundhati Roy's novel. Not only do we have the association of the Kingdom with the vulnerable openness and trust of "little children," as in the Mark 10 passage cited above (vv. 13–16); but we also have the images of the yeast in the flour (Luke 13:20–21), the tiny pearl of invaluable price (Matthew 13:45–46), and perhaps most suggestive and telling of all, that of the mustard seed (Mark 4:30–32)—a minuscule grain that blooms and flourishes into a capacious tree. The kingdom of God, this last text tells us, is "like a mustard seed that, when it is sown in the ground, is the smallest of all the seeds on the earth. But once it is sown, it springs up and becomes the largest of plants and puts forth large branches, so that the birds of the sky can dwell in its shade."

One might be tempted to call this recurring motif of the kingdom as the last or least or littlest of things—a *microtheology* to the extent that it resists the standard macrotheology of the Kingdom as emblem of sovereignty, omnipotence and ecclesiastical triumph. The frequent reference in the gospels to the judgment of the Kingdom being related to how we respond in history, here and now, to the "least of these," *elakhistōn*, is crucial (e.g., Matthew 25:40). The loving renunciation of absolute power by Christ's emptying (*kenōsis*) of the Godhead, so as to assume the most humble form of humanity (the last and least of beings), is echoed by the eschatological reminder that it is easier for the defenseless and powerless to enter the Kingdom than the rich and mighty. And I think it is telling—as Dostoevsky reminds us in the Grand Inquisitor episode of the *Brothers Karamazov*—that the greatest temptation that Christ must overcome, after his forty days in the desert, is the will to become master and possessor of the universe. This is a temptation he faces again and again right up to his transfiguration on Mt. Tabor, when his disciples want to apotheosize and crown him by building a cult temple there on the mountain (Luke 9). Instead, Christ proceeds to a second kenotic act of giving, refusing the short route to immediate triumph and embracing the *via crucis* which demonstrates what it means for the seed to die before it is reborn as a flowering tree which hosts all living creatures. As "King," he enters Jerusalem not with conquering armies but "seated upon an ass's colt" (John 12). He upturns the inherited hierarchies of power, fulfilling the prophecy of Isaiah that he would bring justice to the world, not by "shouting aloud in the street," but as a "bruised reed" that will not break, and "a smoldering wick" that will not quench (Isaiah 42:1–4).

But in addition to these *spatial* metaphors of the Kingdom exemplified by little things—yeast, a mustard seed, a pearl, a reed, an infant, the "least of these"—a hermeneutic poetics of the Kingdom might also look to the *temporal* figures of eschatology. These invariably take the form of a certain *achronicity*. I am thinking here of the numerous references to the fact that even though the Kingdom has *already come*—and is incarnate *here and now* in the loving gestures of Christ and all those who give, or receive, a cup of water—it still always remains a possibility *yet to come*. This is what Emanuel Levinas calls the "paradox of posterior anteriority"; and it is cogently illustrated in an aphorism of Walter Benjamin which combines the spatial figure of the portal with the eschatological figure of futurity: "This future does not correspond to homogenous empty time; because at the heart of every moment of the future is contained the little door through which the Messiah may enter."[1]

As "eternal," the kingdom transcends all chronologies of time. Christ indicates this when he affirms that "before Abraham was, I am" (John 8:58), and when he promises a Second Coming when he will return again. In short, the Kingdom is: (1) *already* there as historical possibility, and (2) *not yet* there as historically realized kingdom "come on earth." This is why we choose to translate the canonical theophany to Moses on Mt. Sinai (*esher ayeh esher*), not as "I am who am" (*ego sum qui sum*), but as "I am who may be" (Exodus 3:14). God is saying something like this: I will show up as promised, but I cannot *be* in time and history, I cannot become fully embodied in the flesh of the world, unless you show up and answer my call "Where are you?" with the response "Here I am." (I explore this eschatological enigma of time in further detail in my concluding remarks, below.)

The Testimonial Circle

Our second hermeneutic circle explores a poetics of the Kingdom in light of a number of religious writers down through the ages, in what we might call the *testimonial* or *confessional* genre. Unlike "metaphysical" thinkers who presuppose an ontological priority of actuality over possibility, these more "poetical" minds reverse the traditional priority and point to a new category of possibility —divine possibility—*beyond* the traditional opposition between the possible and the impossible.

Let me begin with the pregnant maxim of Angelus Silesius: "God is possible as the more than impossible." Here Silesius—a German mystical thinker often cited by Heidegger and Derrida—points toward an eschatological notion of possibility which might be said to transcend the three conventional concepts of the possible as: (1) an epistemological category of modal logic, along with necessity and actuality (Kant); (2) a substantialist category of *potentia* that lacks its fulfillment as *actus* (Aristotle, the scholastics); and (3) a rationalist category of *possibilitas* conceived as a representation of the mind (Leibniz, the idealists). All such categories fall within the old metaphysical dualism of possibility versus impossibility. But Silesius intimates a new role for the possible as a ludic and liberal outpouring of divine play:

> God is possible as the more than impossible . . .
> God plays with Creation
> All that is play that the deity gives itself
> It has imagined the creature for its pleasure.

Creation here is depicted as an endless giving of possibility which calls us toward the Kingdom.

I think the early medieval Jewish commentator, Rashi, also had something like this in mind when he interprets Isaiah's God calling to his creatures —"I cannot be God unless you are my witnesses." He takes this to mean: "I am the God who will be whenever you bear witness to love and justice in the world."[2] And I believe that the Holocaust victim Etty Hillesum was gesturing toward a similar notion when, just weeks before her death in a concentration camp, she wrote: "You God cannot help us but we must help you and defend your dwelling place inside us to the last."[3] Both Rashi and Hillesum were witnessing to the *dunamis* of God as *the power of the powerless*. This, clearly, is not the imperial power of a sovereign; it is a dynamic call to love which possibilizes and enables humans to transform their world—by giving itself to the "least of these," by empathizing with the disinherited and the dispossessed, by refusing the path of might and violence, by transfiguring the mustard seed into the kingdom, each moment at a time, one act after an other, each step of the way. This is the path heralded by the Pauline God of "nothings and nobodies" (*ta mē onta*) excluded from the triumphal preeminence of totality (*ta onta*)—a kenotic, self-emptying, crucified God whose "weakness is stronger than human strength" (1 Corinthians 1:25, 28). It signals the option for the poor, for nonviolent resistance and revolution taken by peacemakers and dissenting "holy fools" from ancient to modern times. It is the message of suffering rather than doing evil, of loving one's adversaries, of "no enemies," of "soul force" (*satyāgraha*). One thinks of a long heritage ranging from Isaiah, Jesus, Siddhartha and Socrates, to such contemporary figures as Gandhi, Vaclav Havel, Dorothy Day, Jean Vanier, Ernesto Cardenal, Tich Nhat Hahn and Martin Luther King. The God witnessed here goes beyond the will-to-power.

Nicholas of Cusa offers some interesting insights into this eschatological God when he declares that "God alone is all he is able to be."[4] Unlike the God of metaphysical omnipotence, underlying the perverse logic of theodicy which seeks to justify evil as part of the divine will, this notion of God as an "abling to be" (*posse* or *possest*) points in a radically different direction. Let us pause for a moment to unpack the phrase, "God is all he is able to be." Since God is all good, God is not able to be non-good—that is, non-God—defective or evil. In other words, God is *not* omnipotent in the traditional metaphysical sense understood by Leibniz and Hegel. The Divine is not some being able to be all good *and* evil things. That is why God could not help Etty Hillesum and other victims of the Holocaust: God is not responsible for evil. And Hillesum understood this all too well when she turned the old hierarchies on their head and declared that it is *we* who must help God to be God.

Was Hillesum not in fact subscribing here to a long—if often neglected—biblical heritage? After all, if Elijah had not heard the "still small voice" of God in his cave, we would never have received the wisdom of his prophecy. If a young woman from Nazareth had said "no" to the angel of the Annunciation, the Word would not have become Flesh. If certain fishermen, tax collectors and prostitutes had not heard the call to follow the Son of Man, there would have been no Son of God—and no Gospel witness. So too, if Hillesum and others like her had not let God be God by defending the divine dwelling-place of *caritas* within them, even in the most hellish moments of the death-camps, there would have been no measure of love—albeit tiny as the mustard seed—to defy the hate of the Gestapo. For if God's loving is indeed unconditional, the realization of that loving *posse* in this world is conditional upon our response. If we are waiting for God, God is waiting for us. Waiting for us to say "yes"—to hear the call and to act, to bear witness, to answer the *posse* with *esse*, to make the word flesh—even in the darkest moments.

I think Dionysius the Areopagite could be said to add to our understanding of this great enigma when he speaks, in book 7 of the *Divine Names*, of a "possibility beyond being" (*huperousias dunameos*) which engenders our desire to live more abundantly and seek the good. "Being itself," he writes, "only has the possibility to be from the possibility beyond being." And he adds that it is "from the infinitely good *posse* (*dunamis*) of what it sends to them (that) they have received their power (*dunamis*)."[5] I am tempted to relate this notion of an infinitely good possibilizing of God to another extraordinary passage in the *Divine Names*—this time book 9, section 3—where Dionysius writes of the God of little things:

> God is said to be small as leaving every mass and distance behind and proceeding unhindered through all. Indeed the small is the cause of all the elements, for you will find none of these that have not participated in the form of smallness. Thus, smallness is to be interpreted with respect to God as its wandering and operating in all and through all without hindrance "penetrating down to the division of the soul, spirit, joint and marrow," and discerning thoughts and "intentions of the heart," and indeed of all beings. "For there is no creation which is invisible to its face" (Hebrews 4:12). This smallness is without quantity, without quality, without restraint, unlimited, undefined, and all embracing although it is unembraced.[6]

Is this extraordinary passage by Dionysius not a passionate invitation to embrace a microtheology of the Kingdom? Is it not a solicitation to embrace an eschatology of little things—mustard seeds, grains of yeast, tiny pearls, cups of water, infinitesimal everyday acts of love and witness? It appears so.

Moreover, I think it is just this kind of microtheology that Gerard Manley Hopkins had in mind in "Pied Beauty." He records God's grace in small and scattered epiphanies of the quotidian when he speaks of "dappled things" from "finches' wings" and "rose-moles all in stipple upon trout that swim," to

> All things counter, original, spare, strange;
> Whatever is fickle, freckled (who knows how?)

For Hopkins, it is not the mighty and triumphant monarch that epitomizes the pearl of the Kingdom ("immortal diamond") but, contrariwise, the court fool, the joker in the pack, the least and last of these. Here is Hopkins's take on the eschatological kingdom:

> In a flash, at a trumpet crash,
> I am all at once what Christ is, since he was what I am, and
> This Jack, joke, poor potsherd, patch, matchwood, immortal diamond,
>   Is immortal diamond.

Hopkins's deity is one of transfiguration rather than coercion, of *posse* rather than power, of little rather than large things.[7] But in our shift of registers from theology to poetry we are already embarking on our next circle of readings.

The Literary Circle

In our third and final hermeneutic circle—the *literary*—I include a number of passages which offer more explicitly poetic epiphanies of the possible. This amplification of our investigation to embrace a literary poetics extends the range of reference to take in soundings of *posse* which transcend the confessional limits of theism or atheism, enjoying as they do a special liberty of imagination—a poetic license to entertain an unlimited variation of experience. As Emily Dickenson rightly observed, "possibility is a fuse lit by imagination," a belief which informs her imaging of the eschatological possible.

Rabelais had his eye on a similar paradise when he affirmed the possibility of life through death, yea-saying to his last moments as he jubilantly declared: "*J'avance vers le grand possible!*" In his remarkable novel, *A Man without Qualities*, the Austrian writer Robert Musil offers a further perspective on the eschatological *posse* when he claims that "possibility is the dormant design of God in man"—a design waiting to be awakened by our poetic dwelling in the world. Our true vocation in history, for Musil, is one of utopian invention. It involves an audacious surpassing of given reality toward imagined possibility. Here is the passage in full:

> One might define the meaning of the possible as the faculty of thinking all that *might be* just as much as what is . . . The implications of such a creative disposition are huge . . . The possible consists of much more than the dreams of neurasthenics; it also involves the still dormant plans of God. A possible event or truth is not just the real event or truth minus the 'reality'; rather it signals something very divine, a flame, a burning, a will to construct a utopia which, far from fearing reality, treats it simply as a perpetual task and invention. The earth is not so spent, after all, and never has it seemed so fascinating.[8]

The metaphor of fire—with its allusions to both the burning bush and the Pentecostal flame of speaking tongues—is also explored by Wallace Stevens in a poem addressed to George Santayana entitled, "To an Old Philosopher in Rome." Here again the correspondence between the simple (indigent, small, inconsequential) and the eschatological (the Kingdom) is conveyed by the figure of a candle flame which illumines the real in the light of the "celestial possible." The pneumatological call to speak in tongues commits itself here to a poetics of the poor and unremembered.

But it is doubtless Rainer Maria Rilke who composes one of the most inspiring invocations of the gracious power of *posse*, in the conclusion to his

Letters to a Young Poet. Here the eschatological promise of a coming God is combined with the erotic expectancy of a waiting lover. He asks his youthful correspondent,

> Why don't you think of him [God] as the one who is coming, one who has been approaching from all eternity, the one who will someday arrive, the ultimate fruit of a tree whose leaves we are? What keeps you from projecting his birth into the ages that are coming into existence, and living your life as a painful and lovely day in the history of a great pregnancy? Don't you see how everything that happens is again and again a beginning, and couldn't it be *His* [God's] beginning, since, in itself, starting is always so beautiful?

Then Rilke poses this crucial question:

> If he is the most perfect one, must not what is less perfect *precede* him, so that he can choose himself out of fullness and superabundance?—Must not *he* be the last one, so that he can include everything in himself, and what meaning would we have if he whom we are longing for has already existed? As bees gather honey, so we collect what is sweetest out of all things and build Him.

Rilke ends this remarkable passage with a call to vigilant attention and expectancy. Messianism at its best. The metaphor of the flowering, flourishing mustard seed is brought to a new poetic intensity. "Be patient," he counsels the young poet, "and realize that the least we can do is to make coming into existence no more difficult for Him [God] than the earth does for spring when it wants to come."[9]

Here we might look to the "pregnant sense of the possible" in Kierkegaard —the interweaving of the divine and the human in patient prayer and longing. And this eschatological desire, as Rilke vividly reminds us, is not confined to human existence but involves, by extension, the entire expanse of the terrestrial universe as it awaits, yearns and prepares itself for the coming *prima vera*.

My daughter, who brought this Rilke passage to my attention, told me this was a God she could believe in! Could I object?

* * *

So much depends, then, on what we mean by the *possible*. If one defines possibility according to established convention as a category of modal logic or metaphysical calculus—then God is closer to the impossible than the possible. But if one seeks, as I do, to reinterpret the possible as eschatological *posse*, from a postmetaphysical poetical perspective, the stakes are very different. For now we are talking of a *second* possible (analogous to Ricoeur's "second naïveté") *beyond* the impossible, *otherwise* than impossible, *more* than impossible, at the *other side* of the old modal opposition between the possible and the impossible. And here we find ourselves closer to the Kierkegaard's "passion for the possible" as the portal to faith.

I think it is crucial to recall, here, the telling distinction between two competing translations of the Greek term *dunamis*. On the one hand, we have the metaphysical rendering of the term as *potestas/potentia*, that is, as a potency understood in terms of an economy of power, causality, substance—what Levinas calls the economy of the Same (or Totality). On the other hand, we have an eschatological rendering of *dunamis* as *posse/possest*, that is, as a gracious and gratuitous giving which possibilizes love and justice in this world. It is this later interpretation of *dunamis* that I have been seeking to promote in my three hermeneutic detours through the poetics of the possible (and, in more depth and detail in *The God Who May Be*, Bloomington: Indiana University Press, 2001).

In triumphalist accounts of the Kingdom, the advent of the Messiah on the last day is often described in militaristic terms—as sublimely apocalyptic rather than lovingly vulnerable, as almighty rather than solicitous, as coercive rather than caring. By contrast, the divine *posse* I am sponsoring here is more healing than judgmental, more disposed to accept "the least of these" than to meet out punishment and glory. If God can prevent evil from happening by recreating the historical past, as a theologian like Peter Damian once suggested, He is by implication a God of theodicy—namely, a God who has the power to decide whether history unfolds as good or evil. To me, this sounds like *potestas* rather than *posse*. A far cry from the divine power of the powerless Etty Hillesum invokes, when she summons us to help God to be God in the face of violence and war. A world away from the God of little things.

Sometimes I have been asked what would happen to the God of the Possible if we were to destroy the earth? How can God's promise of a kingdom on earth be fulfilled if there is no earth to come back to? What might be said of the existence of God in such a scenario? There are a few observations I would like to make here by way of conclusion, surmises which claim the poetic license of a free imaginative variation!

First, I would say that as eternally perduring and constant (that is, as faithful and attentive to us in each *present moment*), God would live on as an endless *promise* of love and justice. This would be so even if we fail or frustrate this covenant by denying its potential for historical fulfillment *on earth*. In this case, God would be like a spouse abandoned by a spouse—to take up the bride/bridegroom analogy from the Song of Songs. A lover forsaken. Or to borrow a metaphor from Hildegard of Bingen, the *posse* would be like a tree deprived of its greening (*viriditas*).[10] If denied its ultimate incarnation in the last days, the possible God would be like a flowering seed arrested before it could come to its full flourishing and fruition on the earth. It would still be *adventurus,* but no longer *futurus.* The divine advent would be deprived of an historical, human future but would remain, in each moment, enduringly faithful in spite of all. It would still be a "yes" in the face of our "no."

Second, as eternal *memory* (past), the divine *posse* would preserve all those eschatological "moments" from the past where the divine was incarnated in the flesh of the world every time (as Christ and Isaiah taught) someone gave a cup of cold water to someone else. In kairological as opposed to merely chronological time, these instants would be eternally "repeated" in divine remembrance. This would mark a revaluation of a line from Shakespeare's *Julius Caesar,* such that the good that men do lives after them—the evil is interred with their bones. It would be in keeping with the repeated assurances of the biblical deity to remember the faithful who lived and died in history, for example: "Can a mother forget her infant, be without tenderness for the child of her womb? Even should she forget, I will never forget you" (Isaiah 49:14–15). And it would also be consonant with the contrary commitment to erase the memory of evil: "The Lord is close to the broken hearted / The Lord confronts the evildoers / To destroy remembrance of them from the earth" (Psalms 34:16–19). There is then a deeply eschatological character to the biblical injunction to "remember" (*zakhor*). And this character is what translates God's mindfulness of creatures into a form of "anticipatory memory" (the term is Herbert Marcuse's) which preserves a future for the past. As Psalm 105 tells us, "He remembers forever his covenant / which he made binding for a thousand generations / which he entered into with Abraham" (vv. 8–9). In other words, the promise made at the beginning of time is kept by the divine *posse* as an "eternal" remembrance of both the historical past and present right up to the parousia.

Thirdly and finally then, qua eternal *advent* (future), we might say that even though world annihilation would have deprived the divine *posse* of its future realization as a kingdom *come on earth,* we could not, by such an act of self-destruction, deprive God of the possibility of starting over again. Nothing *good* is impossible to God; and rebirth in the face of death is good. As in any nuptial promise or pledge, each partner can speak for him/herself only: God can only promise for God, not for us. We are entirely free to break off *our* part of the promise at any time. And if we do, if we engage in collective self-destruction (God forbid!), why should God not have a "second chance"? Is not *posse,* after all, the possibility of endless beginning?

Of course, the *posse* of the Kingdom is not just a promise for humanity as a universal community (to be reassembled as the mystical body of Christ on the last day, according to the patristic notion of *anakephalaoisis,* recapitulation). *Posse* is also and equally a promise for each unique self whose singular good, but not evil, will be preserved eternally in the recollection of the *deus adventurus*—like each glistening speck of dust in a comet's tail or each glint of plankton in the nocturnal wake of a ship. But if we destroy the earth we also refuse the possibility of each of these recollected and resurrected selves returning to a "new heaven as new earth" on the last day. Such selves would return with *posse*—as part of the eternal promise—but without the *esse* of a Second Coming.

Several of the above remarks and conjectures find textual support, I believe, in the "Palestinian formula" of eschatological memory (*eis anamnēsin*) prevalent in late Jewish and early Christian literature. The formula finds one of its earliest inscriptions in psalm 112, "the righteous will be for eternal remembrance" (v. 6); and again in psalms 37 and 69, where the memory of God refers not just to creatures remembering their Creator in rituals and liturgies, but also to the Creator recalling creatures, making the past present before God in a sort of eternal re-presentation which endures into the future and beyond. Likewise in Ecclesiasticus we find the repeated prayer that God might mercifully remember his children. As the biblical commentator, Joachim Jeremias, observes, such remembrance is an

> effecting and creating event which is constantly fulfilling the eschatological covenant promise . . . When the sinner "is not to be remembered" at the resurrection, this means that he will have no part in it (Ps. Sol. 3.11). And when God no longer remembers sin, he forgets it (Jer. 31.34; Heb. 8.12; 10.17), this means that he forgives it. God's remembrance is always an action in mercy or judgment.[11]

The notion of eschatological memory is, as noted, also frequently witnessed in New Testament literature where it takes the form of a double "repetition"—looking to past and future simultaneously. In the Eucharistic formula— "do this in remembrance of me, *eis tēn emēn anamnēsin*" (Luke 22:19 = 1 Corinthians 11:24)—the proper translation of the repetition-injunction, in keeping with the Palestinian memorial formula, is this: "Do this so that God may remember me."[12] The appeal to divine memory during the Eucharistic sharing of bread and wine may be seen accordingly as an echo of the third benediction of the grace after Passover meal, which asks *God to remember the Messiah*—a benediction which is followed in turn with a petition for "the remembrance of all thy people": "May their remembrance come before thee, for rescue, goodness . . ."[13] The remembrance of past suffering is thus tied to the hope for the advent of the parousia—for Jews the entry of the Messiah to Jerusalem; for Christians the return of Christ on the last day. The petition for repetition—in the *kairological* rather than *chronological* sense—may be translated as: "God remembers the Messiah in that he causes the kingdom to break in by the parousia."[14]

This allusion to a bilateral temporality whereby divine memory recalls the *past as future*, is further evidenced in Paul's gloss on the Eucharistic remembrance formula: "For as often as you eat this bread and drink this cup, you proclaim the Lord's death *until he comes, akhri ou elthēi*" (1 Corinthians 11:23–26). Indeed the use of the subjunctive term *akhri* refers often in the

New Testament to the arrival of the eschaton (Romans 11:25; 1 Corinthians 15:26; Luke 21:24). The crucial phrase here—"until he comes"—may thus be read in light of the liturgical *maranatha* (Come, Lord!) invoked by the faithful in their prayers for the coming of God. So rather than remembering the death of God as no more than a historical event of the past, the remembrance formula can be said to celebrate it as an eschatological advent—that is, as the inauguration of a New Covenant.

> This proclamation expresses the vicarious death of Jesus as the beginning of the salvation time and prays for the coming of the consummation. As often as the death of the Lord is proclaimed at the Lord's supper, and the *maranatha* rises upwards, God is reminded of the unfulfilled climax of the work of salvation until [the goal is reached, that] he comes. Paul has therefore understood the *anamnēsis* as the eschatological remembrance of God that is to be realized in the *parousia*.[15]

It is with this in mind that Luke speaks of the eschatological jubilation and "gladness" (*agalliasis*) which characterizes the mealtimes of the earliest Christian communities (Acts 2:46).

In sum, the close rapport between the Eucharistic request for repetition and the Passover ritual, suggest that for both Judaism and Christianity the Kingdom advent is construed as a *retrieval-forward of the past as future*. The remembrance formula might be interpreted accordingly as something like this: "Keep gathering together in remembrance of me so that I will remember you by keeping my promise to bring about the consummation of love, justice and joy in the parousia. Help me to be God!" Or as the Coptic version of the formula goes: "May the Lord come . . . If any man is holy, let him come. *Maranatha*. Amen."

The above conjectures operate, for the most part, in the realm of hermeneutical poetics which enjoys a certain imaginative liberty vis-à-vis the strictures of theological dogma, speculative metaphysics and empirical physics. Though, I hasten to add, a fruitful dialogue remains open with all three disciplines.

Let me end with a final eschatological image from the poetics of the Kingdom—the invitation to the feast. "I stand at the door and knock, says the Lord. If anyone hears my voice and opens the door, I will come in and sit down to supper with him, and he with me." The great thing about this promise of an eschatological banquet is that no one is excluded. The Post-God of *posse* knocks not just twice but a thousand times—nay, infinitely, ceaselessly—until there is no door unopened, no creature, however small or inconsequential, left out in the cold, hungry, thirsty, uncared for, unloved, unredeemed. The Post-God keeps knocking and calling and delivering the word until we open ourselves to the message and the letter becomes spirit, the word flesh. And what is this message? An invitation to the Kingdom. And what is the Kingdom? The

Kingdom is a cup of cold water given to the least of these, it is bread and fishes and wine given to the famished and un-housed, a good meal and (we are promised) one hell of a good time lasting into the early hours of the morning. A morning that never ends.

NOTES

1. Walter Benjamin, "Theologico-Political Fragment" (1921), in *One Way Street* (London: New Left, 1979), p. 155f.

2. *The Torah: With Rashi's Commentary* (New York: Mesorah, 1997). It would be interesting to relate Rashi's rabbinic interpretation with Isaac Luria's kabbalist reading of God in terms of a generous withholding, or "withdrawal" (*zimzum*), which invites human creatures to subsequently retrieve and reanimate the fragments of the "broken vessels" of divine love which lie scattered like tiny seeds throughout the created universe. This reading, which exerted a deep influence on Hassidic thinkers as well as on philosophers like Simone Weil, seems to confirm my account of God's refusal to impose himself on creation—as some kind of omnipotent fulfilled being (*Ipsum Esse subsistens*), Sufficient Reason, or Supreme Cause (*ens causa sui*)—preferring to relate to humans in the realm of the "possible," rather than the purely "actual" or "necessary." I am grateful to my Boston College colleague, Marty Cohen, for bringing the insights of the Lurianic kabbalah to my attention; see in particular his article "Sarach's Harp," *Parabola* 22/3: pp. 38–41.

3. Etty Hillesum, *An Interrupted Life* (New York: Owl, 1996), p. 176.

4. Nicholas of Cusa, *Trialogus de Possest*, in J. Hopkins, *A Concise Introduction to the Philosophy of Nicholas of Cusa* (Minneapolis: University of Minnesota Press, 1978), p. 69. The original Latin is: *Deus est omne id quod esse potest.*

5. Pseudo-Dionysius the Areopagite, *The Divine Names and Mystical Theology*, trans. J. D. Jones (Milwaukee: Marquette University Press, 1980), p. 182.

6. Ibid., p. 188. For a further exploration of the link between negative theology and micro-eschatology, see Stanislas Breton, *The Word and the Cross*, trans. Jacquelyn Porter (New York: Fordham University Press, 2002), pp. 8–11, 49–50, 60–70, 80–91, 112–114. See in particular Breton's radical claim that we must give to God the being he has not, qua thirsting, kenotic, crucified stranger (pp. 121–122). The *dunamis* of God is here identified with the *germen nihili* or "power of nothing" which reveals itself as a "double nothingness" and powerlessness which liberates those oppressed by the power of *ta onta*, sowing the seed of nonbeing epitomized by the Beatitudes so that the eschatological tree of love and justice may flower and flourish (pp. 80–84, xxiv–xxvi). For it is in and as a "seed of nonbeing" that, in Eckhart's resonant phrase, "God becomes verdant in all the honor of his being" (cit. p. 80). (See also here Hildegard of Bingen's notion of divine "greening" or *viriditas*, n. 9, below.) A more postmodern take on this notion of a micro-eschatology is hinted at by Slavoj Žižek in *Fragile Absolute, or, Why Is the Christian Legacy Worth Fighting For?* He writes, "The ultimate mystery of love is that incompleteness is a way *higher than completion* . . . Perhaps the true achievement of Christianity is to elevate a loving (imperfect) Being to the place of God—that is, of ultimate perfection" (emphasis in original; London: Verso, 2000, pp. 146–147).

7. The lines are from Hopkins's poem "That Nature Is a Heraclitean Fire, and of

the Comfort of the Resurrection"; see the illuminating reading of Hopkins in Mark Patrick Hederman, *Anchoring the Altar: Christianity and the Work of Art* (Dublin: Veritas, 2002), p. 131ff. It is important to note that this microtheological emphasis on God as less rather than more is not confined to the Judeo-Christian tradition. It is also to be found in much of the Hindu and Buddhist wisdom literature; see for instance the following passage from Krishnamurti: "The silence which is not the silence of the ending of noise is only a small beginning. It is like going through a small hole to an enormous, wide, expansive ocean, to an immeasurable, timeless state" (*Freedom from the Known*, San Francisco: Harper, 1969, p. 109). Interestingly, one of the *siddhis*—the powers that a yogin/yogini may acquire—is to become as small as an atom.

The Taoist master Lao Tse spoke from a similar perspective in *Tao Te Ching* when he wrote:

> Know the high
> But keep to the low;
> Become a valley
> To all under heaven.
> As a valley provides in abundance,
> Give in constant Virtue;
> Return to natural simplicity. (chap. 28)

Or again when he wrote:

> The Great Way flows everywhere . . .
> It clothes and feeds all things,
> Yet does not claim
> To be their lord.
> It asks for nothing in return.
> It may be called the Small . . .
> So too the wise may become great,
> By becoming small. (chap. 34)

8. Robert Musil, *A Man without Qualities*, cited in Richard Kearney, *Poétique du Possible* (Paris: Beauchesne, 1984), p. 4.

9. Rainer Maria Rilke, *Letters to a Young Poet*, trans. Stephen Mitchell (New York: Vintage, 1986), pp. 61–63. The emphasis here on the earth as correspondent for divine eros highlights, once again, the incarnational tendency of theo-eroticism. The earth is full of the seeds of the divine (what Augustine called *rationes seminales*, borrowing from the Stoics' *logoi spermatikoi*), incubating within the finite historical world like latent potencies waiting to be animated and actualized by the infinitely incoming grace of God as transcendent *posse*. If one removes transcendent *posse* from this equation, one relapses into a purely immanentist dialectic (evolutionary materialism or, at best, process theology). On the other hand, if one ignores the immanence of terrestrial and human potencies, one is left with an inordinately inaccessible and abstract deity—a sort of acosmic alterity without face or voice (e.g., deism or deconstruction). A hermeneutical poetics of divine *posse* tries to preserve a delicate balance between these opposite extremes.

10. I am grateful to my wise friend and teacher, Peggy McLoughlin, for this reference and the quotes below. Here is one verse in which the term *viriditas* appears (from *Translations of Hildegard* at www.scot-art.org/semc/trans.htm):

O most noble greening power (*O nobilissima viriditas*)
Rooted in the sun,
Who shine in dazzling serenity
In a sphere
That no earthly excellence
Can comprehend.
You are enclosed
In the embrace of divine mysteries,
You blush like the dawn
And burn like a flame of the sun.

And a general comment on *viriditas* in Hildegard:

> For her, the energy that drives the universe—which she calls *viriditas*, or the greening force—is also the power of the Living Light, which is Love-*caritas*. The expression of this in the creation is music. The original creation was a miracle of equilibrium, of perfect harmony, which the Fall disturbed; the incarnation restores a new harmony—indeed the Word of God is music itself, and the soul of mankind if symphonic: *symphonialis est anima* . . . Here she finds the dynamic expression of the love of God and his promise to bring mankind back to him, the expression in the body of the green-growing grace of *viriditas*. (*Great Spirits 1000–2000: The Fifty-Two Christians Who Most Influenced Their Millennium*, ed. Selina O'Grady and John Wilkins, New York: Paulist, 2002)

11. Joachim Jeremias, *The Eucharistic Words of Jesus*, trans. Norman Perrin (Philadelphia: Fortress, 1977), p. 249. I am indebted to two of my colleagues at Boston College, Gary Gurtler and John Manoussakis, for bringing the passages I cite in Dionysius and Jeremias to my attention.

12. Ibid., p. 252.

13. Nahum N. Glatzer, *The Passover Haggadah* (New York: Schocken, 1953), p. 63.

14. Jeremias, *Eucharistic Words*, p. 252. One might see a repetition of this eschatological forgetting and remembering from the finite human perspective, in Dante. In canto 28 of the *Purgatorio* the pilgrim encounters the two inexhaustible streams of the garden, Lethe and Eunoè, of which the former washes away all memory of sin while the latter retrieves the memory of good deeds and life-giving moments (ll. 121–144).

15. Jeremias, *Eucharistic Words*, p. 253.

four
Trinity and Transcendence

Michael J. Scanlon

In the classical understanding of Christian faith we find the distinction between *fides quæ creditur* (faith as belief) and *fides quā creditor* (faith as trusting obedience). The value of faith as belief is orthodoxy; the value of faith as trusting obedience is orthopraxy. Both are necessary for the full reality of faith, but the first is ancillary to the second. Ideally, faith as belief (stemming from communal confession) functions to enlighten the path of faith as trusting obedience (personal or communal). In classical terminology, again, faith is understood as the human response to divine revelation—the enlightenment comes from revelation. The ultimate goal of our enlightened faith-praxis is salvation, and, thus, revelation has always been understood as soteriological—what God has revealed is for our path to salvation. As the Bible witnesses, revelation occurs in historical events, discerned by a community as God's "mighty acts," and received as such.

The language of revelation is primarily symbolic or metaphorical—as symbolic, "it gives rise to thought." And thought here is theology (God-talk)—theology is a second-order conceptual language whose purpose is the partial elucidation of the first-order symbolic language of revelation (e.g., biblical language). Concepts are never adequate to symbols; and symbols, while richer than concepts, are themselves ambiguous and are never adequate in their attempt to express the ineffable reality of God, the eternal Mystery. While never adequate, however, symbols enjoy the semantic/pragmatic power of participating in the reality symbolized. Trinitarian symbolism will be discussed below.

In the Christian tradition doctrine has always enjoyed a special place because of its ecclesial function in service to the unity of faith, which goes through the doctrine to the Mystery expressed in it. As the Trinitarian theologian, Catherine Mowry LaCugna, put it in relation to the doctrine of the Trinity:

> To be sure, doctrines intend to *refer to* holy mystery, or to the experience (collective or individual) of mystery, but no doctrine is itself the mystery. Strictly speaking, then, Christians do not 'believe in' doctrines but freely assent to them (Newman) insofar (and only insofar) as they elucidate and helpfully articulate *experience*.[1]

All doctrines were once someone's theology; they became doctrines as a result of some crisis of interpretation in the history of the Church. Doctrine emerges as a result of the mystery of "reception." Reception is mysterious because it is a pneumatic phenomenon—it is an example of discernment in the power of the Spirit who vivifies the Church. Doctrines receiving the highest degree of Church recognition are called dogmas. A good example of this movement from theology to doctrine (dogma) would be the decision of the Council of Nicæa to reject the Christology of Arius in favor of the Christology of Athanasius, in 325. Another example of this process of reception would be the doctrine of grace, the center of the theology of St. Augustine.

The doctrine of the Trinity received its dogmatic form in the creeds of the Council of Nicæa on the divinity of Christ, and the First Council of Constantinople on the divinity of the Spirit in 381. Major theological works were written on the Trinity by the Cappadocian Fathers in the east and by Augustine in the west. Greek philosophy supplied the austere language for the theological formulations of this doctrine in the patristic and medieval periods. St. Thomas Aquinas brought this philosophical theology of the Trinity to its classical metaphysical formulation in the thirteenth century. Through all of this theological work, a distinction emerged between the "immanent" Trinity and the "economic" Trinity. The former focused on the eternal, immanent life of God as triune, while the latter referred to the New Testament story of God the Father sending the Son and the Spirit into the world for us and for our salvation. The movement from the economic to the immanent Trinity was a logical one—the God who *acted* triunely for us in the biblical story did so because that God *is* triune. Accordingly, in the one God there are three *hypostases* (the Greek formulation) or three *personæ* (the Latin formulation).

In the modern period Friedrich Schleiermacher, the Protestant father of modern theology, nicely summarizes the legacy of Trinitarian theology while he poses a task for its future.[2] In his classic, *The Christian Faith*, Schleiermacher discussed the doctrine of "the divine Trinity" in his conclusion as "the coping-stone of Christian doctrine."[3] Properly understood according to Schleiermacher, the Trinity affirms that "nothing less than the Divine Essence" was present in Christ and is present in "the common Spirit who indwells the Christian Church."[4] Schleiermacher was critical of the further elaboration of this doctrine in terms of the immanent Trinity of the eternal divine life, since this could not be an utterance concerning "the religious consciousness"—his way of saying that this further elaboration has no practical or salutary role in Christian life. In addition, it seemed to Schleiermacher that discussions of the immanent Trinity lead to subordinationism (of Christ and the Spirit to the Father) despite the orthodox intentions of theologians, so that "our living fellowship with Christ as well as our participation in the Holy Spirit would not be fellowship with God"—a conclusion which contradicts the fundamental significance of the doctrine of the Trinity. Instead, Schleiermacher held strongly to the "original intention of the doctrine, namely, to make it clear that it is no hyperbolical expression of our consciousness of Christ and of the common Spirit of the Church to assert that God is in both."[5] Observing that we have no formula for the being of God in Himself as distinct from the being of God in the world, and that the doctrine of the Trinity has remained so long stationary, Schleiermacher looked to the future development of Trinitarianism —"there must be in store for it a transformation which will go back to its very beginnings."[6] Contemporary systematic theologians are rising to this difficult task of transformation. As one theologian put it, "the widespread inability of Christians today to relate to this concept (the Trinity) should alert theologians to the magnitude of the task which faces them if they wish to commend a Trinitarian answer to the major contemporary questions about God."[7] This essay will focus on the contributions of two Catholic theologians, Karl Rahner and James Mackey, to current efforts to retrieve Trinitarian theology.

Rahner's Rule

Karl Rahner discusses the Christian Mystery in an important series of lectures on "The Concept of Mystery in Catholic Theology."[8] In the first lecture he clarifies his use of the term: Mystery refers, not to doctrines, but to the reality of God as God relates to us. Mystery is the eternally incomprehensible, ineffable God as God draws near to us. In the second lecture he focuses on the addressee of the Mystery, the human being for Whom Mystery is the "Whence" and the "Whither" of human transcendence—God is simultaneously the way and the goal of human transcendence. In the third lecture, Rahner focuses on the fundamental Christian doctrines which articulate the core of the gospel, the Self-communication of Mystery to the world. Three doctrines constitute the "hierarchy of doctrine"—the Trinity, the Incarnation, and Grace as the divinization of humanity.[9] In these three doctrines, according to Rahner, the concern is not with the traditional understanding of divine efficient causality as God works *ad extra*, but with what he calls quasi-formal causality: Through Christ, God gives God to us as historical beings; and in the Spirit, God gives God to us in our transcendence. In his later writings Rahner drops the modifier "quasi" from "formal causality" (its use was to avoid a pantheist interpretation of the God-world relationship), as he moves in the direction of what is called today "panentheism" (nicely phrased in Acts 17:28, "in him we live and move and have our being"). Rahner's formulation of the "two ways" the one God gives God away, is reminiscent of early portrayals of the Trinity where the Word and the Spirit are God's "two hands" (according to Irenæus). Thus, the Trinity is *the* fundamental doctrine as we unfold it as the Self-gift of God to the world through Jesus Christ and in the Holy Spirit.

In one of his early essays on the Trinity, Rahner laments that this supreme mystery is also the most obscure. In terms of the development of doctrine he observes that since the Council of Florence in 1439, there has been no progress in the understanding of this mystery—it has indeed been "stationary" as Schleiermacher put it. Like Schleiermacher, he insists that it is the task of theology to present the doctrine of the Trinity in such a way that it can become a reality in the life of Christians.[10] As it stood at the time, it seemed that this mystery appears to have been revealed for its own sake. In the general theological curriculum the tract, *De Deo Trino*, followed the tract, *De Deo Uno*, with formal and very abstract assertions about the three persons, the four relations, and the two processions—a reality entirely centered on itself, a Trinity which is not open to anything outside of it, an "immanent Trinity," outlining the eternal constitution of God *in se*. Something is wrong, Rahner exclaims—the thing is impossible, for the Trinity is a mystery of salvation!

Rahner's Rule

In response to this situation, Rahner insists that the basic thesis which constitutes the link between all the theological treatises, and shows "the reality and not just the doctrine of the Trinity as a mystery of salvation for us, may be formulated as follows: the Trinity of the economy of salvation *is* the immanent Trinity and vice versa."[11] The first part of this statement is traditional—God *acts* salvifically for us in three ways, because God *is* in three ways or hypostases or persons. Like Augustine, Rahner is cautious about the use of the term "person." As Augustine put it,

> So the only reason, it seems, why we do not call these three together one person, as we call them one being and one God, but say three persons while we never say three Gods or three beings, is that we want to keep at least one word for signifying what we mean by trinity so that we are not simply reduced to silence when we are asked three what, after we have confessed that there are three.[12]

Michael J. Scanlon

Not much content there for "three persons"! Obviously, the word person did not mean in Augustine's day what it has come to mean in the modern and contemporary world.

Like everything else we know, language changes. The modern meaning of the word connotes a centered human being with consciousness and freedom. But this meaning of the word renders it inapplicable to the Trinity—it would affirm tritheism (three centers of self-conscious freedom). With his deep respect for the traditional language of the Christian tradition, Rahner does not call for dropping the word person from the Trinitarian doctrine, while he does call for nuance and clarification when it is used. For him, the word is used analogically for the Three in the immanent Trinity.

Now let us return to what has become known by all contemporary Trinitarian theologians, Catholic and Protestant, as "Rahner's Rule"—the economic Trinity is the immanent Trinity and vice versa.[13] Yves Congar declared that the first half of this statement is "beyond dispute," while he suggests that the "vice versa" be dropped in order to protect "the free mystery of the economy and the necessary mystery of the Tri-unity of God."[14] But it is precisely the "vice versa" that has proven to be the most fruitful part of Rahner's Rule for contemporary Trinitarian theology. Maybe we should take a new look at what Congar speaks of as what is "free" and what is "necessary" in God. I propose that the key to the doctrine of the Trinity is God's freedom.

The God of the Bible is the God of freedom. He freely elects Israel as his people, and the Old Testament is the story of God's history with God's people. This is the theology of the *shekinah*, a term which first appeared in postbiblical Judaism to refer to the biblical narrative of "the indwelling of God" in God's people.[15] God is the One who exists, walks, and suffers with his people. When the Old Testament speaks of God, it also speaks of Israel, the partner of YHWH. Unlike classical philosophy which articulated what seemed to be necessary to an appropriate understanding of *Deus in se*, the God of the Bible is always in free association with humans, always a *Deus pro nobis*. And for the New Testament this God is the same God who freely decides to become one of us for all of us in his Son, Jesus of Nazareth. This biblical story of God with humanity, this wonderful story of divine freedom is what is "distilled" into the doctrine of the Trinity.

The doctrine of the Trinity flows from New Testament Christology as the early Christian church reflected on the identity of Jesus, the man for others. There is a progression of Christological titles, identifying Jesus on the basis of God's endorsement of him in the resurrection experience—he is given Old Testament soteriological titles such as Son of Man, Son of God, Christ, Savior and explicitly divine titles such as Lord, Wisdom, Word. For Christians the reality of God cannot be affirmed without including in that reality *the* human partner of God, Jesus. A "binatarian" theology of God emerges and is officially received as the doctrine of the divinity of Christ at the Council of Nicæa in 325. A few decades later, in 381, at the First Council of Constantinople a full-blown doctrine of the Trinity is affirmed as the divinity of the Spirit of God—who in the New Testament had become the Spirit of Christ, and who indwelt Jesus and is indwelling the Church—is recognized officially. "We may confidently look for an access into the doctrine of the trinity in Jesus and the Spirit, as we experience them through faith in salvation history. For in these two persons the immanent Trinity is already given."[16]

The Vice Versa of Rahner's Rule

Karl Rahner did not develop the "vice versa" of his rule, but he left a way of speaking about God's Wisdom/Word and Spirit that has proven highly suggestive for further development by others. The following is perhaps Rahner's most suggestive statement, bearing directly upon his "vice versa":

> The unoriginated God (called 'Father') has from eternity the opportunity of an historical self-expression (the divine Wisdom/Word) and likewise the opportunity of establishing himself as himself the innermost center of the intellectual creature as the latter's dynamism and goal (the divine Spirit). These two eternal possibilities (which are pure actuality) are God, are to be distinguished from each other, and are to be distinguished by this distinction also from the unoriginated God.[17]

We are aware of these divine possibilities because we know them to have been actualized in the Incarnation and in Pentecost. To speak of possibilities in God implies a divine freedom to become something different from a distant and remote origin of the world, to become radical nearness as Self-gift to the world in two ways corresponding to the twofold structure in the world, where the world opens in receptivity to the divine gift—the human being of history and of transcendence. This proposal makes it possible to claim that the key to the doctrine of the Trinity is God's freedom, as narrated in the Bible. Again, this is *God's* freedom so that in his radical Self-communication to the creature, Rahner insists that the mediation of this Gift must be a divine and not merely a creaturely mediation. "But this means first of all in the dimension of the salvific economic Trinity that the statement that the Logos and the Holy Spirit are God himself is not an attenuation or obscuration of monotheism rightly understood, but its radicalization."[18] When God gives God, God gives God through God (the divine Word/Wisdom) and in God (the divine Spirit).

At this point it might be helpful to be more precise about the meaning of freedom in Rahner's anthropology as the place where he finds an analogy for divine freedom. Human freedom for Rahner is not merely free will, the capacity to choose, but the ability to determine oneself, to construct oneself over the course of a lifetime of self-enactment. Time becomes the fuel of freedom as the human being turns time into history, into a narratable story which is one's life. As long as there is time, the human being is becoming his/herself in freedom. And, for Rahner, this is a theological anthropology—a Christian anthropology, since the human being, doing self, is all along empowered by the divine "co-doer" of the self, the Spirit of God, the Spirit of Christ (2 Corinthians 3:17). Thus, the self, forged in time and empowered by the Spirit, becomes an eternal self in the resurrection. Employing this understanding of human freedom as an analogy for divine freedom (while we recall the caution of the Fourth Lateran Council (1215), that we are more unlike than like God), we can say fallibly and tentatively that God, too, has a history: God becomes the kind of God God wills to become by using all of time, with eternity as its fruition. God becomes actually triune in a divine history—an insight which transposes the reality of the Trinity from a "protological" frame to an eschatological reality. While he always affirmed the "immutability" of God in accord with "natural theology," Rahner was ever-wary of allowing Athens to be tutor to Jerusalem. Aware of the difference between the biblical witness to the everlasting fidelity, reliability and steadfastness of God and the unchangeability of God affirmed by Greek philosophy, Rahner dared often to speak of "the history of God," "God changing or becoming in his other," or Jesus as the eschatological "Self-deed of God." And his historical consciousness led him to reject the traditional understanding of eternity as timelessness —eternity is, rather, the fruit, the issue of history, the fullness of time. As we recall, his monotheism was not the abstract monotheism of the philosophical One, but the biblical witness to the One who chose Israel as covenant partner and who raised Jesus from the dead.[19] And that One is indeed the origin, the Creator of the world, but, more emphatically, the Future of the world whose Name is promise, "I *will be* there for you."[20] A profoundly radical affirmation of God's Self-giving love for the world is found in a statement Rahner made in a lecture just three years before his death: "Only when . . . within a concept of God that makes a radical distinction between God and the world, God himself is still the very core of the world's reality and the world is truly the fate of God himself, only then is the concept of God attained that is truly Christian."[21]

Biblical Symbols of Divine Potential

Karl Rahner's protological portrayal of the Second and Third dimensions of the divine Trinity as God's real "possibilities" finds biblical warrant in the central symbols of divine immanence in the Old Testament, and specifically in the wisdom literature of late Judaism. With "the quenching of the prophetic Spirit," the prophetic eschatology of Israel yields to its Jewish issue, apocalyptic eschatology. The emphasis on God's transcendence becomes increasingly more austere, and this experience of divine silence evoked a renewed effort to find affirmations of God's nearness to his people. An utterly transcendent God cannot nourish that hope without which religion dies. The most significant symbols of Hellenistic Judaism were three—Spirit (*Pneuma*), Wisdom (*Sophia*) and Word (*Logos*). Often used interchangeably, these symbols of divine immanence in the world supplied the language for the later development of the Christian doctrine of God as Trinity. The problem is that in the doctrine of the Trinity, these Jewish symbols of *God's immanence in the world* became two *hypostases* (Word/Wisdom, and Spirit) *in the eternal, immanent life of God*—thus, they become transcendent! Returning to the biblical roots of the doctrine of the Trinity raises the question: Were these "intermediary beings" between God and the world distinct hypostases in late Judaism, modifying Old Testament monotheism before their Christian usage? To answer this question we must consider contemporary scholarship on the use of these symbols in the development of the New Testament Christology which is the basis for understanding the doctrine of the Trinity. We begin with the Spirit, where continuity of thought between Hebraic and Christian understanding is generally recognized.

From the earliest stages of pre-Christian Judaism the literal meaning of "spirit" was wind or breath, and the symbolic meaning when applied to God was divine effective *power*—awesome like the wind, life-giving like breath. Given this symbolic understanding, "the Spirit of God *is in no sense distinct from God, but is simply the power of God, God himself acting powerfully in nature and upon men* [*sic*]."[22] As mentioned above, there was a lament in Judaism concerning the seeming withdrawal of the Spirit with the end of prophecy (see 1 Maccabees 4:46; 9:27). For the Jews, Torah was the voice of the Spirit. In the New Testament the Spirit takes on a special association with Christ through the Easter experience which anticipates the universal outpouring of the vivifying Spirit (Joel 2:28–32). The relationship between Jesus and the Spirit of God is evident in his consciousness of inspiration and of divine commissioning behind his preaching, and of divine power in his healing ministry (Matt 12:28 = Luke 11:20). The prophetic Spirit has "returned" in the person of Jesus, the "eschatological prophet" (Isaiah 61:1). For Paul, the risen Jesus is now the pneumatic Christ, "the life-giving Spirit" (1 Corinthians 15:45), in some sense the mediating "form" of the Spirit. The Spirit, the power (*dynamis*) of God, has taken definitive form in the earthly Jesus (Romans 8:15ff.) and in the exalted Christ (Romans 8:29; 1 Corinthians 15:49).

For the Old Testament, the world would return to formless chaos without the continuous creative activity of God. This presence of the Creator in the world, implanting meaning, is expressed in Judaism by the symbol of the Wisdom of God. This divine Wisdom (*Sophia*) is often presented poetically in the form of personification, but never as an entity or hypostasis distinct from God. In the New Testament, Christ is presented as a teacher or envoy of Wisdom, and Paul identifies him as the Wisdom of God. In his death and resurrection Jesus revealed God's original purpose for creation and for humanity in a normative way—so much so that Christ crucified is the Wisdom of God (1 Corinthians 1:24, 30). Since Wisdom is not conceived of as a preexistent divine hypostasis, Jesus, as the Wisdom of God, is the incarnation of the divine plan for creation. In the New Testament "the thought is primarily of Christ as the eschatological embodiment of the wisdom of God, as the one through

Michael J. Scanlon

whom the creator God in all his fullness had revealed himself most clearly and definitively for man's [*sic*] salvation and creation's renewal."[23]

The same questions arise in connection with the Johannine symbol of Word (*Logos*), identified with Jesus. Here there is a major figure of Hellenistic Judaism, Philo of Alexandria, whose work was published several decades before the Gospel of John and for whom the divine Logos was a central concept. While there is no evidence of direct influence of Philo on John, the work of Philo is a clear illustration of interesting developments in the thought of Hellenistic Judaism in conversation with Platonic and Stoic philosophy.

Philo was a contemporary of Jesus and Paul. He is famous for his explorations of the affinity between biblical revelation and Platonic philosophy—indeed, he is the father of the long history of mutual interaction between the traditions of Athens and Jerusalem. While his influence on rabbinic Judaism after the Council of Jamnia was minimal, his work was very influential on the development of Christian theology throughout the patristic period. The very survival of his writings was entirely dependent on their reception by Christian theologians, beginning with Clement of Alexandria (with whom also begins the legend of *Philo Christianus*). By the end of the patristic period he had virtually achieved the status of a church father.[24] The figure of the Logos, whose role in the Johannine prologue was the point of departure for the development of the Christian doctrine of the Trinity, was central to Philo's interpretive mediation of philosophy and theology. The following summary of Philo's doctrine of the Logos is pertinent both for understanding the Johannine Logos (whose background in Hellenistic Judaism is not in question), and for interpreting the Trinitarian thought of that great eastern theologian of the church prior to the first ecumenical councils, Origen of Alexandria.

> The Logos, or Reason-Principle, in Philo's thought may be described as that aspect of God which is turned towards creation. The question rises as to whether it is separable from God himself. Philo appears to vacillate on whether he should regard it as a separate hypostasis or not. Most often (but not always) he considers the Logos at the most conceptually separate from God.[25]

While Origen will overcome Philo's vacillation on the hypostatic status of the Logos, strongly in the affirmative, it seems that the Logos in John remains a symbol of God's involvement with creation. James D. G. Dunn, whose New Testament scholarship has so significantly contributed to our understanding of the development of Wisdom Christology, holds that, while Paul and the other Wisdom Christologists understood Wisdom (and Spirit) in the same way as their Jewish predecessors, John's Logos Christology is different. He maintains that "for John the pre-existent Logos was indeed a divine personal being" who became incarnate in Jesus.[26] I see no convincing reason for this exception. If we stay with our understanding of the Logos as symbol of God's creative and revelatory word addressed to humanity now in its definitive, eschatological form as enfleshment in Jesus, *the* Image of God, we may in a fully realistic way affirm that "in Christ God was reconciling the world to himself" (2 Corinthians 5:19). The incarnation is *the* manifestation of "the humanity of God," the revelation of *Deus Humanissimus*, a radical affirmation of divine Self-definition as *Deus pro nobis*.[27] The traditional presupposition of a preexistent divine hypostasis as *Verbum Incarnandum* is a confusing form of theoretical dualism.

Philo's works were part of the personal library of Origen, who brought them with him from Egypt to Palestine. Like Philo, Origen sought to reconcile his biblical faith with his Hellenistic philosophical education. Perhaps the most brilliant of the Greek fathers, Origen supplied the language for the doctrine of the Trinity. He was the first theologian to speak of three hypostases: From eternity the Logos hypostasis is begotten by the first hypostasis, God, the Father (Godself = *autotheos*), as perfect though subordinate image (second God = *deuteros theos*) but "one in being" (*homoousios*) with the Father. The Spirit proceeds as third hypostasis, subordinate to the Logos. At the same time in the west, Tertullian spoke of three "persons" in the Godhead.[28] Remove the subordinationism and you have the doctrine of the Trinity. The presupposition of Origen's theology is the Platonic-Gnostic scheme of fall and subsequent ascent, and the dualistic separation of eternal idea and temporal manifestation. Hans Küng speaks with great respect of Origen as a person and as a saintly Christian, but ends his observations with the following:

> As a Christian one can speak of Father, Son, and Spirit without having to follow Origen in taking over the Middle Platonic/Neoplatonic doctrine of hypostases. That Origen attempted this in his time is his greatness. But we would be poor things if in our time we did not make the same attempt in our own way. Origen would have had the greatest understanding of this.[29]

The Trinitarian Theology of James Mackey

James Mackey's enmity toward all forms of dualism in philosophy and theology is evident from his contribution to this collection (chap. 5, below). Given the theme of the present volume and the conference on which it is based, his paper focuses on the reifying of analytic abstractions such as the transcendent and the immanent. He has also addressed the reification of symbols into abstract concepts in his major work on the theology of the Trinity, *The Christian Doctrine of God as Trinity*.[30] In chapter 6 of that work, Mackey discusses "the pre-existence of the Son" as the theme which, once literalized, "leads directly into the main difficulties encountered in all incarnational and trinitarian theology."[31] He concludes that the basic meaning of the title, Son of God, refers to "the lived relationship of Jesus of Nazareth to the God he called Father."[32] Chapter 7 follows with a discussion of the Spirit (including the Johannine Paraclete) in terms of the poetic "personification of intermediaries and not a separate *hypostasis* at all."[33]

In a later work, *Modern Theology*, Mackey again takes up the doctrine of the Trinity. Again he confronts the trouble which lies at the root of the two major problems about which theologians have argued—the preexistence of the Son and the preexistence of the Spirit. This trouble "surely concerns the disembodied, the discarnate, status of the second and third personae."[34] While conceding that God's revelation in Jesus—and the ensuing Spirit that makes us its receptive embodiment—does allow us to believe that there is some self-differentiation in the divinity, Scripture does not allow us to understand this possible self-differentiation "in the least."[35] Concretely, this means that for Christians, Jesus of Nazareth is the second persona; and the Church, the Body of Christ indwelt by the Spirit, is the third persona of God.[36]

In his latest discussion of Trinitarianism, "Are There Christian Alternatives to Trinitarian Thinking?," Mackey offers a good critique of contemporary efforts to produce an immanent "social Trinity" as paradigmatic for ecclesiastical and social structures that might enhance human intersubjectivity.[37] Indeed, he suggests his own interpretation of the Trinity as providing a far more concrete model for whatever is to be gained from a "social Trinity." His model is concrete because he rejects the traditional dualist world-view with its ideal/empirical divisions, characteristic of Christian borrowings from Platonic religious philosophies for constructing a metaphysics of the Trinity. Radicalizing "Rahner's Rule," Mackey moves from a protological to an eschatological account of the immanent Trinity. Given the fact that we are still pilgrims on the way to the promised future,

> it follows that there is not now available to us any 'immanent' Trinity on which we could model our changing relationships; in fact there will be no immanent ('remaining in') Trinity properly speaking until all has returned 'in' to God, and God also, after a real history, will finally be all 'in' all of a real body, that of Jesus, and that of his extended 'body of Christ' in the world, and that of the extended body of those who make up the body of Christ, the physical world. Meanwhile, the only Trinity that is, and the only Trinity that can be known, is that of the dynamic (the economy) in which the God that Jesus prayed to as Father, came into Jesus ('I am in the Father and the Father is in me'; 'God was in Christ reconciling the world to himself') and is still active in the world as the risen Lord Jesus, the life-giving Spirit (as Paul calls him in 1 Cor. 15:45—just the phrase used to describe the 'divinity' of the Holy Spirit in the creed: the Lord and giver of life).[38]

Obviously, this eschatological Trinity entails a reinterpretation of eternity as determined from the future, as the fullness of time rather than a protological timelessness "preceding" creation.

A Trinitarian Eternity

Just as the infinite cannot exist in juxtaposition with the finite, if it is really the infinite; so eternity cannot exist in mere juxtaposition with time, if eternity is the fulfillment of time. Eternity must be the everlasting fruition of time, if the not-yet future of the world is the Kingdom of God anticipated, in time, in the resurrection of Jesus. It is this biblical symbol of the Kingdom of God which serves in the meantime as the Judeo-Christian paradigm for the transformation of sociopolitical structures in practical anticipation of the peace and justice to come. I say "practical" anticipation, because the Catholic theology of grace has traditionally understood the gift of the Spirit as empowerment for "building the City of God" as we await its ultimate arrival. Granted the ultimate discontinuity between history and its fulfillment in the reign of God, Catholic theology has maintained a mysterious continuity between history and its future on the basis of the presence in history of the Power of the Future, the Spirit, as the "Whence" of that not-yet "Whither." The Trinity becomes the supreme soteriological doctrine as we witness, in faith and hope, the unfolding of God's Self-gift to the world in Jesus and the Spirit in the history that we share with God. If we humans inherited, inhabited and created a history wherein we were the only agents, we could never expect anything but more of the same—the tragic inhumanity of humans toward humans. But given God's vivifying presence to creation as Spirit, we share the conviction in faith that we are not alone. We believe that Christology is the revelatory moment in a universal Pneumatology—that God's creative Spirit took definitive form in Jesus of Nazareth, whose historical impact on his followers produced in the power of that same Spirit a community that has continued his form of life in varying degrees of fidelity up to the present day. This community called Church is idealized by St. Paul as the Body of Christ, but its symbolic form as Church is not identical with the institutional reality of the church. This community is indeed the "gifted community" (St. Augustine often refers to the Spirit as *the* Gift), and this Gift empowers its task in the world. In a basic sense this task is always the same—bearing witness to and collaborating for a comprehensive human community of peace and justice—while its specific mission takes on different priorities, given the historical situation of the world for which its exists. Today this task must be one of resistance to the monstrous Mammonism which reduces human persons and their communities to commodities in a distorted "globalization."

This "historicization" of the doctrine of the Trinity recalls the teaching of the twelfth-century Calabrian monk, Joachim of Fiore, for whom the progressive history of the world unfolds in three ages under the signs of the Father, Christ and the Spirit. This, too, was a pneumatic Trinitarianism with the third age as the flourishing of freedom.[39] Among contemporary theologians Jürgen Moltmann, Wolfhart Pannenberg, Robert Jenson and Ted Peters offer similar interpretations of the Trinity as the fullness of history.[40]

One of the obvious global tasks facing Christian theology today is "the broader ecumenism," dialogue with the non-Christian religions toward new possibilities of collaboration in service to the world. Another illustration of the current tendency to historicize the doctrine of the Trinity with significant import for the broader ecumenism is the work of Protestant theologian Peter

Hodgson, a theologian deeply influenced by Hegel. Seeking to overcome the traditional subordination of the Spirit, which he sees as having led to the marginalization of women and the exploitation of nature, Hodgson proposes "a transition from an anthropocentric to a holistic Pneumatology—one that embraces the whole creation and recognizes the Spirit as the symbol of wholeness, relatedness, energy, life."[41] Spirit is intimately connected with language, those "little explosions and transmissions of air" by which human beings communicate and which is "the most mysterious and powerful of all invisible forces."[42] The essence of the human spirit is relationality, and the divine Spirit seeks otherness also, as it is embodied in what is other than God—the natural and human worlds. Like Rahner, Hodgson speaks of "potentials" in God rather than preexisting persons. Thus, the Spirit is an "*emergent* person (not an individual but a social person), generated out of the interaction of God and the world, in the process of which the world is liberated and God is perfected."[43] For Hodgson the inner-Trinitarian relations become personal subjects only in relation to the world, and Spirit is the prominent figure. "If Christ is the figure of God's objective and individual presence, then the Spirit is the figure of God's intersubjective and communal presence."[44] The perfection of the God of freedom and the consummation of the world are two aspects of the same reality.

In a very recent article, "The Spirit and Religious Pluralism," Hodgson singles out Rahner's Pneumatology as a basis for a pluralist theology of religions.[45] Hodgson refers us to one of Rahner's last essays, in which he remarked that the time may have come to reverse the perspective that has given Christology its priority over Pneumatology in western theology. In light of "the universal salvific will of God and in legitimate respect for all the major world religions outside of Christianity," Rahner predicted that Pneumatology in the sense of "a teaching of the inmost divinizing gift of grace for all human beings" will become the fundamental point of departure for a new eastern theology. Scriptural passages that prioritize Christ over the Spirit will be less suitable than those that "let the Spirit speak through all the prophets and know that the Spirit is poured out on all flesh."[46] Similar to the flow of Rahner's Trinitarian theology is the following from Hodgson: "The difference between Christ and the Spirit is not, in my view, the difference between two distinct hypostases in the Godhead, but the difference between God's concrete historical presence and universal indwelling power, between fixity and fluidity, history and mysticism, incarnation and communion."[47]

Rahner is famous for his summary statements like "all theology is anthropology." The theology of the Trinity presented in this essay is an elaboration of Rahner's summary—the Trinity is God as Father, Jesus his incarnate Son, and the Spirit vivifying the Church and the world. The goals of Christians are to witness to and cooperate with this God at work for us and for the world. The doctrine of the Trinity tells us how God is—not exhaustively, not exclusively, but truthfully—and "being Christian . . . is believing the doctrine of the Trinity to be true, and true in a way that converts and heals the human world."[48] The doctrine of the Trinity is all about salvation!

NOTES

1. Catherine Mowry LaCugna, "Philosophers and Theologians on the Trinity," *Modern Theology* 2/3 (April 1986): 175, LaCugna's italics.

2. I refer here to Schleiermacher because there is a genuine affinity between the structure and the spirit of many Catholic and liberal Protestant theologians. In this regard, see David Tracy, *The Analogical Imagination: Christian Theology and the Culture of Pluralism* (New York: Crossroad, 1981), p. 379.

3. Friedrich Schleiermacher, *The Christian Faith*, trans. H. R. Macintosh and J. S. Stewart (New York: Harper & Row, 1963), vol. 2, p. 739.

4. Ibid., p. 738.

5. Ibid., pp. 747–748.

6. Ibid., p. 747.

7. Werner Jeanrond, "The Questions of God Today," in *The Christian Understanding of God Today*, ed. James Byrne (Dublin: Columba, 1993), p. 10.

8. Karl Rahner, "The Concept of Mystery in Catholic Theology," *Theological Investigations*, vol. 4, trans. Kevin Smyth (Baltimore: Helicon, 1966), pp. 36–73.

9. At the Second Vatican Council the Catholic Church accepted the notion of "the hierarchy of doctrine" in its decree on ecumenism, *Unitatis Redintegratio*.

10. Rahner, "Remarks on the Dogmatic Treatise 'De Trinitate'," *Theological Investigations*, vol. 4, p. 78.

11. This is the famous "Rahner's Rule" which he elucidated in his short book, *The Trinity*, trans. Joseph Donceel (New York: Crossroad, 1977); the name Rahner's Rule was given it by Ted Peters in his *God as Trinity* (Louisville, Ky.: Westminster/John Knox, 1993), p. 22.

12. St. Augustine, *The Trinity*, trans. Edmund Hill (Brooklyn, N.Y.: New City, 1991), pp. 228–229.

13. For a comprehensive overview of contemporary Trinitarian theology, see Stanley Grenz, *Rediscovering the Triune God* (Minneapolis: Fortress, 2004).

14. Yves Congar, *I Believe in the Holy Spirit*, trans. David Smith (New York: Seabury, 1983), vol. 3, p. 13.

15. Bernd Janowski, "The One God of the Two Testaments," *Theology Today* 57/3 (October 2000): 310.

16. Rahner, *The Trinity*, p. 39.

17. Rahner, "Oneness and Threefoldness of God," *Theological Investigations*, vol. 18, trans. Edward Quinn (New York: Crossroad, 1983), p. 118. The original German, translated here as "opportunity," is *Möglichkeit* (possibility). This is not a mere "potential" in God, but a "power" (Latin *potestas*, rather than *potentia*); and indeed, Rahner uses *Möglichkeit* and *Macht* (power) interchangeably. In his articles on the Trinity and the Incarnation in *Sacramentum Mundi*, he speaks of *Gottesselbstaussagbarkeit*, with *barkeit* italicized in the original: God's ability to speak himself outwardly. Since God is pure actuality (*potestas*) and has these two eternal real possibilities (*Logos*

Michael J. Scanlon

and *Pneuma*) of getting out of himself, God can give Godself outwardly and "become" God-for-us more and more and more—can become not more God, but more *our* God or God-for-us.

18. Ibid., p. 116.

19. See Rahner, "Theos in the New Testament," *Theological Investigations*, vol. 1, trans. Cornelius Ernst (Baltimore: Helicon, 1961), p. 79.

20. In the Septuagint the divine name of Exodus 3:14 is translated as "I Am Who Am"; but see recent exegesis of the tetragrammaton, YHWH, in André LaCocque and Paul Ricoeur, *Thinking Biblically*, trans. David Pellauer (Chicago: University of Chicago Press, 1998), pp. 307–329, where the Hebrew Name is interpreted as *theophanic and performative*. This interpretation claims that "God, as it were, 'stands and falls' with his people" (p. 316), a claim which launches the thesis of Richard Kearney in his *The God Who May Be: A Hermeneutics of Religion* (Bloomington: Indiana University Press, 2001).

21. Karl Rahner, "The Specific Character of the Christian Concept of God," *Theological Investigations*, vol. 21, trans. Hugh M. Riley (New York: Crossroad, 1988), p. 191.

22. James D. G. Dunn, *Christology in the Making*, 2nd ed. (Grand Rapids, Mich.: William B. Eerdmans, 1989), p. 133, Dunn's italics.

23. Ibid., p. 211.

24. David Runia, *Philo in Early Christian Literature* (Minneapolis: Fortress, 1993), p. 3.

25. Ibid., 41.

26. Dunn, *Christology in the Making*, p. 244.

27. The phrase "humanity of God" reminds us of Karl Barth's later emphasis on God *with* us. See *Karl Barth: Selected Writings*, ed. Clifford Green (London: Collins, 1989); see also Philip Kennedy, *Deus Humanissimus: The Knowability of God in the Theology of Edward Schillebeeckx* (Fribourg: Fribourg University Press, 1993).

28. See Hans Küng, *Great Christian Thinkers* (New York: Continuum, 1994), p. 51.

29. Ibid., p. 67.

30. James P. Mackey, *The Christian Doctrine of God as Trinity* (London: SCM, 1983).

31. Ibid., p. 51.

32. Ibid., p. 63.

33. Ibid., p. 84.

34. James P. Mackey, *Modern Theology: A Sense of Direction* (New York: Oxford University Press, 1987), pp. 128–129.

35. Ibid., p. 129.

36. Ibid., pp. 129–130.

37. James P. Mackey, "Are There Christian Alternatives to Trinitarian Thinking?" in *The Christian Understanding of God Today*, ed. James Byrne (Dublin: Columba, 1993), pp. 66–75.

38. Ibid., p. 68.

39. See the interesting retrieval of Joachim's Spiritual Age in relation to our time, in Gianni Vattimo, *After Christianity*, trans. Luca D'Isanto (New York: Columbia University Press, 2002).

40. See Stanley Grenz, *Rediscovering the Triune God* (Minneapolis: Fortress, 2004), pp. 72–116.

41. Peter Hodgson, *Winds of the Spirit: A Constructive Christian Theology* (Louisville, Ky.: Westminster/John Knox, 1994), p. 277.

42. Ibid., p. 278.

43. Ibid., p. 283, Hodgson's italics.

44. Ibid., p. 291.

45. Peter Hodgson, "The Spirit and Religious Pluralism," *Horizons* 31/1 (Spring 2004): 22–39.

46. Karl Rahner, "Aspects of European Theology," *Theological Investigations*, vol. 21, trans. Hugh M. Riley (New York: Crossroad, 1988), pp. 97–98.

47. Hodgson, "The Spirit and Religious Pluralism," p. 29; see Rahner, "Experience of the Holy Spirit," *Theological Investigations*, vol. 18, trans. Edward Quinn (New York: Crossroad, 1983), pp. 189–210, esp. 192–193, 195–199.

48. Rowan Williams, "Trinity and Pluralism," in *Christian Uniqueness Reconsidered*, ed. Gavin D'Costa (Maryknoll, N.Y.: Orbis, 1990), p. 13.

five

Transcendent Immanence and Evolutionary Creation

James P. Mackey

The aim of this piece is to bring together a critical account of the Christian doctrine of divine creation with an equally critical account of some relatable elements of the best of postmodernist thought, and then to see, to put the matter perhaps too bluntly, if prospects of collaboration emerge or if we are still in the more familiar war-torn territory of recent decades. Now the reader will notice that this brief account of the intended content of this essay does not contain any mention of the term "transcendence," even though that term defines the topic of this volume and occurs also in the title of this essay. This is because, as David Wood's contribution to this volume amply illustrates (chap. 9, below), all known deployment of that term and its derivatives could be adequately accounted for in a godless universe; and, further, because many all-too-common usages of the terms "transcendence" and "the transcendent" as straightforward ciphers for divinity are examples of the sin of onto-philosophy, as that latter term is to be defined and argued against later. Transcendence then will be talked about, as the theme of the volume requires, but only in such a critical manner, and in the context of discussing from the point of view of a particular, indeed foundational piece of Christian theology—namely, the

Christian theology of creation, and the relationship of religion and postmodernism. In sum, the task undertaken by this piece would be all the less compromised if the term "transcendence" were not used at all. So then, to the Christian theology of creation.

Creation

The Christian doctrine of creation, as commonly presented, is bedeviled by two related and equally questionable assumptions. The first is that this act of divine creation consists (or rather consisted) in a one-off act, or one-off series of acts of naked power, imagined as acts of unconditional and irresistible command; from which there resulted what a contemporary scientific cosmologist would call a space-time singularity, that is to say, a state or stage of the universe brought about by processes different from those that govern its continuous coming-into-being as experienced in all other stages; a space-time singularity from which in turn the universe we now know derived.[1] The second is that this doctrine of divine creation can be caught properly and accurately only in a highly abstract conceptual formulation of the theme—*creatio ex nihilo*. The standard unpacking of the connotation of that abstract conceptual formulation of the phrase yielded little, if anything at all, in addition to the following two negatives: (1) that the world was not created out of parts of the divine being or substance itself, that is to say, out of the divine *ousia*; and (2) that it was not created out of any material that could be thought to have coexisted with, or even preexisted the divine act of creation. Despite the almost entirely negative yield of this abstract conceptual formulation, those mythic formulations of belief in the divine creation of the universe so freely available in the age of Genesis were commonly refused consideration, on the grounds that they represented nothing more than illusory and unedifying imaginings from the wayward childhood of the race. The creation stories in the opening chapters of Genesis were then loudly proclaimed not to be myth, and their obvious similarities to the creation myths of surrounding civilizations in the ancient Near East were explained (away) as the clever inclusion of elements, symbols and themes of this ambient mythology precisely in order to counteract the false impressions and bad examples inevitably conveyed in their own context, by including these elements now in the context of the serene omnipotence of a divine creator who brought all things into being, each in its own place and in all its pristine goodness, without struggle or compromise.

If that second assumption above, concerning the adequacy of the abstract conceptual formula for divine creation and the inadequacy of mythic formulations is considered first, then it does not take a great deal of critical and literary-critical acumen to see how eminently challengeable it is. The case against the assumption can be made in both general and particular terms. In general terms it can be maintained that imagination is the prime heuristic "faculty" of the human mind, and everything from the image to the metaphor, through the poem, to the fully-fledged myth forms both its tools and its express products. In particular terms, the Genesis creation stories can be read wholly and precisely as myth, so as to reveal a fuller and more proper understanding of divine creation than the abstruse conceptual formulation of the theme, *creatio ex nihilo,* could ever attain.

The confines of this essay will not permit me to argue in general terms for the permanent primacy of concrete imagery over abstract conceptualizing in the human quest for knowledge. So, in order to take the shortest route to that desired conclusion, let us focus for a moment on an epistemological principle accepted by Aquinas, though by no means first invented by him: *Nihil est in intellectu quod non prius fuerit in sensu;* nothing is in the intellect that will not have been present previously in sense perception. Such a strong and un-qualified claim for the place of imagery as the prime heuristic power of the human mind has seldom exercised its due influence in western epistemology. Indeed it reached its nadir in the course of the Enlightenment, the arid ra-tionalism of which has left few if any academic disciplines undamaged to the present day. Nevertheless, it is true, as the principle in its most unqualified sense implies, that the image, and thereby the imagination—in the attempt to construe reality at all its ranges and levels, in response to reality's most concrete and comprehensive self-revelations—is ever and always the prime heuristic process. For imagination deals in living, organic, or at least structured wholes. Whereas the analytic function of the mind, which abstracts certain features of such whole structures and organisms, thereby forming ideas or definitions, and then perhaps tries by synthesis to put these back together again—usually with as much success as can be expected by the one who tries to reassemble a frog after vivisection—deals in aspects, features, parts, qualities and quantities, which are never in fact found wandering about on their own, like the grin of the Cheshire cat.

And if the universe is itself a unified structure, perhaps in some respects reaching the status of an organism, in which all things act and react for the maintenance and, in addition, the further development of each and all; and if the would-be knower in fact learns all she will ever know precisely through that co-operation with other entities (as the best of pragmatist epistemologies in essence maintain); then the profusion of imagery required for the most basic cognition of such a universe of being will of necessity be very complex indeed. For instance, the knowing-by-engaging-with other persons and things will in-volve envisaging how certain developments can work to the benefit of one and all; and that simple fact engages automatically the creative and indeed the ethical exercises of imagination, and the optimal form of the complex imagery which then forms the seedbed of all possible knowledge may well then be the story; and the conventional term for stories that operate at the broadest com-munal or cosmic, that is, metaphysical dimension is—myth.

In addition, any particular heuristic excursus of the human mind, en-fleshed as it is in a human body and inevitably embodied also in the language in which its research is essayed and its results expressed, will commonly reveal an inextricable mixture of image and abstract idea or—perhaps a better way of putting this point—a kind of continuum in which imagery and abstract ideation fade almost imperceptibly into each other. For this distinction between image and abstract concept is itself an example of abstract analysis, and as liable as any other to fall foul of the characteristic temptation of its kind—the temptation, that is to say, to take to be separate and independent entities what it abstracts from reality in the course of its analytic efforts; whereas what actually exists in all human discourse is the more or less imaginative and the more or less conceptualized.

Yielding to this characteristic temptation of the analytic mind produces, at one level of our analysis of reality, what is often nowadays called onto-theology. Presumably it is commonly called onto-*theology* because those who identify instances in which the abstractions of the analytic mind are reified, treated as separate and independent entities (e.g., Logos, Reason), commonly assume that such reified concepts fall within the traditional category of the divine, or within the traditional category of the metaphysical which these days is often presumed to be, if not coterminous with, then conflated with the category of the divine.

But there are many examples in modern philosophy of what we may have to call onto-philosophy, for they involve the same reifying of what are in reality analytic abstractions—concepts of the kind that from the earliest exponents of western philosophy were to be preferred to the categories of myth—yet the reifications of which do not result in anything we would normally call divine. And these go quite unnoticed, and certainly uncriticized in the Age of Heroic Materialism, as our age has been aptly called. There is the example of the analysis of the human being into the ideas of spirit and body, mind and matter, inner and extended substance. The abstracted terms of this dualistic analysis are regularly treated as if they named two separate and distinct—though often allegedly conjoined—substances. The resulting onto-philosophy can be blamed as much on those who deny the very existence of one of these "substances"—usually the mental or spiritual one—as on those who assert the existence of both.[2] And there are other examples of onto-philosophy that we have yet to meet among the postmodernists, incurred in their analyses of language, signs and texts; and perhaps even others still, incurred by those who operate such analytic dualisms as that of the transcendent and the immanent. But more of this later.

It is sufficient for the moment to end this opening move in the present argument with the observation that imaginative investigation of and discourse about reality—and not just the abstract, analytic investigation of and discovery about it—can result in its own kind of onto-philosophy, or in this case perhaps onto-mythology of the merely imaginary. For imagination's forte is to envisage and describe how things interact in this unified universe—not only for continued wellbeing but for development, for betterment. In this creative reach of its remit the imaginative can easily end by positing the merely imaginary—powers or processes, things that do not at all exist as depicted, that are merely creatures of wishful thinking or exaggerated fears. And what all of this amounts to, in effect, is the interim conclusion that both the imaginative and the abstract-analytical responses and approaches, insofar as they can be adequately distinguished in any domain of human discourse, are equally capable of similar degrees of truth and falsehood in construing the real. And indeed, each is as capable of correcting its own shortcomings as it is of improving the other's performance. All of the great leaps forward even in the most physical of sciences — most recently, relativity theory and quantum theory—are in origin leaps of imagination in construing anew the dynamic fabric of reality. Yet Einstein, for instance, could never quite bring himself to believe that the quantum picture of the physical world would turn out in the end to be anything other than imaginary. Which simply goes to show that it is often difficult to determine whether one is in the presence of a piece of onto-philosophy or onto-mythology or what is more usual, due to the mixed nature of human discourse, some hybrid of the two. Only the constant creative and critical engagement with reality can keep the truth a step ahead of the malign posse of conceptual and imaginative illusions.[3]

Genesis

A more particular argument against the sole adequacy of an abstract-analytic conceptualization of *creatio ex nihilo* and its logic can be raised upon an interrogation of the actual text of the opening chapters of Genesis. This will lead to a challenge to the first assumption mentioned above, namely, that that text depicts a one-off act or activity that created the world—an act that constituted a space-time singularity as physicists would call it—by means of something resembling a peremptory command from the omnipotent.

"In the beginning of God's creating (*bārā*) the heavens and the earth, the earth was without form and empty (*tōhû wā bōhû*) and darkness covered the face of the abyss" (Genesis 1:1–2). The root meaning of the Hebrew *bārā* signifies "to cut, to cut out," hence "to shape or form." The verb is used in Isaiah 43:1, 15 in order to depict Yahweh forming or fashioning a nation. At the other end of the Bible, a more literal translation of Hebrews 11:3 gives us: "the world [more literally still, 'the ages'] has been framed by God's word, to the end that that which is seen be known to have arisen not from things which appear." The key image for divine creation, then, is that of shaping, framing, forming, and not of some act of now irresistible force or power. *Tōhû* connotes emptiness, the void; *bōhû*'s connotation is more elusive—something unsubstantial, shall we say, something unreal. Darkness is absence of light where no form can appear; the abyss is the very symbol of formless chaos. A great collusion of images to evoke—with far more power and effect than an abstract and empty concept like nothingness could evoke—a formless, unsubstantial unreality. Add to this an understanding of temporal references characteristic to myth, and in particular of those grand metaphysical myths that deal in the ultimate origins or sources, as well as in the final goals of all things: In the beginning, *en archē*, in the principle itself; *in illo tempore*, once upon a time, long, long ago, or at the end, in the consummation. No dates are given or are possible here for, as Eliade so often says, this mythic time is time out of time—a time contemporary with all calendar times—in short, eternity as the opposite of linear or even circular time. The story you now hear is a story of acts without sequence, of a sequence that belongs to the structure of the story and not to the (divine) activity as such.

Further, not only is the activity of the great cosmic/metaphysical myths contemporaneous with all points of empirical time (as pre-Christian Irish religion, for instance, illustrated by spreading versions of their creation myths and commemorations of what these connoted over the four quarterly rituals of each year), but the creation of the formless, unsubstantial unreality, the no-thing, is a contemporaneous byproduct of the very forming in which the activity of divine creation essentially consists. Further still, the contemporaneous bringing-into-being of this formless no-thing as a byproduct of the formation of finite things (quite comparable to the Greek image/idea of prime matter, that is, matter-without-form which the Greeks actually called *to mē on*, "the no-thing," for only *forms*-of-matter are things, *ta onta*, and prime matter cannot be found on its own), prevents neither the possibility of talking of created things being formed out of this no-thing (just as in physics measurable formations such as fields of energy can be said to emerge in or out of space-time, even though in reality space-time is the byproduct of the emergence of such entities), nor even the possibility of the no-thing being depicted as ever threatening the good divine creation. This latter possibility is at least suggested by flood stories in which the abyss, the chaos, returns to destroy a divine creation already compromised by evil. It is more than suggested in some Hebrew Scriptures references to monsters of the deep, in myths as old as Genesis and as recent as Moby Dick; forces that, though created by God, albeit as byproducts, are adversarial to good; forces that God can deal with but cannot in the activity of creation entirely avoid or simply eradicate, it would appear. And it is still more than suggested in Isaiah 45:7, a chapter sprinkled with references to the opening creation scene of Genesis: "Forming light and creating darkness, making peace/prosperity (*shālōm*) and creating evil—I am the Lord who does all these things." The verb translated "creating" here is the same word found in the creation story of the opening of Genesis, *bārā*; and the Hebrew word translated "evil" here is the same word found in the phrase about the tree of the knowledge of good and evil, in Genesis 2:17 and 3:5.

So God forms all the things that make up the world, and forms them so as to make a universe, and in the process calls up unreality round the edges, as it were, of this reality, just like darkness inevitably emerges at the limits of light, whenever a source of light sends out light. This darkness, this abyss, this formless no-thing-ness is sometimes depicted as engulfing or threatening to engulf the formed world. Flood stories, for instance, are in themselves creation or re-creation stories: The dry land has to be formed (separated) and furnished (once again) from the chaos/abyss in order that life should be possible. And this nothingness in turn may be interpreted either as an undifferentiated—that is, as Hegel argued at the outset of his *Phenomenology of Spirit*—an abstract nothingness in which we may be totally swallowed; or, as Hegel would prefer to see it, a determinate nothingness—the "nothinging," the negation, the limiting in space-time—the deprivation (a *deprivatio boni*, which in Platonic thought became the essence of evil) of particular forms or stages in the on-going formation, so that higher states are achieved; an example, in short, of the patient labor of the negative in bringing all of reality, including the creator, to its absolute form and state.

The abstract concept of nothingness that characterizes the most analytic-conceptual version of the *creatio ex nihilo* theme results most frequently in the commission once again of the sin of onto-philosophy: That which is in actual fact an analytically abstracted element in a complex project—no less than the whole concrete project of cosmic creation/evolving reality as we know it—is treated as if it were an entity, a thing in its own right, giving the very odd impression of "nothing" then also as a something, out of which the world is created. It is this impression which then necessitates the correction of confining the connotation of *creatio ex nihilo* to the two negatives outlined at the outset of this essay. (And as we will see shortly, this is just one example of a failure of this abstract conceptual version of *creatio ex nihilo* which some theologians—in ignorance or forgetfulness of the rich variety of kinds, versions and interpretations of *creatio ex nihilo* advertised from Greeks to Christians—attribute to the theme of *creatio ex nihilo* as such.)

Evolution of the *Creatio*

But how did this purely abstract conceptual version of *creatio ex nihilo* come about and take its place among the others? What follows offers one partial historical explanation. For the rest it is a matter of (what Whitehead described as) a "retro-projection" by caesaropapist authorities in the Christian church, of the autocracy of the Roman emperor onto the creator God; or more generally, a prejudicial-style replacement of the imaginative-mythic by the abstract-analytic-conceptual.

The agencies directly involved in this creative forming of reality, according to the Genesis myth, are God's word ("God said") and God's spirit. The latter image is of the spirit as a great bird brooding over the abyss—a conventional image of forming in a womb and birthing, or bringing into being a world. The former, however—the image of the word—is more ambiguous. It could convey an image of word as an expletive, more especially a command, thus initiating a raw command scenario of creation. Such a reading gives us the *Dieu Fabricateur*, as Sartre called him, who further issues with all thus-fabricated entities, instructions for use with equal power to command the obedience of any who might be tempted to use the creation for any purpose they choose. This total image of creation and creator is much favored by those who prefer their morality in the form of obedience to explicit divine commands (mediated, naturally, through their own good offices), and yielding, finally, ideas of divinely initiated yet humanly exercised autocracies. But the imagery of God's word could equally convey an intelligible *form*, once again realized either in the thing and world formed by word; or in the representations of these in words and other signs and symbols; or in all of these. This latter option is offered particularly by the Greek word, *logos,* and was taken up explicitly into Jewish and Christian theology of creation especially during the period of Middle Platonism which coincided with the tragic separation of Christianity from the religion of the one it calls its founder.

A brief visit to pre-Christian origins of a philosophical theology that formed almost the whole of the theology which Christians borrowed and adapted to their own message—change a few words and phrases, Augustine said of the Platonists, and they might be Christians—would be enough to convince any student of *creatio ex nihilo* of the variety of its versions and interpretations, and the forms of myths or the forms of abstract-analytic conceptualizations, and especially the forms of philosophical commentaries on Plato's myths, in which it was available for borrowing.[4]

So from at least the Middle Platonists (roughly, over three centuries stretching from first-century BC to early third-century AD), this philosophizing about creation often took the form of commentary on Plato's inspired scriptures and most frequently on the myth of the *dēmiourgos* in the *Timaeus* (esp. 28ff). This story was of a world ordered and realized by means of forms (or *logoi*) which (now, in the Middle Platonic period, are seen to) exist within the divine, creating Logos. A world formed in or out of what? In imaginative terms—a receptacle, a space, a disorder, an emptiness of forms and of their ensuing order. In more conceptual terms, "material" or "matter"—these words in quotes because they cannot refer to matter as we know it, for that is already formed, created matter. Such "matter" is similar rather to something like the "prime matter" of Aristotle's hylemorphic theory, which never exists on its own like a formed thing, a *phusis* or nature. And then some commentators characteristically debate whether Plato's myth implied a creation in time or not: Those who say yes, inevitably imply that there was matter, a resistant, formed and evil force awaiting the *dēmiourgos* and its best efforts (examples would then be those Gnostic dualists so sternly and lengthily denounced by Plotinus, for instance, in *Enneads,* bk. 2, sec. 9); those who say no, imply that talk of a beginning refers to a necessity of the narrative form, but that in reality the world we know came, not from a moment in linear time, but from eternity. In that case, that which is depicted as chaotic flux, receptacle-space, prime matter, darkness (in which no form appears), comes into existence with the creative outpouring of the good creator (see Plotinus, *Enneads,* bk. 4, sec. 3.9; bk. 3, sec. 9.3)—just as Einstein would say that space is a function of the

James P. Mackey

forming of "fields" rather than a receptacle which preexists or exists independently of them, and parts of which may still lie empty of them. Yet it is still possible to think, imagine and say that the world-forming activity takes place in or out of this prime matter, this no-thing which is symbolized by images of formless, chaotic abyss, and of darkness—*creatio ex nihilo.*[5]

And it is also possible to say that this byproduct of divine creation then acts as adversary to the creator and all creatures. For with the exception of the raw-command model of divine creation and the abstract-analytic versions of it in which that model finds a home, the *creatio ex nihilo* theme does not entail any of those extreme conceptions of divine omnipotence which are so objectionable to modern theologians—particularly to feminists (even when they seem to support or invoke images of God as doing even the impossible, or of divine love as insuperable?)—and which are thought to be the source of a divine autocracy then claimed by Christ's vicar on earth, and so on. On the contrary, those early creation-out-of-nothing accounts that make such integral use of imagery and idea, always make clear the limits of what even a creator God can do. This is blindingly clear in the *Timaeus*, where it is claimed only that the creator makes everything good, and not bad, "insofar as this was attainable" in face of the resistance of something called "necessity." Translate that however one likes into ideas of "the materiality of things," this inevitably entails the finiteness of space-time and the consequences of flourishing at others' expense, disintegration, death and accompanying loneliness, grief, and above all a fear that makes one grasp at finiteness to sustain oneself (as Kierkegaard once put it), with ensuing damage to finite things—especially persons who cannot bear up under such expectations. Add to this powers that turn, in their created freedom, to destruction—instead of co-creating as they are designed to do—and one just begins to get a sense of the loving impotence of a God who formed forms of existence to generate, in turn, all that would evolve in this wonderful and potentially ever-more wonderful world. Such a God cannot avoid being the ultimate source, both directly and indirectly, of evils natural and moral; and can only—and only with the co-operation of creatures—keep on creating, out of what Plato called the creator's overflowing goodness, Eros, love. Omnipotence, then, need not and does not connote absolute autocracy, but rather the ability to create all that is created: Father Almighty *means* creator of heaven and earth.

The Stoicized Platonism, then, that Christians of that early period borrowed to form the substance of their own theology, envisaged the divinity called Logos continually forming and reforming the universe in and through the derivative "seed-words"—the *logoi spermatikoi* or *rationes seminales.* Hence the Stoics also named this divine Logos, by whom all things are made, Physis or Nature, after Aristotle's definition of *phusis* as the *form* of things that have in themselves the source of their own motion or development. (The Stoics also named this divine creator Zeus, of course, to whom Cleanthes wrote a memorable hymn.) This was, and is, a story of continuous creation. And this story is quite compatible with the Genesis account of God creating things that contain the seeds of their own future within themselves; and creating one species in particular which, being in the image of the creator, knew (named) the creatures and was therefore placed in a position of co-responsibility for the future of all. This idea of the human species as the husbandman of creation—the form of creature which was informed of itself and of the others and hence could continue to guide the continuing formation of all—translated quite easily into the Stoic system in which the characteristic *logos spermatikos* of the human was conscious both of itself and, potentially, of all other *logoi spermatikoi*, and was therefore in a position to participate more fully than the others in the nature and work of the divine creator Logos. Or, to put the matter the other way round, to have the divine Logos work its continuous creation in and through the co-operation of the human logos.

Such thoughts about the creation myth in Genesis, together with its more philosophical exposition from the beginnings of Christian theology, constitute the outline of a Christian concept of divine creation which is fully compatible with the contemporary concept of evolution:

- What the myth describes is what happens at all times.
- The act of divine creation is an act of forming, rather than an act of raw power which, on the analogy of a command, brings a thing or state of affairs into existence instantly and fully formed.
- The divine form-giver of things, and of the relationships between things that make them a universe, works through these forms toward their fuller or future development.
- Due to the materiality, plurality, and hence finitude of created things (which is an inevitable byproduct of even divine creation) the life of any creature, and especially its advance in life, involves the expense of some part of that creature's own life and also, most likely, expense of the lives of other creatures—and this is true whether we consider individuals or species.

Evolution is then the visible trace, seen from the short-lived and limited view of the creature, of the universal continuously creative power that drives the formation and continual re-formation of this ever-changing universe, through the mutual information, transformation and, yes, deformation which the created forms exercise upon each other. Creative evolution; evolutionary creation.

That is not to say, of course, that the post-Darwinian concept of evolution can be found in Genesis or even in the Stoicized Platonism adopted by early Christians as their philosophical exposition of Genesis. But it does allow us to take contemporary evolution theory fully into our Christian doctrine of creation, if only as the best account available to date concerning that inherent developmental capacity which for Aristotle characterized *phusis*—the natural form(s) of the creation—and which both Genesis and the Stoic philosophy of divine creation presented under the image of the seeds. (We should perhaps note that the Stoic philosophy saw this development as involving much more than the Genesis idea of reproduction, and much less than the vast complexity and range of development that modern evolutionary science opens up to our still somewhat astonished gaze.)[6]

Creatio and Onto-philosophy

Two things need to be said concerning the choice and deployment of dynamic form and forming as that which reality reveals to be the master-image for continuous creation, the sheer cosmic dimensions of which suggest traces of the divine. First, a word about mind and matter again, and how some ultimate source of space-time and of all that evolves in it, while conceived as of the nature of mind or spirit, could give rise to the evolving forms of space-time without these incurring the suspicion of being simply carved from its own *ousia* (Greek, translatable as either "being" or "substance"); and, second, a word about transcendence and immanence.

Sartre objected to the Christian idea of a divine mind creating the universe on many grounds, but first and foremost because he maintained that no conceivable act of such an entity—if such an entity existed—could result in anything that could then be deemed to have broken out of its own absolute subjectivity. Now, of course, it is easy to retort: He would say that, wouldn't he? For his own philosophy is both exponent and victim of a completely dichotomous dualism of *pour-soi* and *en-soi*, the complete counterpart of that equally dichotomous dualism of two substances falsely attributed to Descartes, though Sartre himself preferred to talk of two dichotomously distinct realms of reality. But it is more important for present purposes to realize that Sartre is just one of a group of philosophers and assorted scientists of the modern and postmodern eras who commit the sin of onto-philosophy in their dealing with the "substances" of mind and matter. Many of these then go on to assume that the *res cogitans* of "Cartesian" dualism is just another name for a material brain, so that there really is only one substance—the *res extensa*. Others struggle to see how mind or spirit or consciousness and activities that result thereof could derive from the known evolution of the purely material, extended substance— with so little success that John Searle sighs for a second Newton.

So immersed are these moderns in their version of the sin of onto-philosophy, so biased toward the resulting crudity of their materialism, that it could possibly never occur to them to consider how the *res extensa* could derive from mind or mind-like being. And this, paradox of paradoxes, despite the fact that Kant (as crude a dualist in his way as the modern age has produced), with his distinction of noumenon and phenomenon, yet equivalently declares at one critical point of his first great *Critique* that the defining features of matter, of material substance—namely, its extension in space and time—did derive from mind. For space and time, he said, were a priori forms attributable to mind in the process of sense experience. Einstein thought that Kant could hardly be taken seriously in his suggestion that space-time (a term now used by scientists for the "objective" universe as such) could be a purely subjective experience. Yet Einstein also insisted that, first, matter has lost its role as a fundamental concept in physics, as the model of field proves a potential replacement for the model of particle or material point. By carrying this replacement to its logical conclusion, space-time becomes a structural quality of a field. Now the idea of a field—the representative of reality, as Einstein calls it—a field of force expressed in mathematical form or formulation, is much more of the nature of a mind-like entity, or at the very least something formed or fashioned by mind-like entities. Certainly, with this demotion of the crude idea of matter that was characteristic of the equally crude, putatively Cartesian dualism, the prospect of a world as we know it deriving from mind becomes much more promising for philosophical investigation—and much, much more promising than the prospect of mind deriving from the cruder conceptions of matter. And in any case that dualism called "Cartesian," consequent as it is upon the sin of onto-philosophy, is to be rejected in favor of a much more subtle metaphysic of mind-in-matter and matter-in-mind.[7]

Such mutual in-being of mind and matter brings us to immanence, and to our second and final word in this section, concerning immanence and transcendence. Both of these terms have a basic connotation construed from spatiotemporal imagery—remaining within or outside of; going, or being borne beyond. Their metaphorical use, however—which is the usage at issue in the kind of contexts we consider in the present volume—does not need to carry with it the mutual opposition between immanence and transcendence inevitably suggested by the most literal, that is to say spatial, connotation of that imagery. For according to that most basic connotation: To the extent that something remains within, to that precise extent it is not (gone) outside or beyond; immanence is at the expense of transcendence, and vice versa. But when these terms are used metaphorically, in a usage that carries them beyond our more primitive experiences of the spatiotemporal relationships of bodies, such mutual exclusion need not at all apply. Certainly this is the case when they are used of a creative power that forms a world of things as formings of the forms of space and time; a creative power that makes these forms interrelated and interdependent to the point of forming universe, so that they are taken up into its continuous creativity, in that each species-form through its individual members is empowered to inform, reform, or deform, and in any case to transform both itself and the others. Then, certainly, such a foundational creative power—whether it be named a gene or a god—can be said to be at all times and places immanent in space-time as it continually transcends each stage in the evolution of that same universe.

Yet so much talk of immanence and transcendence (and not just popular talk but apparently talk of a high philosophical tenure) sounds as if it takes "immanence and transcendence"—used now not of simple bodies and their simple spatiotemporal relationships, but as names for abstract concepts, for two concomitant and intrinsically interrelated features of reality-in-the-process-of-becoming—and reifies them. Such talk treats them, that is to say, as concepts for separately existing entities or separate and distinct regions of being: One within space-time, the immanent; and the other beyond or outside of space-time (whatever "beyond" or "outside" could mean in this context), the transcendent. This is surely another form of the sin of onto-philosophy.

The anthropologist Lévi-Strauss, who thought of cultures as texts, once famously remarked that incest is bad grammar. And one cannot help thinking that a little lesson in grammar would prevent much of the current talk about immanence and transcendence from misleading philosophical discussion in the way it too often does. "Transcendence" is an abstract noun, connoting a process in which a variety of entities are known to engage—a process of over-reaching or going beyond certain current limits or limitations. "Transcendent" is an adjective for entities as they engage in this process and, as with any adjective, the noun it qualifies should be added or clearly implicit in the discourse. In short, whenever the phrase "the transcendent" is used, it should be accompanied by a noun which answers the question: The transcendent *what*? The transcendent mind? The transcendent gene? The transcendent process of natural selection? Use of the noun "transcendence" or of the adjective "transcendent" with nothing but the definite article in attendance is likely to give rise to much mystifying gobbledegook, especially in a context in which the expectation seems to be that transcendence or the transcendent may be taken automatically to denote divinity, even if no reason has been supplied for the existence or character of any entity or region of being that could reasonably be deemed divine. Therefore, far too much talk about transcendence or the transcendent in fact provides instances of onto-philosophy which are in the precise form of that onto-theology so frequently complained about in modernist and postmodernist texts.

Creation, of course, in all the most obvious instances of it, involves a process of transcending in that it brings about new forms of things or of processes in which they engage and from which they result. And if people believe they can detect *within* all this pullulating and pulsating universe a unified and unifying power that forms space-time and forms the other natures that take up or make up space-time, continually combining them so that they participate in that perpetual transformation which is seen from this side as evolution; then they may well claim that they are in the presence of the traces of a being which, as the constant creative source of cosmic or universal reality, can be deemed divine. Transcendence and immanence will be seen then not as contraries but as coordinates used to locate these agencies that, in their mutual co-inherence, bring about those states of disrupting, exceeding and so on which David Wood so well describes (chap. 9, below).

Such are the end-results of analyzing what we call creation through the master-image of creating as forming or shaping; and there are similarly interesting results for the understanding of the relationship between the creator and the creatures. These may best be seen from a brief revisit to the other master-image of creation mentioned previously—the command-of-an-irresistible-power image, more crudely known as the shouting-it-into-existence model. On the latter model, God would need to shout again to tell us about the first shout, since we were not there to hear it; and then would need to shout again—more than once, given our persistent waywardness—to tell us how to behave ourselves in and with the creation. This succession of shouts yields the model of divine revelation as verbal communication, and the model of moral code or pontiff issuing commands that require childlike obedience as the first virtue. Further, the command model of revelation (telling us what to believe), of morals (telling us how to behave), and of existence itself, suggests a creator God who operates from outside the creation. Whereas the forming and re-forming model of creation used from Genesis onward opens onto the model of the *archē anarchos*—the beginning in the sense of origin or source-without-source, ever creatively, transcendentally active *within* the evolving cosmos. This model of knowing the divine through the traces of this continuous creativity—and more precisely through the experience of being oneself both passive and active with respect to this cosmic creative evolution—is essentially a pragmatist model of revelation and knowledge, informing by creative forming. And this model of revelation yields a model of morality as cooperative envisaging-of and attempting better being, more fulfilled life and existence for all inevitably interlinked creative creatures: Real responsibility, with all the damage and all the guilt, yet all the fulfillment and all the dignity this can bring.[8]

Postmodernism

It is best to begin this section as well with some common assumptions—and mainly, once again, with critical intent. It is commonly assumed, even when it is not being trumpeted by prominent postmodernists themselves, that post-modernism dispenses with metanarratives—those grand narratives about being which attempt to tell the truth, the whole truth, and nothing but the truth of "whatever is begotten, born and dies . . . of what is past, or passing, or to come," as Yeats would put it. Or, in another formulation of the same assumption, that postmodernism finally dispenses with metaphysics. The first formulation of the assumption (and I think it is the same assumption), is best dismissed by a simple tu quoque; although it would take another book by Sean Burke to do it properly. Burke's book *The Death and Return of the Author*—the best book on postmodernism by one who does not profess philosophy—shows how the author, also ushered out the front door by postmodernists, always surreptitiously re-enters their scenarios by the back door and operates all the more effectively for not being any longer noticed.[9] This, incidentally, is an author who, when noticed, looks suspiciously like divinities of the old metanarratives that sit outside the world, subject to none of its changing conditions—eternally and infallibly and immutably knowing, quite literally, all about it. A companion

James P. Mackey

volume by Burke could make a similar case concerning the much-advertised demise and surreptitious return of metanarrative.

Vicissitudes of Metaphysics

A similar critique of the premature advertisement in postmodernist publications of the demise of metaphysics, can bring the important philosophical matters at issue here under an even closer scrutiny. But what do we mean by metaphysics? In his work of that title Aristotle is engaged in what he himself called *philosophia prōtē*, first philosophy, and in this he included both the study of beings precisely as being and the study of that which could be found to be the foundation, cause, or source of this being of all beings: All of this duly entered into the connotation of metaphysics in the tradition of western philosophy. Heidegger however preferred the term "ontology" for the study of beings in respect, not now of their various particular forms or natures, but of the condition of their being as such; and for that part of traditional metaphysics that studied the supreme being, alleged to found the very being of the beings, he used the term "onto-theology." For (as he argues at the outset of his *Was ist Metaphysik?*) those who think they have sufficient reason for believing in the existence of a supreme being which founds, and thus guarantees, the being of all empirical beings, cannot even engage with the very question which the being of all such empirical beings puts to them (and which yields the whole substance of the discipline of ontology or metaphysics). The question, namely: Since the being of all space-time entities seems to be a being-unto-death, a being-unto-nothingness, why are there *essenzen*? Why is there anything at all rather than nothing? Those for whom an answer to that question is already available—whether through rational proof or special divine revelation—cannot experience as a real question that question that is at the heart of all finite existential experience. It can only be for them an "as if" question, and the pursuit of it a pure philosophical charade. And the onto-theological tag comes into play because these so-called proofs and their results are simply instances of an abstract conceptual analysis and logical argument, the terms of which are then taken to represent realities defined by the analytic and argumentative process itself.

So for instance, abstract concepts of omnipotence, omniscience and so on (all the omni's) are assembled, with ideas of personality and of "that than which nothing greater can be thought" thrown in for good measure (Kant was correct is suggesting that the so-called ontological argument was actually assumed in all of the so-called cosmological proofs, though he failed to notice that it would have to be equally assumed in his postulating a god on moral grounds); abstract concepts of contingency and necessity are then added to the mix in order to provide what seem like logical steps in an argument; these abstract concepts are then substantivized, and of course capitalized as the Omnipotent, the Omniscient, the Necessary (and, of course, the Transcendent) Being; *et voila!*

Something similar to Heidegger's strictures upon any return to metaphysics are encountered again in recent reaches of the Humean skepticism that has for so long masqueraded as empiricism. Ousted as plain nonsense by the nonsensical over-simplicity of A. J. Ayer, his logical-positivist predecessors and linguistic-analyst successors, metaphysics has recently made a comeback to these otherwise rather barren philosophical regions. At first, the comeback was condoned only under such straitened conditions as those imposed by Quine: Only those entities necessarily referred to by the most advanced scientific theories should be deemed to make up the fabric of reality as such. Or, as Strawson put it: Metaphysics must remain descriptive, that is to say, confined to articulating and making explicit, from within, views of the world's deepest and most universal existential structures that we ourselves inhabit; metaphysics must never become revisionary, by pretending to compare and criticize different views of the world's existential structures as if from a viewpoint outside the world somehow made available to us. And yet, recently, British metaphysics has since gone beyond the strictures imposed by Quine—has gone further, one might say, into the deep existential structures of the world and the vistas of possibility allegedly opened up there. It has still, in general, not gone quite so far as to envisage the existence of a supreme being, source and ground of all the other beings in the world and of its deepest structures.

What is noticeable about these various versions of reemergent metaphysics is this: The supreme being envisaged, if only for purposes of rejection, is always one which squats outside the world—an image used by Heidegger, but which goes back to the Feuerbachian-Marxist critique of religion—a supreme being that fits with Strawson's view-from-outside and that is often adopted for purposes of a revisionist as opposed to a descriptive metaphysic. This supreme being is reminiscent of the shouting-it-into-existence imagery of one reading of the Genesis myth, and also reminiscent of crude (though common) views of transcendence as likewise referring to something outside, rather than within the entity or event with respect to which the process of transcendence is deployed. That is not to say that this outsider status for the creator was invented by those who criticized it. Quite the contrary. In the west, at least, it was suggested by Christianity's insistence on a kind of faith in God which itself placed God beyond the range of investigative reason, and hence beyond the range of Strawson's descriptive metaphysics. And even though certain Catholic traditions in Christianity seemed to place God's existence well within the range of investigative reason, they did this mainly by adopting what became known as proofs of God's existence. Then, particularly since the dawn of the Age of Reason—or rather, the Age of Rationalism—philosophy of religion took these odd pieces of reasoning to be its first and main preoccupation. Odd pieces of reasoning? Yes. Because, as hinted just now, they proceeded by first defining the kind of entity something called God must be, and then set out to prove that that particular and extra entity or person actually exists—an absolutely classic piece of onto-philosophy. The puzzlement as to how one could

James P. Mackey

name and define some entity one had not yet encountered, even in the traces in which it presents itself, remains unrelieved. For if one had encountered it, one would not need to prove its existence. Just as, when I stood before my colleagues at the Villanova conference and read this paper aloud, I left so many traces (in the form, perhaps, of increasingly convoluted and boring argumentation) that it would have been as unmannerly as it would have been unnecessary, for them to engage in trying to prove my existence before my face. (I borrow the latter phrase from Kierkegaard, who uses it in a context more appropriate to the face of God.)

In light of this contemporary status of metaphysics, then, what now is the relationship of postmodernism to metaphysics? Well, first of all, the postmodernists and their followers chant the mantra of the overcoming, or of the end of metaphysics, as ritually as any others. Yet Sartre was quite correct in observing that any metaphysics implies a theory of knowledge, an epistemology, that is, a theory of how reality is known, and then of how is the knower known; just as any theory of knowledge, even in the form of theory of text or language, implies a metaphysic, that is, a theory about the characteristics and conditions of being as such, a theory that seeks to go beyond the more particular theories that deal with specific kinds of forms of reality which Aristotle called *phusikē*, natures. In Aristotle particular forms of being contain within themselves the source of their development (so kinds of particles, for instance, or species), so that the effort to describe and explain the characteristics or conditions of the whole of empirical reality—characteristics and conditions common to all natures, all *phusikē, le tout ensemble*—could be called *meta ta phusikē* (that which goes beyond the individual natures, species and classes), metaphysics. And in both cases, that of the epistemology and of the metaphysics necessarily implied from the beginnings of the scientific quest for knowledge of the fabric of reality, it is philosophy's task to make the implicit critically explicit. Quine says no more and no less when he insists that hard science, in order to secure the truth of its best theories, needs *both* an ontology and an epistemology, and that it is philosophy's task to do its best to supply these. That Sartre and Quine are correct in these views—together with so many others who take all this talk about the end of metaphysics to be about as effective as whistling in the wind—can be shown by reflecting for a moment on a deep and serious fault line that runs through Derrida's metanarrative.

Signs and the Death of Wonder

The fault line in Derrida's thought can be best described as a serious metaphysical deficit; and it can be most easily detected by closer inspection of that Saussurean semiology which Derrida imports into his system, and more particularly the Saussurean definition of sign. The sign is defined by Saussure as the associative totality of signifier and signified, where the signifier is some image of the psychic order (acoustic perhaps or visual, a word heard or read), and the signified is something of the order of an idea. The signifier itself is empty; only the associative totality of itself and the signified has and gives a meaning. And from here Derrida takes off into his theory of *différance*, invoking simultaneously the ideas of differing and deferring: For signifiers are never anchored by the signified, but only by other signifiers, by their very differences; and so any final meaning or truth for any of them is infinitely deferred; and so on.

Now unless one's critical faculty has fallen asleep, something must immediately be said about a sign so defined. And it is this: Signs exist only as part of a well-known and quite distinctive actual, existential process and one which, incidentally, is by no means confined to human beings. The real, existential process in which alone signs exist—in which alone signs *are* and are *signs*—is a process in which one communicates with another about something; even if that something be only the one or the other communicator, or things with which the one and the other communicator have to do. Outside of that actual, active, living process—marks on paper, sounds in the air, images and ideas of mind, or any and all combinations of these *are not signs*, or parts of signs, or anything to do with signs. As Wittgenstein observed, there is and can be no such thing as a private language. Or, to put the same point more positively: Language, in order to be and to be language—whether in textual, oral, or any other form—must be public, that is to say, instantly usable in the most public forum; and in order to be public it must be both objective and subjective—or, rather, intersubjective—that is to say, it must denote and connote objects in the world that are available to at least two consciousnesses-in-communication.

In order to be persuaded of all of this it is necessary only to explicate a little further the process by which signs are and are signs, the process by which languages, being sign systems, come into existence. As the ancient Latin poet put it, with that awesome power of precision that poetry alone possesses: *Sunt lacrimæ rerum, et mentem mortalia tangunt,* "tears are of things, and mortal things do touch the mind." For "tears" say "signs" (and tears too are signs), and then what is being said is this: Things are intelligible forms (*logoi*) of matter, hence finite and mortal; and being such they inform minds, and minds then know and can judge them. The Stoics were wise enough to know and say that our emotions are judgments, primary means of apprehending what objective reality reveals, and of communicating this to others: In this case, the metaphysical condition of the mortality of material things touches the mind, is apprehended in our sadness and communicated in our tears—part and parcel of the commonest semiological currency of our kind.

So the intelligible forms—the in*form*ations that come from reality in its constant self-revelation, in the course of our constant interaction with it—are then communicated in signs: Signs in their vast variety range from signals that simply draw attention to something, accompanied perhaps by expressions of emotion that interpret what is signaled (as fear does in pointing at a predator); through pictorial representations (cave paintings at Lascaux); through the special sign that is known as a symbol, because it participates in the reality it signifies and is thus frequently performative (the Christian Eucharist where bread and wine, both gifts of nature and human products, are broken and poured to others, to show that we live by giving life, that is, by dying for each other, as life and its supports are constantly poured out unstintingly to each and all from their original source); to the more arbitrary, conventional kinds of signs that form these extremely complex examples of languages that all peoples evolve, comprised of words spoken or written, or gestures (as in so-called sign languages) and themselves ranging from most concretely imaginative ("radio has the best pictures") to the most analytically abstract (*Transcendence and Beyond: A Postmodern Inquiry*).

Perhaps this is to go on a bit much about such an elementary matter, but it never fails to be surprising how difficult it seems to be to get certain post-modernists and their followers (and indeed, assorted phenomenologists also) to see what appears to be so obvious—namely, that signs exist and can exist only in the existential context of intersubjective communication concerning *ta onta*, the things that are. Leave out of the account of signs, then, either or both of the following: (1) the things that in their self-revelation offer the first forms from which signs may be developed, and (2) the subjects who can both develop sign systems from these and communicate them to each other. The loss thereby suffered comprises both signs themselves and, since texts are made up of signs, the loss also of all text—a loss for which no amount of reference to some mysterious ur-text can in the least compensate. All that remains is a prime piece of onto-philosophy which treats an analytic abstraction from the full descriptions of the sign—the associative totality of signifier and signified (like sound and fury) that signifies nothing beyond itself—as if it could exist in its own right, when in fact it does not and cannot.

The loss from this account of reality of subjects and things, of their informative interactions among themselves and with each other, as the existential context in which alone signs are and can be signs—that is the enormous extent of the metaphysical deficit in Derrida's philosophy. It is a metaphysical deficit which he himself seemed to acknowledge—though still not fully and completely—in that most pretentious and oft-quoted declaration of his: *Il n'y a pas de hors-texte*, "there is nothing outside of or beyond text."[10] And despite the number of times he and his expositors have tried to reinterpret that statement so as to prevent its plain connotation from coming across, all such moves are futile, for the metaphysical deficit is entailed by the very importation of the fatally flawed Saussurean definition of sign into the heart of his system.

It might be possible to suggest that the ur-text to which Derrida refers is comprised in fact of that inherently evolutionary reality that continually comes into being precisely by the natural forms (idea-like entities) that constitute the natural cosmos by forever informing, reforming, deforming, transforming themselves and each other in an open-ended, infinite process. So that the very truth we tell about this evolutionary universe—as indeed whatever truth we may be able to tell about any ultimate source which we can only see and describe in terms of our present images and ideas about that universe[11]—is consequently subject to continual revision. But if that is the case, it would still be necessary to say that Derrida's system is more of a caricature than an accurate picture of such a cosmic text. A caricature exaggerates in order to draw attention to some facets of the thing depicted, but this caricature does this to the point where other equally important facets of the reality in question disappear entirely from view. The facet which appears in Derrida's picture of reality exaggerates the mental nature of the reality portrayed—signifiers and signifieds as conscious, mind-like creations. The facet which does not appear at all in his picture—thereby undermining the value of a caricature by an equal and opposing falsification—is the process in which this multiform, ever-transforming reality is expressed and emerges in the actual, material, existential conditions of space-time, in which other minds can contemplate, as well as to some extent re-create it in both mental and extra-mental terms.[12]

Agir les choses

Roland Barthes's epistemology and accompanying metaphysics is not so inadequate. Of course he also uses Saussure's inherently inadequate semiology, in order to rightly rid the world of those onto-theological systems whose conceit it is to describe reality in immutable and obligatory categories which are allegedly available in or through some being who squats outside the world. But Barthes then, without giving any notice of this, moves to what is in fact an adequate epistemology and metaphysics.

Barthes's semiology-epistemology and (at the very least, implicit) metaphysics is essentially comprised of two axioms. The first, derived from Marx, states that the world we know bears everywhere the traces of humanity's intentional and active presence in it.[13] As Barthes puts it: The most apparently "natural" thing in the world retains a trace—however faint, in some instances—of a presence of human being and of human acts of producing, managing, using, subsuming or even rejecting those things of which the natural world is constructed. The second axiom states that language is, in essence, designed to do things (*dresse . . . a les agir*; one recalls Heidegger's word for things, the old Greek term, *pragmata*, "things with which we have to do"). Put the two axioms together and the resulting epistemology-metaphysics is as follows: We know things, and each other, in the process of acting together on and with them and being acted on by them. Knowledge *is* our consciousness of the forms of selves and things as these are informed, reformed, deformed and in all cases transformed in that ubiquitous and permanent process. Add only that this epistemology-metaphysics needs to be broadened from its overly anthropomorphic focus, not only in Barthes but in most modern philosophy: For all other things also have the forms, the in-form-ations, by which all engage in these mutual transformations that constitute the evolution, that is to say, the

James P. Mackey

continuous creation of the universe. And it is by engaging in this process that all know themselves and all others to be equally and daily engaged in cosmo-genesis—whether each is conscious of this, or not.[14]

It is in this kind of philosophical context—and not in the context of that desiccated Humean skepticism which has for so long masqueraded as empiricism—that linguistic analysis provides access to the means and sum of our knowledge of reality, since it is by language that we communally (that is to say, in communication) think how we do, and are to *agir les choses*. (It is unnecessary to add so-called "sign languages" here, since any system of signs constitutes a language; but it is necessary to remember, once again, that other species use languages.) That having been said, there is little if any conceptual difference between language designed to do things and the idea of word as the operative process of continuing creation; provided, once more, that word is not taken in the sense of expletive-like commands, but rather in the sense of intelligible forms or formulations inscribed in various ways within, and ex-pressed in various ways by, all things that make up the creation.

Put in these terms, the question that lies in wait for all truly critical, unprejudiced analysis of the languages by which we investigate all that is engaged in the cosmogenic process named *agir les choses*, is this: What num-ber or kind of such cosmogenic agents do we encounter through the traces they leave as they continually co-create this universe? As we pursue this un-avoidable question, this quest, we do of course notice how the very language games by which we both discover and co-create this evolving universe—in both the primal, imaginative and the more derivative, analytic forms—betray us out of their very own strengths and lead us astray. Imagination in its attempts to construe the world, in both senses of that word, construe—to represent and to co-create—can easily overstep its limits and imagine unreal and unrealiz-able states of being; the imagination carrying us toward the merely imaginary. Analytic, that is to say, abstract thought, on the other hand, can mistake its abstractions and some of their logical developments for whole and concrete realities. Then, in forgetfulness of the fact that these have been abstracted from the concrete, ever-changing flux of being and nonbeing that characterizes the universe (Heidegger's "forgetfulness of being"), these can easily come to be thought of as things-in-themselves, immutable and universal forms, and some-times as existing outwith the universe as really real, ideal and regulative reality. The Pre-Socratics pointed to the characteristic failure of imagination in an-cient myth, and thus began the development of the analytic, logical reasoning known as philosophy, to ameliorate matters. Postmodernists and some of their predecessors pointed to the characteristic failures of philosophy, particularly at its metaphysical depths; and since many of these failures involved the reifica-tion of abstract forms or ideas as godlike entities squatting outside the world, they were denounced as onto-theology. But there are many other examples of the reifying of the abstract fruits of analysis and its accompanying logic, such as those found in "Cartesian" and equivalent kinds of dualism; and although some of these do not seem to be examples that would fit the category of the divine, they need to be denounced also—this time as onto-philosophy, even and perhaps particularly when they occur in the works of the postmodernists themselves.[15]

The real question behind and within this piece concerning creation and transcendence, is not: Is there (a) god? But, rather: What or who, if anyone or anything, among all the entities that present themselves through the traces they continue to leave all around you, and indeed in you, do you think could reasonably be called divine? The answer from the Christian theology of creation—and the extent to which that is primarily what is called a natural theology, that is to say, one accessible to natural imagination and reason has strong Biblical backing[16]—the answer is: Some forming-reality that forms, like minds form words, but that is not itself formed; that is to say, is not shaped, cut out, limited as are all the formed entities in and through which it continues to act. Some forming-reality that is producing the endless play of formed entities among themselves who in turn produce the ever-evolving universe; orchestrating their play so that the evolving *universe* continues to be co-created by them; and so is always and everywhere accessible to all through such cosmic traces.

At the beginning of his quest for *Being and Nothingness*, Sartre accessed an entity in some respects similar to the Christian creator: A consciousness-type being in itself contentless—that is, without form or forms—which he calls an absolute, the *pour-soi*. But then, as already remarked, Sartre denied that this or any other such consciousness-type being could ever function as creator of the world, since nothing to which this *pour-soi* could give rise—if it ever could give rise to anything—could escape from its absolute subjectivity and so be described in any manner or form as an objective reality. There are many things that could be said about this position, and some have been said already. But just one more thing needs to be said about it in order to bring this long analysis and argument to some conclusion: Subjectivity and objectivity are here assumed by Sartre—as by so many others who bandy these terms about—as dichotomously distinct and opposite, whereas they are in fact correlates or coordinates, like immanence and transcendence. All knowledge is subjective in that it is essentially a function of a subject; and is simultaneously objective insofar as that which is known, insofar as it is truly known, exists independently of current instances of our awareness of it. Or, as Hegel pointed out at the beginning of his *Phenomenology of Spirit*, the distinction between subjective and objective—denoted in the metaphor of inward and outward, and cousin to the duality of immanent and transcendent—falls always within the subject. This is most clearly illustrated in the case of our consciousness of other selves, which can only take place in the context of some shared intersubjectivity.[17] The objectivity of these other subjects, these other subjectivities, is not only the most assured instance of our sense of objectivity—in that their freedom and independence assures us that they are not merely parts or extensions of our selves—it is also the ground and principal guarantor of the objectivity of other things that we jointly know. Add now the consideration, already canvassed, that it is much more feasible to imagine mind-like beings giving rise to matter—in that it is our scientific experience that forming (shaping and thus limiting) gives rise to space-time, and thus to what might be called the materiality of things—than to try to imagine, on a cruder materialist conception of the world, how mind-consciousness could derive from this, and the answer to Sartre is complete.

So, if the traditional Christian ideas about divine creation were to be put in the manner already outlined, and if we were to opt for the epistemology-metaphysics of, say, Barthes rather than, say, Derrida—traces continually left everywhere by agents forever active and acted upon in the process of cosmogenesis, and continually read by those agents who are thereby conscious of all engaged in the task defined as *agir les choses*—then it would be difficult indeed to understand why religious folk and some postmodernists[18] are prevented from making common cause in the quest for the ultimate source and conductor of the grand enterprise of being.

NOTES

1. On the idea of a space-time singularity and scientists' natural antipathy toward it, see Stephen Hawking, *Black Holes and Baby Universes* (London: Bantam, 1994), esp. 39–41. On the alignment of space-time singularity with the one-off command model of divine creation; the alignment of the forming-model with the conviction of continuous creation; and hence the possibility of natural theology as a possibility for scientists also (as physics opens quite naturally onto metaphysics for them); there is insufficient space-time within the confines of this essay, but see, e.g., the interrogation of David Deutsch's "The Fabric of Reality" in James P. Mackey, *The Critique of Theological Reason* (Cambridge: Cambridge University Press, 2000), p. 120ff.

2. Descartes himself was not guilty of the crude dualist metaphysics that is nowadays summoned up under his name. Matter and spirit to him were "incomplete substances" of the *une seule personne*. Spinoza represented Descartes's position much more accurately than most when he wrote, "mind and body are one and the same individual conceived now under the attribute of thought, now under the attribute of extension" (Spinoza, *Ethics*, trans. G. H. R. Parkinson, Oxford Philosophical Texts, 2000, bk. 2, p. xxi, note; see also Mackey, *Critique of Theological Reason*, p. 11ff.)

3. For an introduction to scientists like Gould who see science as essentially story, in opposition to postmodernists like Lyotard who see narrative as the very opposite to the experimental knowledge of science, see Stephen Prickett, *Narrative, Religion and Science* (Cambridge: Cambridge University Press), 2003.

4. Many other terms for images/ideas of origins, such as "emanating from, taking origin from, being brought forth, being formed by," and so on, are fully interchangeable with "being created by, or made by"; not least in that all of these—receiving as they do their humanly accessible connotations from such actions/experiences as are characteristic of creatures—need to be treated to the "ways" of negation and eminence *simultaneously* with the "way" of affirmation. The Greeks insisted on this (see the *Di-*

daskalikos of Albinus), once again, before Christians began to philosophize—that is to say, to theologize—their faith, and that not just in imitation of the Greeks, but by borrowing the Greeks' theology wholesale. In any case, simplistic and misleading contrasts between emanation and creation should not be allowed to lessen our appreciation of the amount of borrowing in which our ancestor-theologians engaged.

5. When I referred, in the spoken version of this piece, to Plotinus and Porphyry (and in particular to the latter's commentary on the *Timaeus*) as exemplars of the creation-out-of-nothing theme, I was taking these as the best examples of this theology among the Greeks. I did not feel it necessary to illustrate how in this respect they were Neoplatonic exponents of a long tradition that went back through Middle Platonism. Those who would still wish to assure themselves of this long tradition should read Philo, a contemporary of Jesus, a Middle Platonist in philosophical terms and a thoroughly orthodox Jew who, particularly in his *On the Creation of the World*, offers this kind of version of creation-out-of-nothing, but now by also exegeting his favorite creation myth, that of Genesis. And it is well known that his future influence was among early Christian theologians, rather than among his fellow Jews.

6. This creative-evolution model of the divine creation of the universe has existed from time immemorial, and in contexts far different from certain readings of Genesis or the Platonized Stoicism of early Christian theology. But it was kept out of the mainstream, as is so often the case with aspects of the Christian truth that were lost to the sight of those who, in pursuit of tight orthodox definitions of the faith, adhered ever more closely to a model of command by omnipotence. So from Ovid's *Metamorphoses* to the *Mahabharata*, to pre-Christian Irish shape-changers, the theme of divine power within—taking the shapes of and changing the shapes of different creatures—has been universal; and with the advent of modern evolutionary theory the metamorphosis of the whole of natural reality is secured (see Marina Warner, *Fantastic Metamorphoses, Other Worlds*, Oxford: Oxford University Press, 2002). A related arena for the survival of this more rounded idea of divine creation as continued exercise of immanent creative evolutionary power—"the force that through the green fuse drives the flower," as Dylan Thomas described it—consists in that esoteric European tradition rather disparagingly known as the Occult. Deriving from a variety of ancient sources—instanced by Heracleitus, Pythagoras, and Neoplatonism (including the great Irish philosopher, John Scotus Eriugena's *Periphysion*)—the adherents of this persisting movement, from Jewish kabbalah to the Christian William Blake, sought by conative as much as noetic means to achieve a unity with the divine creative impulse throbbing not only through their own souls, but through all the changing forms of the whole universe, and thus developed a religion of creative cooperation and of an ethic uninterested in merit (B. J. Gibbons, *Spirituality and the Occult*, London: Routledge, 2001; Shimon Shokek, *Kabbalah and the Art of Being*, London: Routledge, 2001).

7. See Appendix V in Albert Einstein, *Relativity: The Special and the General Theory*, 15th ed. (London: University Paperbacks, 1954). For a fascinating piece on Spinoza and Weil which incidentally illustrates the actual equivalence of saying that the natural world is outside the mind and that it is inside the mind—and vice versa, presumably—see David Cockburn, "Self, World and God in Spinoza and Weil," *Studies in World Christianity* 4/2 (1998): 173–186.

8. It is hardly necessary to produce and itemize a full list of instances in which the Bible alternates images of immanence from God-in-creatures to creatures-in-God: "in

Him we live and move and have our being"; "I live now, not I, but Christ lives in me." And it is interesting to note that the same alternation would apply to Dawkins's selfish gene, which some of his critics see as a creative agent modeled upon a post-Enlightenment, Logos-type creator divinity (see Steven Rose, *Lifelines: Biology, Freedom, Determinism*, London: Penguin, 1977).

9. Sean Burke, *The Death and Return of the Author: Criticism and Subjectivity in Barthes, Foucault and Derrida* (New York: Columbia University Press, 1998).

10. I realize that in the original, oral presentation of this paper I relied too heavily on that (in)famous declaration of Derrida's, "*Il n'y a pas de hors-texte*" (*Of Grammatology*, trans. G. C. Spivak, Baltimore, Md.: Johns Hopkins University Press, 1997, p. 158). I did so in order to make the case concerning the metaphysical deficit in Derrida. It is always possible to try to wriggle out of the plain meaning of one's words, by continually insisting that one did not mean *that*, and then go on to say what one did mean (but did not quite say?). And indeed, in the following paragraph of the paper I look at a possible meaning for the declaration which might allow it an acceptable meaning—but at a cost Derrida might not wish to pay.

11. Joseph O'Leary argues most convincingly in "Ultimacy and Conventionality in Religious Experience" (unpublished manuscript) that although the Ultimate is referred to and comes to be known by us as simply Emptiness, Unconditionedness, Unformed, No-thing-ness, and so on, our knowledge of it is still necessarily characterized by the conditions or forms which we perceive it to transcend. As he puts the point, with reference to Madhyamika thought:

> 'Emptiness' is always 'emptiness of'; ultimate truth has as its basis some conventional truth; the unconditioned dawns on a conditioned mind, and emerges as the dissolution of just those conditions already in place . . . in practice emptiness emerges on each occasion as a deconstruction of a given construction. Not the endless deconstruction of Derrida's *différance*, to be sure, but a deconstruction that finds something unconstructed, unconditioned at the heart of the constructed, conditioned. Ultimacy is always known as a conventionality deconstructed.

Apply this to Christian Neoplatonic quests for the Ultimate—as indeed to all other religious traditions—and it is easy to see that knowledge of the Ultimate must develop and differ as one moves forward within a tradition in one's knowledge of the conditioned, formed universe; so also if one moves between traditions.

12. A good illustration of what is meant here can be found in Richard Southwood's recent book, *The Story of Life* (Oxford: Oxford University Press, 2003). The book recounts the steps through which the secret of life's origins and persistence is explained: Darwin's primordial soup; inorganic molecules leading to complex carbon molecules, to "protocells" and then to living organisms; organic molecules spontaneously emerging from elements already around in the early history of the earth; and, finally, the model of DNA, an information system complete with strategies for at once transmitting and altering itself. At that last stage many felt life's secrets were finally in the open, until some more critical minds realized that progressive theories in chemistry showed only the raw material in and through which the process called life occurred. And that, in Southwood's view, still left us with one large question to answer: How do organisms know how to form and re-form the information they pass on? Clearly in posing this question he rightly considers the organisms to be knowers. But that means that further investigations need to be made. Does each have to know how to organize itself and

others so as to keep the whole on track in that process of continuous creation known as evolution? Or is there present in this process some cosmic knower organizing and transforming the whole through all individual organizers, transcending all from within? And how is that knower to be known? Derrida's epistemology-metaphysics is clearly inadequate to the task outlined in such scientific-cosmological quests for knowledge.

13. The world is humanity's extended body according to Marx. Which prompts one to suggest that some Christian ecologists who have pressed into service the idea that the world is God's body, should perhaps produce the metaphysics which would at once clarify and justify that concept. One can perhaps see that they need it, but not quite see their title to it.

14. Recall Southwood's question in n. 11, above: How do organisms know how to form and re-form the information they pass on?

15. Fuller details on this critique of onto-philosophy/theology are provided in James P. Mackey, *The Critique of Theological Reason* (Cambridge: Cambridge University Press, 2000), esp. chap. 2. An earlier criticism of an instance of onto-philosophy occurs in Marx's *Theses on Feuerbach*. Accepting what he thought to be Feuerbach's reductionist move—that of retrieving the attributes of divinity for humanity—Marx then complained that Feuerbach's humanity thus defined still seemed to squat outside the world, rather than seem an immanent cooperative part of it. What Marx failed to see through the smoke and flames of this latest blast at an implicit onto-philosophy, was this: The attributes which Feuerbach retrieved *were* such as identified divinity—from his opening attribution of transcendence-infinity to human consciousness—and would become no less so in Marx's corrective resort to full immanence, since the world to Marx is humanity's extended body, and humanity, the "species-being," is the world's continuous creator.

16. However one translates John 1:9 in the context of that famous prologue, it is unavoidably obvious that we are being told that the Word which became enfleshed in Jesus of Nazareth is the divine Word that creates the world and that (thereby) enlightens everyone at all times and places in the creation, presumably concerning itself and the world.

17. This perception is an intrinsic part of the other perception already referred to—namely, that signs exist only in the context of consciousnesses-in-communion. The quest for the source of this communion of individual consciousnesses is close to the start of Indian philosophy and its road to the Absolute; see Ananda Wood, "Objective Pictures and Impersonal Knowledge," *Studies in World Christianity* 4/2 (1998): 187–211.

18. For this is a cause common also to an increasing number of contemporary scientific cosmologists who work away at their task of discovering the deepest reaches of the cosmos—in general without paying a blind bit of notice to postmodernism, at least in its extreme Derridean form. For it seems that we are indeed witnessing a relatively new phenomenon in recent times: In defiance of persistent missionaries of allegedly science-based atheism such as Richard Dawkins; but with as little trust in the god-of-the-gaps strategies that some scientists and philosophers, but mostly theologians use in defense of recognizably religious views (for such strategies depend upon the uncertain and unsatisfactory coincidence of finding features of the universe that science does not now explain, with the hope against hope that science never will explain these); an increasing number of scientists express the conviction that when they, in the name of science itself, lift their discussion of the traces of agency from the more specific levels (e.g., the origin of life or of consciousness) to the more generic or universal, that is to

say, to the "meta"-levels which follow in unbroken heuristic sequence (referred to above as the epistemological/metaphysical levels), then the agency engaged in the project, *agir les choses*, may well begin to be perceived, however dimly, to be deserving of religious aura and awe. So that, as my erstwhile colleague at Edinburgh, the physicist Wilson Poon put it, "the commitment to truth which leads a scientist like myself to the laboratory is, ultimately, not different from that commitment which issues forth in the reasonable activity known as worship." See Poon's severe but just critique of Keith Ward's god-of-the-gaps approach, and notice of some writers who adopt a more integrated approach, in his review of Ward's *God, Chance and Necessity* in *Studies in World Christianity* 4/2 (1998): 255–258.

G★d—The Many-Named

Without Place and Proper Name

Elisabeth Schüssler Fiorenza

I approach our topic not as a philosopher but as a feminist theologian. Moreover, my work not only engages a different theoretical discourse—the socio-rhetorical, rather than the onto-philosophical—but also speaks with a different, feminist accent. My goal here is to engender a critical reflection on the sociopolitical location, rhetorical situation, and political-religious function of the very abstract, postmodern, philosophical or theological discourses about the transcendent, the other, or the divine.

Although it is generally not customary in academic circles, I will approach the abstract philosophical topic "transcendence and beyond" with an experiential story that focuses and articulates in a nutshell the thea- or theo-logical problem with which the present volume is concerned. In light of the overall topic such an approach from experience is, however, problematic: According to the dictionary (Encarta) definition, mundaneness and experience are antonyms to transcendence, which carries meanings like "existence above and apart from the material world" or "otherworldliness," "beyond the limits of human experience" and "beyond and above all categories." Such an experiential approach, however, is methodologically demanded by feminist theologies

Elisabeth Schüssler Fiorenza

which begin with the critically reflected and analyzed "mundane" experience of wo/men understood in the inclusive sense.

When my daughter was around five years old she asked one day, after having watched a space program, "Mommy where is G*d?"[1] Busy with something else, I answered quickly, "G*d is in heaven." "But Mommy," she objected, "where is heaven?" I realized that I had a budding the*logian on my hands whose questions were to be taken seriously. So after some thought I answered, "Some people say that G*d is in church, others that G*d is present among the poor, others that G*d can be experienced in nature. Others, in turn, are saying that G*d speaks in the Bible, and others that G*d is to be found deep down in ourselves." Her face lit up and she exclaimed, "Now I understand! That's why boys call G*d he and girls call G*d she."

This episode articulates the theological questions before us: On the one hand, where is G*d to be found if heaven is no longer above? What does "being above the material world or apart from the universe" actually mean? On the other hand, how to speak about transcendence or about the Divine if it/she/he is "beyond comprehension" and "escapes categorization"? How then can we the*legein, which means to speak about G*d? Finally, who is the subject of such G*d-talk and what is its sociopolitical function in a particular historical situation?—These are questions which may be not sufficiently philosophically abstract, but in my view are central to feminist the*logy.[2] I will approach them by looking first at the problem of speaking about G*d, and second, will discuss the rhetoric of such G*d-talk. Third, I will sketch feminist theological interventions in malestream discourses about G*d, and finally, I propose that the the*logical four strategies of traditional G*d-talk could facilitate our speaking of the Divine in a feminist key.

The Rhetorical Problem

Our modern understanding of the world and the universe with its countless galaxies and infinite space no longer allows the imagination to think either in the biblical terms of above and below—of heaven, earth and underworld—or in the philosophical terms of "beyond." In addition, we have become more and more conscious that all discourses about the transcendent or the Divine—including those of the Bible[3]—are socially conditioned and politically interested. Feminist, black power, indigenous peoples or postcolonial movements have radically questioned those white elite malestream theological discourses that have spoken about the transcendent as He, or named G*d in the interest of the powerful.

As is well known, it was Rudolf Bultmann who wrestled with the question of G*d's location in the full awareness that the apocalyptic, mythological language which has shaped the Christian understanding of the place of G*d no longer has a reference-point in experience and imagination.[4] Bultmann's existentialist *Entmythologisierungsprogramm* has been displaced in the past decades through an emphasis on metaphor and image. Both approaches, the existentialist and the metaphorical, locate G*d in a modern understanding of subjectivity, after the natural sciences have

> eliminated God entirely from the order and design of the natural world. Christian theology had long distinguished the traces of God in the sensible and material world from the image of God in the soul, but in modernity this distinction became a rupture, with the locus of God for humans restricted to subjectivity—pious subjectivity without objectivity.[5]

Having located the Divine in human subjectivity, the construction of G*d in language and metaphor becomes central. Resorting to the language of metaphor and symbol, the*logy in modernity has changed the quest for G*d from an ontological or metaphysical quest for the transcendence of G*d into a rhetorical one which asks for both the proper name/representation of G*d, and the sociopolitical rules and contextualizations that have constructed G*d-talk.[6] Rather than to approach the*legein that is speaking about G*d in abstract philosophical or the*logical terms, it is necessary to investigate the practices of such speaking as rhetorical practices.

In a comprehensive article on "God" (see n. 5, below), Gordon Kaufman and Francis Schüssler Fiorenza trace the established white elite western malestream G*d-discourse and its attempts to articulate G*d's proper name (albeit they would not themselves identify such theological discourses in this way). Although they do not explicitly define their approach as rhetorical, they are clearly concerned with the rhetoricality[7] of all discourses about G*d. They begin by analyzing the use of the word "G*d" in contemporary English, and end by arguing that religion studies ought to focus on the interaction of G*d-talk with its sociopolitical, historical location. In this western kyriocentric (i.e., elite male-Lord-centered) tradition, they single out four Christian discourses about G*d which can be distinguished by their different locations—the biblical-mythological, the philosophical-ontological, the modern subjectivist, and the postmodern discourse of negative theology.

The*logical discourses on G*d have named the Divine in interaction with their respective societies: The imperial structures of Rome and of medieval feudal society celebrated G*d, the Father, as an all-powerful king and omniscient ruler of the universe.[8] The absolute power of G*d legitimated the power of princes and overlords, of bishops and popes, of fathers and males. According to Jürgen Moltmann, monotheistic monarchism not only justified the power of a few over the many but also provided a unifying ideology for such imperial power: "One God—one Logos—one humanity, and in the Roman Empire it was bound to be seen as a persuasive solution for any problems of a multi-national, multi-religious society. The universal ruler in Rome had only to be the image and correspondence of the universal ruler in heaven."[9]

Among others, Susan Brooks Thistlethwaite has pointed out that a radical break in this monotheistic-monarchic conceptualization of divinity occurred

in the Renaissance and the Reformation, but that the emphasis on authoritative unity nevertheless continued:

> that watershed period is characterized by the modern emphasis on God as
> Absolute Subject. . . . Thus the experiencing self is the starting point for
> modern white, Western theological reflection. But the emphasis on unity
> remains. Subject can only be considered an identical self, acting in dif-
> ferent ways. This is the modern bourgeois concept of personality.[10]

It is against the absolute and universalized subject of modernity that the
postmodern critique of the subject is advanced. Postmodern theory insists that
to posit an I or a subject forecloses the investigation into its production. How
then does one engage in the naming of G*d as "Absolute Subject" without
ruling out in advance a critical reflection on the sociopolitical rules and cultural practices "that govern the invocation of that subject and regulate its
agency"?[11] How does one speak of G*d without reducing the Divine to a being
like other beings or an object like other objects? The postmodern critique is
not just a critique of epistemology but also of ontology. Jacques Derrida, for
instance, has pointed out that if one argues that G*d is beyond Being one still
resorts to the conceptuality of a Platonic or Neoplatonic onto-theology that
retains "a being beyond Being, a hyperessentiality that is beyond all negation
and positive predication."[12]

While believers may share the conviction that G*d is a reality beyond
Being and claim that they have experienced this reality, just like nonbelievers
they have no adequate language to express that conviction. To say that G*d is a
"being beyond Being" linguistically concedes this lack of a proper name while
at the same time occluding the fact that no adequate language, untainted by
sociopolitical/theoretical frameworks and interests, can be had. Hence, it is
the task of the*legein—in the original sense of the word—to subject all language about G*d to a radical critical ethics of discernment.

The Rhetorics of The★legein

The topic of this essay, "G*d—The Many-Named:[13] Without Place and Proper
Name," therefore, is best approached not in metaphysical-ontological but in
the rhetorical terms of ideology critique.[14] Not an ontological definition but a
rhetorical exploration is called for! While some might want to continue the
ontological-metaphysical search for G*d's Being, I do not wish to engage in it
here. Rather, I am concerned with the rhetoricality of all our speaking about
G*d: The*legein, in the original sense of the word.

If language and images for G*d say more about those who use them and
the society and religion in which they live and envision the Divine, than about
Divinity itself, then the*logy's proper task is to engage in a persistent critical
analysis of all discourses about G*d. The task of the*legein in the proper sense
is best positioned, I argue, not in the sphere of metaphysics and ontology but in

that of ethics and communicative praxis. To say that all language about G*d and all knowledge of the world is rhetorical means to assert that all discourses about the Divine are articulated in specific sociopolitical situations, by particular people, with certain interests in mind, and for a certain audience with whom they share cultural codes and religious traditions. G*d -discourses are not just rhetorical, that is, persuasive address; they are also ideological communication enmeshed in power relations Accordingly, the*logy must focus on the rhetoricality of all language about G*d, whether it pertains to Her place or Its name.

Rhetorical analysis assumes that language produces not just meaning but also affects reality.[15] Moreover, all communication circulates between a speaker and an audience which are both historically and socially determined. For that reason, feminist rhetorical analysis investigates the structures of domination that have produced the exclusion and marginalization of wo/men[16] from the Divine. In other words: Emancipatory-rhetorical analysis is not so much interested in exploring the modern question as to whether G*d exists, but in asking the liberation-the*logical question as to how philosophers or the*logians speak about the transcendent Divine, and what kind of G*d believers confess and proclaim. Do they proclaim a G*d of injustice and dehumanization or a G*d of liberation and wellbeing, a G*d of domination or of salvation? Do we speak about a G*d who sides with the poor who are wo/men, and children dependent on wo/men, or about the Almighty One who is aligned with those who wield oppressive power?

What is G*d's proper name if we all name G*d not only differently but also, often, in pernicious and violent ways? How is our language about the Divine shaped by and in turn shaping the social location of our G*d-talk? Who is the subject of such naming and in whose interest does it take place? These questions are intensified by the experience of multiculturalism and growing interreligious awareness. In problematizing how G*d is best named, feminist and liberationist inquiry seeks to move from a philosophical-ontological to a sociopolitical rhetorical construction of G*d-discourse. It seeks to uncover the hidden frames of meaning that determine malestream as well as feminist discourses about the Divine. What Edward Said has said about the task of the intellectual with respect to human rights discourses, equally applies to that of articulating liberating G*d-discourses:

> For the intellectual to be "for human rights" means, in effect, to be willing to venture interpretation of those rights in the same place and with the same language employed by the dominant power, to dispute its hierarchy and methods, to elucidate what it has hidden, to pronounce what it has silenced or rendered unpronounc[e]able.[17]

It is well known that I approach this critical the*logical task "to pronounce what is silenced" and to elucidate what is submerged in speaking about G*d from a critical, feminist, liberationist perspective. What do I mean by such a feminist perspective? There are many different articulations of feminism and the proliferation of theoretical perspectives indicates the strength of the field. Nevertheless, feminism is still stereotyped and remains for many a "dirty word" which is associated with man-hating crazy wo/men. Hence, it is imperative that one explicates ones own understanding of feminism.

My understanding of feminism is a political one that is whimsically expressed by a popular bumper sticker which says: "Feminism is the radical notion that wo/men are people." This definition echoes the democratic assertion, "We the people." Wo/men are not beasts of burden, sex objects, or ladies, but we are citizens in society and religion with full rights and responsibilities. In short, I subscribe to a sociopolitical definition of feminism rather than simply to a personalistic, anthropological, or psychological one. Theologically speaking wo/men are the people of G*d, made in Her image and likeness, representing the Divine in the here and now. The Divine Image is exemplified by each and every wo/man, especially by those who struggle for survival, justice and wellbeing on the bottom of the kyriarchal pyramid of gradated dominations. If I were to locate the presence of G*d, it would be in the courageous struggles of multiply oppressed wo/men for human dignity and self-determining power. Such a location of the Divine in everyday struggles for justice and wellbeing is thus the opposite of a rhetorics of transcendence.

Since, however, the term "woman" has become as much debated as the term "G*d," I need to explain how I understand this controverted expression. "Woman" as the subject of feminist movements and theories has been problematized and destabilized. While cultural hegemonic discourses construct a universal feminine essence in the interest of domination, feminist theory has critically questioned such a substantive notion of gender and its cultural inculcation.[18] A feminist "politics" of meaning, to invoke a much-used but little understood phrase,[19] must be concerned with the discursive construct "woman," I argue, if its G*d-discourses should articulate what it means to say that wo/men are the image of G*d. Such a politics of meaning investigates the links between feminist the*logical articulations and those theoretical, historical, cultural and political conceptual frameworks that shape malestream as well as feminist G*d-discourses. A critical feminist investigation of the G*d-discourses of the Bible, history and theology is important not just for religious reasons. Rather, as "master narratives" of western cultures, they are always already implicated in and in collusion with the production and maintenance of systems of knowledge and belief that either foster exploitation and injustice, or contribute to a praxis and vision of emancipation and liberation.

In the next part of my reflection I will focus, therefore, on the feminist intervention into G*d-talk in order to show how the*logy as a critical interpretive rhetorical practice, must explore and assess the implications of its own impregnation by kyriarchal knowledge and discursive frameworks that make "sense" of the world and produce what counts as "reality" or "common sense." The*logy must become conscious of the rhetoricality of its own G*d-discourses and critically adjudicate the ethos such discourses promote.

Feminist Thealogical Interventions in Malestream Discourses about G⋆d

The feminist discussion of G*d-language[20] has two focal points: One is the question of how to speak about the Divine in an andro-kyriocentric language system that uses masculine terms such as "man" and "he" in both gender-specific and gender-inclusive ways. The other area of feminist the*logical inquiry is the rediscovery of the Goddess. Both areas of inquiry are contro-verted and their results are challenged not just by traditional the*logians, but also by feminists themselves. I will focus here on these two areas of the feminist attempt to reformulate G*d-language in inclusive or feminine terms, because they are instructive for the methodological problems which a very concrete (rather than abstract) mode of speaking about G*d, transcendence and the Other encounters.

First, the often heated discussions and violent reactions[21] around the inclusive-language translation of the Bible or the liturgy indicate how deeply masculine G*d-language and imagery is ingrained in Christian self-under-standing.[22] Although Scripture seeks to avoid the essentialist reification of the Divine as male by prohibiting any image-making of G*d, biblical and tradi-tional G*d-language is predominantly masculine. Critical malestream and feminist biblical studies have amply documented that the Bible is written in andro-kyriocentric language, as well as written by, addressed to and interpreted by people in kyriarchal cultures.

Although the Bible can speak of G*d in feminine terms and use female images, biblical G*d-language is overwhelmingly kyriocentric and its patri-archal bias is all-pervasive. G*d is imaged as a mighty warrior. He acts like a typical Near Eastern potentate and overlord who destroys not only Israel's enemies but also Israel itself. He is said to demand the wholesale destruction of cities and empires, of men, wo/men, children, animals and all living beings. In his wrath he sends deluges and hailstorms, draughts and pestilence, in order to destroy the people and the earth. Or, G*d is pictured as an abuser of children (cf. Genesis 22), and as a sexual voyeur: For instance, in order to punish David, G*d is said to have vowed to give the king's wo/men to another man for the explicit purpose of rape (2 Samuel 12:11); or, G*d threatens "to lift up Israel's skirts for exposing her genitals" (Isaiah 3:17; Ezekiel 16:35–43; 23:9–10, 28–30).[23]

At the same time it must not be forgotten that the Bible does not speak about G*d in philosophical-ontological but in metaphorical, symbolic, mytho-logical, analogical language. It speaks in a multiplicity of images that are not always gendered, but that draw on all kinds of patri-kyriarchal experiences and cultural concepts. Moreover, the Bible does not just use human imagery for speaking about the Divine, but draws on the experience of the whole creation. It sees G*d as rock, light, roaring lion, water, love—as acting and relating, threatening and consoling—as G*d "with us" and "over and against us"—as Elohim and Yahweh. Biblical the*logy insists on the holiness and total otherness as well as on the embeddedness and likeness of the Divine in human history. It utilizes the symbolic worlds and belief-systems of its surrounding cultures and at the same time insists that it is idolatry to make images of G*d. It knows that human language and images are not able to comprehend and express the Holy One, although believers are always tempted to reduce G*d to limited and distorted human comprehension and conceptualization.

Nevertheless, biblical discourses about G*d have not succeeded in avoiding the danger of reifying monotheism in terms of the western sex/gender system, because they have used predominantly elite-masculine language, metaphors and images in their G*d-talk. The*logy reinscribes such kyriocentric biblical G*d-language when it understands, for instance, the discourse on Divine Wisdom or the Shekinah in metaphorical terms while at the same time it construes the masculine discourse on G*d, the Father and Lord, as descriptive theological language that adequately expresses G*d's nature and being. Such interpretations in masculine terms obscure, however, that according to Jewish and Christian tradition human language about G*d must always be understood as metaphorical or analogical. G*d-language is symbolic, metaphoric and analogous because human language never can comprehend and speak adequately about Divine reality.

Biblical translation therefore has to adopt a theory of language that does not subscribe to linguistic determinism. Kyriocentric language is not to be understood as "natural" propositional language which describes and reflects reality, but rather as a grammatical classification system that constructs reality in kyriarchal terms. Conventional language is not only produced but also regulated and perpetrated in the interest of kyriarchal society and culture. If language is not a reflection of reality but rather a sociocultural linguistic system, then the relationship between language and reality is not fixed as an essential "given." Rather it is always constructed anew in discourse. This is especially true when language speaks about Divine reality, since transcendent Divine reality cannot be adequately comprehended or expressed in human language. The inability to comprehend and express who G*d is prohibits any absolutizing of symbols, images and names for G*d, be they grammatically masculine, feminine, or neuter. Such an absolute relativity of the*logical G*d language demands, on the contrary, a proliferation of symbols, images and names in order to express Divine reality which is humanly incomprehensible and unspeakable.

If language is a sociocultural convention and a tool of power, but not a reflection of reality,[24] then one must the*logically reject any essentialist identification not only of grammatical gender and Divine reality but also of grammatical gender and human reality. Not all languages have three grammatical genders or identify natural gender with grammatical gender. Masculine or feminine identity is not defined by biological gender but it is constructed in and through linguistic, social, cultural, religious, or ethnic conventions.[25] Biological womanhood and cultural femininity have had quite a different meaning, for instance, for a freeborn woman or a slave woman in Athens; for a queen and her serfs in medieval Europe; or for the white lady of a plantation and her black slave woman in North America.[26] Hence, feminist theology must pay attention not only to gender but to the ideology of the White Lady.[27] Wo/men are defined not only by gender but by race, class, and other structures of domination that inflect gender.[28]

In short, the debate around inclusive biblical and liturgical translation requires that the*logy reflect on the inadequacy of andro-kyriocentric G*d-language and problematize it. This debate compels us to continue the struggle not only with conventional masculine language for G*d, but also with the exclusivist authoritarian functions and implications of such language. Feminist the*logy must be joined by malestream the*logy, I argue, in rearticulating the symbols, images, and names of the biblical G*d in the context of the experiences of those wo/men who struggle at the bottom of the kyriarchal pyramid. It must do so in such a way that not only the masculine ossified and absolutized language about G*d and Christ are radically questioned and undermined, but also that the western cultural sex/gender system is entirely deconstructed. Only then will the*logy be able to open up biblical possibilities and visions of liberation and wellbeing[29] which have not yet been historically realized.

But how is it possible at all to think of and to name the Divine differently in a kyriarchal culture and society?[30] How can one speak of G*d in such a fashion that the the*logical symbols for G*d no longer legitimate relations of domination or continue to inculcate the cultural myth of the masculine and feminine in the*logical terms? How can one correct the masculine tradition of G*d-language and ritual in such a way that wo/men can understand themselves theologically as paradigmatic manifestations of the Divine Image? How can one undo the soteriological valorization of the cultural Masculine and Feminine constructs in Christian theology proper?

Feminist the*logy has sought to address these questions by introducing female/feminine images into Christian G*d-language.[31] It has done so either by revalorizing the traces of feminine imagery in the bible such as those of Divine Wisdom, or by recovering lost Goddess traditions.[32] Jewish feminists in turn have reclaimed the female figure of the Shekinah particularly as She was elaborated in kabbalah, whereas Christian theologians have focused on rearticulating the Trinity in terms of relationality[33] and female imagery. Feminists of various persuasions have begun to celebrate the female Divine in liturgy and art. They have sought to rearticulate traditional formulas and rituals not just in inclusive terms, but in terms of wo/men's experience.

To that end, neopagan and postbiblical thealogians have revived Goddess cult and Goddess traditions.[34] They have postulated that patriarchal warrior societies were preceded by peaceful matrilineal societies in which the Goddess was worshipped. They have rediscovered not only so-called prehistoric Goddesses, but have also sought to free those of classic Rome, Greece, or Egypt from their embeddedness in patriarchal myth. Feminists working in the area of comparative religion have made known to western audiences the Goddesses of Asia, the Americas, Africa and those of indigenous peoples around the world. In her now-classic essay, "Why Women Need the Goddess," Carol Christ has summed up this quest for the Goddess as a quest for spiritual female power.[35]

My own work has introduced and elaborated the Wisdom-Sophia tradition as one but *not as the sole* early Christian discourse that might open up hitherto unfulfilled possibilities for feminist the*logical reflection.[36] Jewish sophialogy that is funded by the interactive meaning-making of apocalyptic, prophetic and wisdom traditions, valorizes life, creativity, and wellbeing in the midst of injustice and struggle. These elements of the biblical Wisdom traditions—open-endedness, inclusivity, and cosmopolitan emphasis on creation spirituality as well as practical insight—have been especially attractive not only to feminists but also to Asian liberation-the*logical reflections.

Yet, it also must be pointed out that some feminist G*d-talk is in danger of succumbing to a "romantic" notion of femininity[37] or what I would call the ideology of the White Lady. Thereby it is in danger of reinscribing the western cultural kyriocentric gender binary which either devalues women and femininity or idealizes femininity as representing superior transcendent and salvific qualities. In extolling the femininity of Wisdom or of the Goddess, such a feminist binary-gender approach cannot but reinscribe western cultural kyriarchal systems of domination in theological terms, insofar as it divinizes the hegemonic gender ideology of cultural femininity that is shaped after the image and likeness of the "White Lady." Whenever the*logy is positioned within a framework of essential gender dualism, it cannot but reproduce this ideological frame.[38]

In order to avoid this pitfall, I have argued, one must explicitly read against the grain of the cultural feminine framework and shift the discussion of a Divine female figure from the ontological-metaphysical level to a linguistic-symbolic-rhetorical level of reflection. Such a shift is justified insofar as Divine female and Divine father language are not unified the*logical discourses about the essence and true being of G*d, but rather discourses embodying a variegated "reflective mythology."[39] The grammatically masculine language adopted by ancient Wisdom discourses and modern biblical interpretation has a difficult time to speak adequately of Divine Wisdom in the "preconstructed" kyriocentric framework of Jewish and Christian monotheism. Insofar as this language struggles to avoid turning Divine Wisdom into a second feminine deity who is subordinate to the masculine deity, it also struggles against the the*logical reification of monotheism in terms of western cultural-elite male hegemony.

When speaking about the biblical G*d, scriptural discourses and Christian liturgies as well as malestream the*logies have succumbed to this danger insofar as they have used predominantly masculine language, metaphors and images for speaking of the Divine. Biblical interpretation reinscribes such kyriocentric G*d-language as given or revealed, when it understands female images for G*d in *metaphorical* terms, but identifies the language about G*d as Father, King and Lord as *descriptive* language that adequately expresses G*d's nature and being.

In short, I argue, it is neither patriarchal God nor matriarchal Goddess— neither the Masculine nor the Feminine—neither Divine Fatherhood nor complementary Motherhood, that expresses the Divine. Rather, all kyriarchal symbols—masculinity and femininity, pale and dark skin, domination and subordination, wealth and exploitation, nationalism and colonialism—must be carefully tested out in an ongoing feminist ideology-critique. Such a feminist ideology-critique may neither take its cues from established dogmatics nor from cultural systems of domination. Rather, it must attempt to name and to reflect critically on the negative as well as on the positive G*d-experiences of wo/men. For doing so, it needs to sustain a permanent critical self-reflexivity which on the one hand is able to reject language about G*d that promotes hierarchical masculinity, or an ideal feminine which projects the western cultural sex-gender system into heaven.

At the same time, the*logy and spirituality should not go on to name the heavenly world and the Divine in purely masculine language and kyriarchal images that are exclusive of wo/men. In order to sustain such a persistent critical impetus the*logical reflection, I argue, must transform the traditional rules for speaking about G*d in ontological-metaphysical terms rather than simply complement or replace male G*d language with female/feminine one. It furthermore needs to develop them into a critical method that understands these traditional rules for speaking about G*d as rhetorical strategies of affirmation, negation, proliferation and transformation.

Traditional Rhetorical Strategies for Speaking about G★d in a Feminist Key

Only a the*logical strategy that approaches classic discourses about G*d with a method of deconstruction and proliferation, of symbolic critique and amplification,[40] I suggest, is able to develop a liberating way for engaging and transforming G*d-language, symbols and images. For inquiring into the rhetoricity of G*d-language, a critical feminist rhetorics of transformation can utilize and combine, I suggest, the four ways of speaking about G*d developed in the Christian the*logical tradition:

1. Such a the*logy begins with the assumption that G*d is not a G*d of

oppression but of liberation and seeks to articulate this conviction in a multiplicity of ways. Since G*d is a G*d of liberation and wellbeing, an affirmative the*logical strategy (*via affirmativa* or *analogica*) ascribes to G*d positively all that utopian desires of the liberation and wellbeing of which countless people dream and for which they hope, would seek in G*d. Such an affirmative analogical discourse about G*d may not, however, restrict itself to anthropological individualism but must remain oriented toward the reality and vision of the *basileia* of G*d. Moreover, affirmative discourses about G*d always need to be conscious that their language is only analogical, because G*d transcends human desires for liberation and our images of salvation.

Since the Christian G*d has been understood mostly in masculine terms as father and son, this affirmative strategy of speaking about G*d has the special task of introducing new symbols and images of wo/men into the language about G*d so that the fact becomes conscious that wo/men as well as men, blacks as well as whites, young as well as old, poor as well as rich, Asians as well as Europeans, Christians as well as Jews, Hindus as well as Muslims are made in the image of G*d. As long as the*logy remains conscious of the analogical character of G*d-language and the apophatic character of the Divine, it will be able critically to introduce into Christian G*d-language the images and names of the G*ddess which have been transmitted, for example, in Catholicism in and through mariology.[41]

However, such female images for G*d must not be reduced to abstract principles or restricted to the eternal feminine. They must not be seen as feminine aspects or attributes of a masculine God, or as applied to only one person of the Trinity. Instead, many different images of wo/men and variegated symbols of the Goddess must be applied to G*d generally as well as to all three persons of the Trinity equally. Just as language about Jesus Christ does not introduce a masculine element into the Trinity, female symbolic language must not be used to ascribe femininity or motherhood to a G*d whose essence is defined as masculine. Just as references to the lamb of G*d do not introduce animalistic features into the Divine, or speaking of G*d as light does not suggest a Divine astral element, so also anthropomorphic G*d-language must not be misunderstood as maintaining femininity or masculinity as a quality and attribute of the Divine. Finally, such a critical-affirmative integration of female symbols and G*ddess-images into Christian discourses about G*d would make it possible for the*logy to make clear that wo/men as well as men are images and representatives of G*d.

As Judith Plaskow has demanded for Jewish the*logy, so Christian feminists must also insist that the*logy overcome its "fear of the Goddess."[42] The threat to Jewish and Christian monotheism consists not in Goddess worship,[43] but in monotheism's misuse for religiously legitimating patriarchal domination. This domination has sanctified not only the exploitation of wo/men, but also that of the poor and of subjected races and religions. The salvific power of the biblical G*d of justice and love is not endangered by G*ddess cults but by the (ab)use of Her/Him as an idol for inculcating kyriarchal interests.[44]

2. Since G*d radically transcends human experience, because She/He/It is the X beyond Beyond-Being, no human language, not even that of the Bible, is able to adequately speak about the Divine. Hence the *via negativa* of classic the*logy underscores that we are not able to say properly who G*d is, but must iterate again and again who G*d is *not*. God is *not like* man, *not like* white, *not like* father, *not like* king, *not like* ruler, *not like* lord. She is also *not like* woman, *not like* mother, *not like* queen, *not like* lady. It is also *not like* fire, *not like* womb, *not like* wind, *not like* eagle, *not like* burning bush.

Because Christian tradition and the*logy for the most part have used masculine language for the Divine, the*logy today must especially focus on and elaborate the inadequacy of such masculine language, imagery and titles for the Unnamable, and reject their sole and often exclusive use for speaking about G*d. The same applies to symbolic language and images which identify Divinity with the eternal feminine or with eternal otherness. Such a critical rejection and deconstruction of kyriocentric masculinity and femininity, ruling and subjection, orthodoxy and heresy as determinative for the language about G*d is one of the most important tasks not only of feminist the*logy.

3. The *third* strategy of classic the*logical reflection, the *via eminentia*, presupposes the first two strategies but stresses that neither the rejection of masculine G*d-language nor the mode of speaking about G*d positively as Goddess suffices. Divinity is always greater and always more than human language and experience can express. This "excess" of the Divine calls for a conscious proliferation and amplification of images and symbols for G*d which are to be derived not only from human life but also from nature and cosmological realities.

The *via eminentia* is able to retrieve a rich treasure of symbols and metaphors from the manifold G*ddess images and traditions for the*logical discourse about the Divine. One cannot object to such a method of proliferating and amplifying G*ddess images, that this would mean a remythologization of the Divine. Such an objection overlooks that all language about the Divine utilizes mythic images and symbols. A strategy of mythologization leads with necessity into the multiplicity of myths and mythologies, but does not result in polytheism as long as it remains within the rhetorical boundaries set by the *via negativa* and *via analogica*. Such a strategy of both retrieving the cultural-religious images of the G*ddess from different social and religious locations, and reconstructing or reintegrating them into Christian G*d language, would lead to an articulation of the Divine that is no longer conceptualized as masculinist, exclusivist, or as agent of domination.

4. The last traditional the*logical strategy, the *via practica*, is usually associated with liturgy and spirituality. Yet, a critical feminist the*logy seeks to locate G*d-language[45] in the praxis and solidarity of anti-kyriarchal societal

and ecclesial liberation movements. The creativity and emotionality of Goddess spirituality must be positioned and integrated within these liberation discourses in order not to be misused in a kyriarchal, reactionary way.

Although G*d is "beyond" oppression, Her revelatory presence can be experienced in the midst of the struggles against dehumanization and injustice. Hence, the Divine must be renamed again and again in such experiences of struggling for the change and transformation of oppressive structures and dehumanizing ideologies. G*d is to be named as active power of justice and wellbeing in our midst. It is S/he who accompanies us in our struggles against injustice and for liberation, just as S/he has accompanied the Israelites on their desert journey from slavery to freedom.[46]

NOTES

1. In order to mark the inadequacy of our language about G*d, I had adopted the Jewish orthodox way of writing the name of **G-d** in my books *Discipleship of Equals* and *But She Said*. However, Jewish feminists have pointed out to me that such a spelling is offensive to many of them because it suggests a very conservative, if not reactionary, theological frame of reference. I have begun to write the word **G*d** in this fashion in order to visibly destabilize our way of thinking and speaking about the Divine. Accordingly, I write also the *legein*/the *logy in this way.

2. See Monika Jakobs, *Frauen auf der Suche nach dem Göttlichen. Die Gottesfrage in der feministischen Theologie* (Münster: Morgana Frauenverlag, 1993).

3. See, e.g., Bernard J. Lee, *Jesus and the Metaphors of God: The Christs of the New Testament* (New York: Paulist, 1993).

4. See, e.g., *Bultmann: Retrospect and Prospect*, ed. Edward C. Hobbs (Philadelphia: Fortress, 1985); and James F. Kay, "Theological Table-Talk—Myth or Narrative? Bultmann's New Testament and Mythology Turns Fifty," *Theology Today* 48 (1991): 326–332.

5. Francis Schüssler Fiorenza and Gordon D. Kaufman, "God," in *Critical Terms for Religious Studies*, ed. Mark C. Taylor (Chicago: University of Chicago Press, 1998), p. 146.

6. See Karen M. Armstrong, *A History of God: The 4000-Year Quest of Judaism, Christianity, and Islam* (New York: Ballantine, 1993).

7. This expression is derived from *The Ends of Rhetoric: History, Theory, Practice*, ed. John Bender and David E. Wellbery (Stanford: Stanford University Press, 1990), p. 25:

Rhetoric today is neither a unified doctrine nor a coherent set of discursive practices. Rather it is a transdisciplinary field of practice and intellectual concern. . . . The classical rhetorical tradition rarified speech and fixed it within a gridwork of limitations: it was a rule-governed domain whose procedures themselves were delimited by the institutions that organized interaction and domination in traditional European society. Rhetoricality, by contrast, is bound to no specific set of institutions. . . . It allows for no explanatory metadiscourse that is not already itself rhetorical. Rhetoric is no longer the title of a doctrine and practice, nor a form of cultural memory; it becomes instead something like the condition of our existence.

8. Brian Wren has argued that the metaphorical system which undergirds Christian imagination, worship, prayer, and theology is that of "KINGAFAP: the King-God-Almighty-Father-All Powerful-Protector" (*What Language Shall I Borrow? God-Talk in Worship: A Male Response to Feminist Theology*, New York: Crossroad, 1989, p. 119). In this frame of reference, G*d is worshipped as a powerful king enthroned in splendor who receives homage and atonement for offences against His majesty, rules by word of command, and legitimates the cosmic kyriarchal order.

9. Jürgen Moltmann, *The Trinity and the Kingdom* (San Francisco: Harper & Row, 1981), p. 129ff.

10. Susan Brooks Thistlethwaite, *Sex, Race, and God: Christian Feminism in Black and White* (New York: Crossroad, 1989), p. 122.

11. Judith Butler, *Gender Trouble: Feminism and the Subversion of Identity* (New York: Routledge, 1990), p. 144.

12. Cited in Francis Schüssler Fiorenza and Gordon D. Kaufman, "God," in *Critical Terms for Religious Studies*, ed. Mark C. Taylor (Chicago: University of Chicago Press, 1998), p. 153.

13. At the 1998 World Council of Churches Assembly in Zimbabwe, participants from the four corners of the earth called on the "G*d of Many Names" throughout Assembly events. Some of those names were: "Barefoot G*d," "Center G*d Who Runs Out to the Periphery," "G*d, Our Refuge, Hope and Light," "Liberating G*d, Who Always Frees," "*Kiluba* = G*d of the Multitude of People," "Creator G*d, the One Who Is Modeling," "Loving, Beyond Any Idea of Love," "Spiritual Beautifulness," "Womb G*d," "G*d With *Minjung* Grassroots People," "G*d of Justice," "Weeping G*d Connecting with Our Tears," "Mother G*d" (National Council of Churches, *NCC News*, 18 December 1998).

14. With the feminist theorist Michèle Barrett (*The Politics of Truth: From Marx to Foucault*, Stanford: Stanford University Press, 1991, p. 177), I understand ideology as referring to a process of mystification or misrepresentation. Ideology is distorted communication, rather than simply false consciousness. A fundamental assumption of critical theory holds that every form of social order entails some forms of domination, and that critical emancipatory interests fuel the struggles to change these relations of domination and subordination. Such power relations engender forms of distorted communication that result in self-deception on parts of agents with respect to their interests, needs and perceptions of social and religious reality, see Raymond A. Morrow, *Critical Theory and Methodology* (Thousand Oaks, Calif.: Sage, 1994), pp. 130–149. Theologically speaking, they are structural sin.

15. See Jane P. Tomkins, "The Reader in History: The Changing Shape of Literary Response," in *Reader-Response Criticism: From Formalism to Poststructuralism*, ed. Jane P. Tomkins (Baltimore: John Hopkins University Press, 1980), pp. 201–232.

16. Critical postmodern feminist studies have problematized the function of the signifier "woman/feminine." Critical cultural and liberationist studies, in turn, have warned feminist theoretical gender-analyses not to abstract from their sociopolitical function for reinscribing the cultural ideal of the "white Lady." Such a problematization of the basic categories of feminist analysis have introduced a crisis into the self-understandings and practices of the feminist subject. I have sought to mark this crisis by writing **wo/men** in a broken form that seeks to problematize not only the category of "woman," but also to indicate that wo/men are not a unitary social group, but fragmented by structures of race, class, ethnicity, religion, heterosexuality, colonialism and

Elisabeth Schüssler Fiorenza

age. I have done so because I do not think that feminists can relinquish the analytic category "woman" entirely and replace it with the analytic category of gender if we do not want to marginalize and erase the presence of wo/men in and through our own feminist discourses.

17. Edward W. Said, "Nationalism, Human Rights, and Interpretation," in *Freedom and Interpretation: The Oxford Amnesty Lectures 1992*, ed. Barbara Johnson (New York: Basic, 1993), p. 198.

18. For the location and discussion of this problem in feminist discourses see, e.g., Tania Modleski, *Feminism Without Women: Culture and Criticism in a "Postfeminist" Age* (New York: Routledge, 1991).

19. For a theoretical discussion of the politics of gender see, e.g., the essays collected by Seyla Benhabib and Drucilla Cornell, *Feminism as Critique: On the Politics of Gender* (Minneapolis: University of Minnesota Press, 1987).

20. See Rebecca Chopp, *The Power to Speak: Feminism, Language and God* (New York: Crossroad, 1989).

21. See, e.g., Susan Brooks Thistlethwaite, *Sex, Race, and God: Christian Feminism in Black and White* (New York: Crossroad, 1989), p. 109ff.

22. See, e.g., Donald Bloesch, *The Battle for the Trinity: The Debate Over Inclusive God-Language* (Ann Arbor: Servant, 1985); *Speaking the Christian God*, ed. Alvin Kimel (Grand Rapids: William B. Eerdmans, 1992); and Werner Neuer, *Man and Woman in Christian Perspective* (London: Hodder & Stoughton, 1990).

23. Terence E. Fretheim, "Is the Biblical Portrayal of God Always Trustworthy?," in Terence E. Fretheim and Karlfried Fröhlich, *The Bible as Word of God in a Postmodern Age* (Minneapolis: Augsburg Fortress, 1998), pp. 97–112.

24. On androcentric language, see the diverse contributions in *The Feminist Critique of Language: A Reader*, ed. Deborah Cameron (New York: Routledge, 1998).

25. Cf. Ean Beck, *The Cult of the Black Virgin* (Boston: Arkana, 1985); Martin Bernal, *Black Athena: The Afroasiatic Roots of Classical Civilization* (New Brunswick: Rutgers University Press, 1988); *Black Women in Antiquity*, ed. Ivan Van Sertima (New Brunswick: Transaction, 1988); and China Galland, *Longing for Darkness: Tara and the Black Madonna* (New York: Penguin, 1990).

26. Elizabeth V. Spelman has graphically depicted these relationships in antiquity and in the modern world, in *Inessential Woman: Problems of Exclusion in Feminist Thought* (Boston: Beacon, 1988).

27. For the elaboration of this expression, see H. V. Carby, "On the Threshold of Woman's Era: Lynching, Empire and Sexuality in Black Feminist Theory," in *Race, Writing, and Difference*, ed. Henry L. Gates (Chicago: University of Chicago Press, 1986), pp. 301–328; see also the article by Kwok Pui-Lan, "The Image of the White Lady: Gender and Race in Christian Mission," in *The Special Nature of Women*, ed. Anne Carr and Elisabeth Schüssler Fiorenza (Philadelphia: Trinity, 1991), pp. 19–27.

28. See Susan Brooks Thistlethwaite, *Sex, Race, and God: Christian Feminism in Black and White* (New York: Crossroad, 1989).

29. See, e.g., the practical exercises and liturgical rituals in *Wisdom's Feast: Sophia in Study and Celebration*, ed. Susan Cole, Marian Ronan and Hal Taussig (New York: Harper & Row, 1989).

30. On this question, see the important work of Sallie McFague, *Models of God: Theology for an Ecological, Nuclear Age* (Philadelphia: Fortress, 1987); and *The Body of God: An Ecological Theology* (Minneapolis: Fortress, 1993).

31. See the overview by Linda A. Moody in *Women Encounter God: Theology Across the Boundaries of Difference* (Maryknoll, N.Y.: Orbis, 1996).

32. Silvia Schroer, "Die götliche Weisheit und der nachexilische Monotheismus," in *Der eine Gott und die Göttin: Gottesvorstellung des biblischen Israel im Horizont feministischer Theologie*, ed. Marie-Theres Wacker and Erich Zenger (Freiburg: Herder, 1991), pp. 151–183.

33. See Catherine Mowry LaCugna, "God in Communion With Us," in *Freeing Theology: The Essentials of Theology in Feminist Perspective*, ed. Catherine Mowry LaCugna (San Francisco: Harper San Francisco, 1993), pp. 83–114; and Elizabeth A. Johnson, *She Who Is: The Mystery of God in Feminist Theological Discourse* (New York: Crossroad, 1992).

34. See Carol P. Christ, *The Rebirth of the Goddess: Finding Meaning in Feminist Spirituality* (Reading, Mass.: Addison-Wesley, 1998).

35. Carol P. Christ, "Why Women Need the Goddess: Phenomenological, Psychological, and Political Reflections," in *Women Spirit Rising: A Feminist Reader in Religion*, ed. Carol Christ and Judith Plaskow (San Francisco: Harper & Row, 1979), pp. 273–287.

36. See Elisabeth Schüssler Fiorenza, *Jesus: Miriam's Child, Sophia's Prophet: Critical Issues in Feminist Christology* (New York and London: Continuum, 1994), pp. 131–163; and *Sharing Her Word: Feminist Biblical Interpretation in Context* (Boston: Beacon, 1999), pp. 137–160.

37. See the roundtable discussion in Catherine Madsen et al., "If God Is God, She Is Not Nice," *Journal of Feminist Studies in Religion* 5/1 (1989): 103–118.

38. See, e.g., Christa Mulack, *Jesus der Gesalbte der Frauen* (Stuttgart: Kreuz Verlag, 1987).

39. For this expression, see my article "Wisdom Mythology and the Christological Hymns of the New Testament," in *Aspects of Wisdom in Judaism and Early Christianity*, ed. Robert L. Wilken (South Bend, Ind.: University of Notre Dame Press, 1975), pp. 17–42. I became fascinated with the Wisdom tradition in the Christian Testament in the context of the 1973 Rosenstil seminar on Wisdom in Early Judaism and Christianity, sponsored by the Department of Theology at University of Notre Dame.

40. See Susan Heckman, *Gender and Knowledge: Elements of Postmodern Feminism* (Boston: Northeastern University Press, 1990), pp. 152–190.

41. Such a mode of multifaceted theological association and imaginative amplification comes to the fore for instance in *Akathistos*, a Marian hymn of the Eastern church (see *Der Hymnos Akathistos im Abendland: Die älteste Andacht zur Gottesmutter*, ed. Gerhard G. Meersemann, Freiburg: Herder, 1958). It can serve to show how such biblical language can be appropriated in feminine form:

Gegrüßt, du Meer, das verschlungen den heiligen Pharao;
gegrüßt, du Fels, der getränket, die nach Leben dürsten;
gegrüßt du, Feuersäule, die jene im Dunkeln geführt . . .
Gegrüßt, o Land der Verheißungen;
gegrüßt, du, aus der Honig und Milch fließt.
Gegrüßt, du unversehrte Mutter. . .

42. Judith Plaskow, *Standing Again at Sinai: Judaism from a Feminist Perspective* (San Francisco: Harper & Row, 1990), pp. 121–169.

43. For an extensive annotated bibliography see Anne Carson, *Goddesses and Wise*

Women: The Literature of Feminist Spirituality, 1980–1992 (Freedom: Crossing Press, 1992); for an interreligious discussion, see *The Book of the Goddess: Past and Present*, ed. Carl Olsen (New York: Crossroad, 1983); for a personal thealogical account, see especially Carol P. Christ, *Laughter of Aphrodite: Reflections on a Journey to the Goddess* (San Francisco: Harper & Row, 1987).

44. For the interconnection of G*d-language and self-esteem, see Carol Saussy, *God Images and Self Esteem: Empowering Women in a Patriarchal Society* (Louisville, Ky.: Westminster/John Knox, 1991).

45. Cf. Ruth C. Duck, *Gender and the Name of God: The Trinitarian Baptismal Formula* (New York: Pilgrim Press, 1991).

46. See *Wisdom of Solomon* 10:1–21.

PART 3. RELOCATING TRANSCENDENCE ON THE PLANE OF IMMANENCE

seven

Rumors of Transcendence

The Movement, State, and Sex of "Beyond"

Catherine Keller

Transdisciplinary Transcendence

Like a rumor, transcendence drifts between philosophy and theology. One doesn't know quite where the concept originates. Immanent to both discourses, it emanates elusively, tantalizingly, from each, toward the other. Transcendence—as an other or an alterity that "moves beyond"—thus characterizes an event that exceeds or eludes discourse itself, even as it attracts linguistic attention. But it happens not only at the edge of language itself, but at the boundary between the two traditions of language. Philosophy and theology insistently resist and transcend each other. Yet in their mutual edginess each seems to lure the other toward a certain unsupervised space, a more playful rigor, loosed from the enclosing certainties of a discipline or a dogma. Here, just where they transcend each other, each moves again—in mistrustfully postmodern attraction—toward the other. But in this relation of alterity their mutual immanence precedes them.

Certainly theology as such knows no aphilosophical origin. In the force field of impure beginning—trembling with motley energies, elemental vectors preceding and exceeding every doctrinal exertion—both disciplines pulse, as we shall notice, with certain enfolded, quite untranscended sexualities. Their carnalities or incarnations move beyond each other but never quite detach (however hard some try) from that originary planetarity signified by "the creation." Moving beyond, neither discourse ever quite escapes the flesh of its own language, its own carnal words.

At the edge of our particular discourse, we are called to "transcendence and beyond." An invitation to extraterrestrial journeys? Or another postmodern code for "getting beyond theology"—at least getting over God? (Getting more transcendent, if not holier, than Thou?) But the "beyond" is already contained in the concept of transcendence and is thus, in this call, mysteriously (or redundantly) doubled. Does this "beyond" thus intend something that surpasses the concept of "transcendence"? Or does such a transcendence of transcendence, a beyond of the beyond, work as a double-negative? Would it burst its tautology and deposit us anew amidst the creaturely politics and sexes of the earth? That possibility is the prayer of the present essay. In this it willfully fails to transcend the impure concerns of planetarity, or of what is labeled clumsily, as though in an emergency, ecofeminist theology.[1] Yet this site of material emergence does not lack its concept of transcendence, readable only in the interaction between philosophy and theology. Might both learn to recognize the gendered, mattering folds of any movement "beyond"? Might they explicate these folds also as sites where movement, the very transit of transcendence, is often stopped?

For transcendence can also paralyze the motion of the other—and thereby ultimately of itself. I will try to illustrate this ambiguity at the edge just "beyond" theology. There is a tension within twentieth-century French philosophy that I will dramatize by juxtaposing the radical transcendence developed by Emmanuel Levinas and Simone de Beauvoir (an odd couple, to be sure) with the radical immanence of Gilles Deleuze and Felix Guattari. With some mediation by a teacher they all respected, some interjections by Luce Irigaray, and some un-French philosophical cosmology—the present essay seeks to provoke a bit of *theological* becoming. Why all these philosophers for an ultimately theological effort? Perhaps it is the very alterity, the distance and the withdrawal of philosophy from theology, which permits such a *genesis*. As Levinas says, "the absolutely foreign alone can instruct us."[2] If the mutual immanence of philosophy and theology has always already compromised this "absolute," it need not mitigate the otherness or the instruction.

Unbecoming God

In philosophy the being of the beyond, or of the Other beyond being, has at least been recognized to be a rumor—not necessarily false, but hauntingly unfalsifiable. Theology by contrast has in general treated transcendence as a straight attribute and metonym of God, whose being is set beyond rumor, beyond language, and so beyond question. Not that the nineteenth-century term "transcendence" actually gets thematized much in theology. It is not one of the classical predicates of God. Yet it often swoops down anachronistically to gather and bind the whole bundle of orthodox "omni's." Transcendence (implying then a prehistory of omniscience, omnipotence, aseity, eternity, *creatio ex nihilo* and a noisy "ineffability") serves to protect God's sovereignty against a corollary immanence (creation, spatiotemporality, nature, experience). Classical theism continuously emits transcendence as a warning signal. Above all this God must not be permitted to collapse into immanence. Except perhaps at the saving pinprick of the Incarnation. Christ is revealed as the exception that proves the rule—the rule of this sovereignty in His Name.

Deleuze and Guattari register the force of this rule.

> The idea of transcendence [insists] that immanence is a prison (solipsism) from which the Transcendent will save us. . . . Immanence can be said to be the burning issue of all philosophy because it takes on all the dangers that philosophy must confront, all the condemnations, persecutions, and repudiations that it undergoes.

They mention Cusa, Bruno, Eckhart as instances of those who must "prove that the dose of immanence they inject into world and mind does not compromise the transcendence of a God to which immanence must be attributed only secondarily."[3] Theology still tenses and tightens against any slide (down) toward the heretical condition of boundless immanence called "pantheism." In theology we know little about it—except that it is rumored to be a great threat to God. It could cost him His Highness, His Otherness, His Over- and Aboveness, His Be/yond, its very Be—and oh, even his He-ness. Liberal theology tries politely, almost chemically, to balance the opposites: Too much transcendence here, add some immanence . . . But the dyadic hierarchy will not be balanced out. The superior term is too powerful.

To liberate a space of immanence must we then, with Deleuze and Guattari, resist *every* notion of transcendence? Or only that transcendence which posits its own superiority over against a self-enclosed immanence? Let me suggest that whenever immanence appears as the interior of a sealed and static world—the clammy space of becoming and passing away, of all the rotting and repetitive relations comprising the creation—then a specific *style* of transcendence is taking hold. Already breaking away from any materialized immanence, this transcendence will turn to dominate that from which it separates. We might as well call it a *separative transcendence*.

Rumor has it that feminist theology takes the side of the subjugated immanence, in its mess of flesh, earth, and anger, its nagging interdependences, its struggling histories. That the more ecological it turns, the more it will be tempted toward the Her of heresy. That indeed it moves beyond "transcendence." But when could the women's movement in or beyond Christianity be so simply located? How can a movement of liberation like that of women, which has moved history itself, enacting so much exodus, ecstasy, and difference, be said to lack the *movement* of "movement beyond"—of transcen-

Catherine Keller

dence? Unless of course transcendence has been already defined as a separation from history and its movements. But is it still *transcendence*?

In a certain evident sense, one can no more transcend transcendence than make water wet. One does not move beyond moving-beyond. Yet nonetheless, theology early began to transcend its own *movement*—in favor of a *stasis*, a *state*, indeed an *empire* of God. God was revealed as the great mover and shaker, a God no longer moved or shaken, the Absolute neither transcended nor self-transcending—an unbecoming God. Dominant and separate, transcendence seems to have frozen into a state of being, a state paradoxically more static than the immanence it presumably transcends: into something immutable, its supreme Otherness protected by a moat-like void. Does this state represent the onto-theological captivity of theology?

Theologians are tempted to blame philosophy, or at least Plato. Thus various orthodoxies of the family of Abraham, rightly worried about unscriptural aspects of this stasis, insist that their faith transcends philosophy. They variously repudiate its otherworldly gnosis, its pagan worldliness, its eternal matter, or its historical materialism—its arrogant pseudo-transcendence, or its reductive immanence. Indeed some of the most progressive, feminist, or postmodern theologies return to scripture in search of a prephilosophical origin. But no purity of origin presents itself to a persistent (let alone "more radical") hermeneutic. We cannot help but read our scripture—itself already rent with conflictual impulses—through philosophically ground lenses. But theologians speak philosophy awkwardly, like a foreign language, even as we translate the yet more foreign language of our most immanent, and dangerously familiar, text.

Saline Immanence

Let me back up, then, before not beyond, to the time of scriptures, a space of foreign instruction and familiar rumor. A desert time-space. Here a certain passage of transcendence (*sans* "transcendence," before the concept or the abstraction) has left its narrative traces. Not an entity, a being, or its attribute; not a state but a movement. We notice a passage, a surge, Moses stretching out his rod—a gesture of liberation, desert desperation, insubstantial verb. At the risk of becoming other, these mobile ones encounter the other—not the face but the backside, as Sallie McFague likes to stress, of the unfaceable Other. Moses perishes in the desert. But he was in his element. He dies faithful, that the gift of liberation will survive—transcend?—his own life. He was not the first in this line of past-surpassing personages. Abraham, Lot, whole populations read as dynamos of a prototranscendence. All that is progressive in western history surges out with them, exiting from every oppression, every stagnation. Exodus toward the new, the free, the other.

But something, someone, slows me down. She falls like a shadow across the desert—intimate, anonymous, hardly human. It is Lot's wife. She who fails to transcend. To separate. She who looks back. Who loses her verb. Her verve, her nerve. She who for a moment re/collects—her relations? Herself? She did not obstruct that exodus, she merely glanced back. In loss. In empathy. In grief. In iteration of a past that is no longer, that is already other, that is rendering her an other. The work of mourning requires this repetition. It effects its own slow liberation. But here, as Sodom and the cities of the valley are being consumed in a prototype of apocalypse, grief is forbidden. So she is reduced to a memorial and mockery of her tears—a pillar of salt. History, husband and the holy abandon her without comment. She was *not* in her element; she turned *into* an element. A pillar of pure immanence. A marker and an anachronism of the protest of immanence against a separative transcendence? And of the punishment inflicted by that transcendence?

Some of us return to touch and read such odd formations in the desert, such petrified femininities, tribalisms transcended by the God of history and of the beyond-history. In this returning we also repeat. Precisely not to become this past but to move on. In order not to wander in a great desert circle. For this break-away transcendence has been repeating itself, despite its horror of repetition. Its line in the sand bends into an arid sameness. Might we sidestep this linear circulation? Facing neither straight forward like Lot, nor backwards like his wife. Might we not move *onward*? But in this indirect gaze, we already fail a test of transcendence, that of the Levinasian "face," the epiphany of separation—though not that of an escape from "the unfolding of terrestrial existence" (Levinas, *Totality and Infinity*, p. 52). We are still in the desert, not in heaven. "The face, all straightforwardness and frankness, in its feminine epiphany dissimulates allusions, innuendos" (ibid., p. 264). In merely glancing back at her backward glance, I iterate the failure of Lot's wife—of straightforwardness, of Levinas's ethic of *droiture*, of uprightness in the "separation" of the self face-to-face with the supreme separateness of the Other. Having caught a glimpse of the intolerable losses, I dissimulate in the face of transcendence—the very transcendence by which justice for the losers has been negotiated in western history. So the bonds of love effect a double-bind.

"The metaphysical event of transcendence—the welcome of the Other, hospitality—Desire and language—is not accomplished as love" (Levinas, *Totality and Infinity*, p. 254). Intriguingly, hospitality—a welcome that suggests the gestures of immanence, of extending familiarity to otherness—is here subsumed under the paradigm of transcendence, pushing it free of any feminized interiority. Levinas may be right: "Love does not transcend unequivocally." But when he adds that love "is complacent, it is pleasure and dual egoism" (ibid., p. 266)—it is as though Lot's wife, in her loving glance toward her doomed relations, is condemned along with them; as though she too is guilty of *their* rapacity, their violation of hospitality. Hospitality to the stranger had been upheld by Lot. He had conversed face-to-face with the three angelic visitors, emissaries of God. "The transcendence of the Other," writes Levinas, "which is his eminence, his height, his lordship, in its concrete meaning includes his destitution, his exile, and his rights as a stranger" (ibid., p. 77). Lot—in a superb gesture of prototranscendence—had welcomed the two angel-strangers (all angels are strange, *strangels*, though not all strangers are angels). In his *droiture* he protected the Other from the violent locals.

Recall, however, the test of his hospitality: He offered the mob his two virgin daughters to be gang-raped instead.[4] I do not want to get mired in complaint, grief, and feminist repetition. Yet I feel the salty immanence creeping up on me, slowing, ambiguating the movement of transcendence. "Equivocation," continues Levinas, "constitutes the epiphany of the feminine—at the same time interlocutor, collaborator and master superiorly intelligent, so often dominating men in the masculine civilization it has entered" (*Totality and Infinity*, p. 264). Levinas's association of the feminine with equivocation, with appearance, and as we shall see with alterity itself, may not symptomatize misogyny so much as perplexity in the face of these unexpected interlocutors. Trapped in the contradictions of their desires? Or of his? But first of all I want to confess: Yes, this equivocating love (akin to a Derridean undecidability?) does indeed permeate theology, if it remembers that it cannot even know its own object. Doesn't the very transcendence of the divine require a speech of the unspeakable—thus allusion and innuendo, parable and midrash? It is a version of this apophasis, a more flagrant equivocation, that both enables and troubles what is called feminist theology.[5]

Let me put this hermeneutical aporia as *straightforwardly* as possible. We love this forward exodus and its messianic nomadisms, risking the unknown, transgressing boundaries for the sake of justice, reaching out to the strange, the stranger, the strangest. And we refuse its brutal separativity—hospitality as sacrifice of the daughter; salvation as betrayal of the mother; justice as apocalyptic conflagration; God as sovereign dictator. Yet the biblical prototranscendence never ceased to move and to *be moved*. YHWH appears rent with equivocations, indeterminacies, reciprocities. (In our very text, for example, he wonders to himself whether to tell Abraham his plans for Sodom; and lets Abraham, who argues "Shall not the Judge of all the earth do what is just?" bargain down the collateral damage.[6]) Feminist theology moves between these texts, where justice does sometimes mingle with mercy—and "beyond" them, in a hermeneutical loop that does not transcend but transforms the biblical tradition. It cannot conceive of a hospitality that would sacrifice the daughter for the stranger—or immanence for transcendence.

Yes, love does not transcend unequivocably. But neither does God. Or at least any God worth her salt.

Transcendence of the Second Sex

One might lodge one's gender analysis in this imbalanced opposition of gestures: Between the masculine transcendence, the straightforward thrust, the surge upwards and onwards, irruption and separation, the trail and trace of the absent father; and a bound and binding feminine immanence, down and under, a past-present, absorbing the shocks and breaks of transcendence. One might take up the cause and cry of immanence, its interiority so archaically embodied in anatomy. But if this transcendence signifies the only alternative to Lot's nameless, speechless wife—who would not prefer *his* way?

Within the French philosophies of transcendence, let us glance back at the work of a contemporary and collaborator with the mid-century Levinas, Simone de Beauvoir (too easily relegated to the already past).

> Now what peculiarly signalizes the situation of woman is that she—a free and autonomous being like all human creatures—nevertheless finds herself in a world where men compel her to assume the status of the Other. They propose to stabilize her as object and to doom her to immanence *since her transcendence is to be overshadowed and forever transcended by another ego* (conscience) which is essential and sovereign.[7]

Thus, a sovereign male transcendence reduces its Other to immanence.

> The domestic labors that fell to her lot because they were reconcilable with the cares of maternity imprisoned her in repetition and immanence; they were repeated from day to day in an identical form, which was perpetuated almost without change from century to century; they produced nothing new. (Beauvoir, *The Second Sex*, p. 71)

With its Sartrean transcendence *sans Dieu*, this most influential text of the women's movement produced much that is new indeed—including, by one calculation, feminist theology itself.[8] At this point, feminist theology has less reason to stumble on her atheism than on her unintended God. Minus the divine subject, transcendence is apotheosized in its opposition to immanence —as repetition, sameness, the stagnation of a self-enclosed transience. Indeed, as a feminized incarnation: "In no domain did she create: she maintained the life of the tribe by giving it children and bread . . . she remained doomed to immanence, incarnating only the static aspect of society, closed in on itself" (ibid., p. 22).

The contrast to all this procreative and nurturing work, merely incarnational and repetitive, is straightforward indeed: "Man went on monopolizing the functions which threw open that society—war, hunting and fishing represented an expansion of existence," she writes admiringly. "The male remained alone the incarnation of transcendence" (Beauvoir, *The Second Sex*, p. 23). Indeed. One does not know, however, whether she intended the Christological echo. "For it is not in giving but in risking life that man is raised above the animal." Never mind that nonhuman animals risk life; or that giving life entailed, then, as great a risk as taking it. She is in the grip of a divine predication —of him who creates by destroying, the warrior god of the desert, modernized, existentialized. And yet this humanistic transcending, very much in touch with its verb, energized the women's movement. It made a way for women in the desert of patriarchy. But it defines liberation as separation from both nature *and* nurture. "To transcend" is at once exposed and embraced in its dynamism —as a killing verb, a work of war.

A Wound Was Needed

Levinas moves in direct opposition, however, to any killing transcendence. He offers his eschatological metaphysic as the very alternative to war. "The eschatological, as the 'beyond' of history, draws beings out of the jurisdiction of history and the future; it arouses them in and calls them forth to their full responsibility." Eschatology in this sense frames transcendence, and so enables the "full responsibility" that is the human response in *language* to one another. "Peace is produced as this aptitude for speech." (No wonder that the U.S. president, at the time I write, lacks this aptitude.) "The eschatological vision breaks with the totality of wars and empires in which one does not speak" (Levinas, *Totality and Infinity*, p. 23). Indeed, no peace movement in the west lacks the eschatological vision, the messianic anti-empire. Of course apocalyptic eschatology fuels the rhetoric of every holy war, manifest destiny and messianic conquest in history. Given the passionate concern for historical suffering, it is striking that Levinas places the eschatological "beyond history," in the pure exteriority of transcendence—in what he calls "the infinite."

When he opposes "to the objectivism of war a subjectivity born from the eschatological vision" (Levinas, ibid., p. 25), he seems to invoke the movement rather than the state of transcendence: "Infinity overflows the thought that thinks it. Its very infinition is produced precisely in this overflowing." Like Kierkegaard's expansion of subjectivity, this transcendence effects neither a self-abjection nor a self-totalization: the infinity *in* the finite subject opens it beyond its capacity. "To contain more than one's capacity is to shatter at every moment the framework of a content that is thought, to cross the barriers of immanence" (ibid., p. 27). Like Beauvoir he marks the immanent as the other of transcendence, its opposite and barrier. Furthermore, it is "*implantation* in the other and a confusion with him." The "confusion" that Levinas decries is the fusion of the other with the self, as the homogenizing ontology of totalization. But does his "implantation in the other" not inadvertently mirror pregnancy, with its fluid border between self and other, inner and outer? Indeed if the empire is a speechless totality, the intimate interiority constituted by "the feminine" is similarly called by him "a society without language."

In other words, quite in accordance with Beauvoir's analysis, femininity is constituted in a realm of immanence, as incapable of "full responsibility." In these terms one might be hard-pressed to distinguish ethically between Lot's speechless wife and the gang-rapists of Sodom. Transcendence simultaneously cuts free from history and cosmos, nurture and nature. But transcendence for Levinas does not signify a supernatural escapism or otherworldly abstraction. According to Tamara Eskenazi, "he reclaims the body and resists abstractions."[9] Alterity infuses life with ethics. But "separation as life"—as a relationship of a being that "in relation absolves itself from the relation"—defines the Levinasian transcendence.[10] And so one must question a "confusion" prior to that of self and other—that of "separation" with difference, alterity, life. In this opposition of transcendence to immanence—where existentialism teams up with eschatology—Levinas establishes a postmodern dichotomy of exterior and interior, charged with a premodern, theo-sexual hierarchy.

In Levinas the existential binary of a free transcendence opposed to an imprisoning immanence seems to run parallel to that of Beauvoir. To Beauvoir "woman" has been not just an other sex, but as the second sex, The Sex, sex itself. Similarly for Levinas she is not just an other, but otherness itself. But his view of sexuality veers in a very different direction. Whereas Beauvoir's woman is called to revolt from her alterity of mere immanence and claim her transcendence, transcendence itself now entraps the Levinasian woman in her alterity—she is not only interiority but "difference itself," the origin of the transcendent alterity.[11] Never however can she appear as a fully ethical subject of transcendence, equivalent to man in her difference. Expounding upon a rabbinic reading of the Genesis 2 creation of woman, Levinas seems unable to escape the logic of her inferiority:

> Humanity is not thinkable on the basis of two entirely different principles. There had to have been a sameness that these *others* had in common. Woman is set apart from man but she came after him . . . Real humanity does not allow for an abstract equality . . . Subordination was needed, and a wound was needed. . . .[12]

Accordingly the only alternative to gender monism or gender dualism is a violent subjugation of the woman. Perhaps reacting against Beauvoir's call for equality (as did Karl Barth, in almost identical terms, during the same period), a patriarchy of the biblical desert circles back in sameness. If ethics however flows from "the origin of the very concept of alterity," which he had identified as "the feminine," then the "wound" inflicted upon woman by the male God festers at the heart of his ethics. And so the very resources for justice, which presumably opposes any subjugation of an other (even a female one) to a self, remain *originally* compromised. While alterity and thus femininity make transcendence—that is, ethics itself—possible, his gender analysis quite consistently fails precisely as ethics.[13] But it suggests to us that indeed in the case of sexuality, there is not a clean break but a wound.

Differential Transcendence

Beauvoir and Levinas both, with their notions of transcendence, perform the separative transcendence. Thus they resist any interstitial indeterminacy, any fluidity of uncertain—equivocal—boundaries. Yet while the one demands an equal-opportunity transcendence for women, the other subjugates woman as the origin of difference. But what if sexual difference partakes of the radical alterity of transcendence, not in a primal dualism but as its elemental instance? What if that very difference illumines difference itself—at least a difference that finds incarnation—as born in the interstices? What if not only interhuman ethics but intercreaturely ecologies take place in the uncertainty of the between? Theologically, would we find ourselves renegotiating the very boundaries of what we call "the creation"?

"Indefinitely open and closed, she unfurls this strange world where outside and inside unite in a light embrace." Thus Luce Irigaray designates her feminine subject the subject of a next wave of French feminism, "Never set out, the contours wed each other in overflowing growth that never quits the medium that gives rise to it. That never abandons the body that gives it life."[14] This overflowing of an unfinished *infini*, in which it is precisely the barrier between inner and outer that is crossed, cannot be identified with the Levinasian overflow, which crosses the barriers of immanence like the walls of a prison. Her "sensible transcendental" does not resemble his Cartesian "idea of the infinite." But Levinas reads infinity after all "in the sensible appearance of the face." Surely there is some common *sensibility* here influencing, however fitfully, her *infini*—the unfinished, open infinity produced in the overflowing. This shared sensibility appears perhaps only from an interstitial perspective, eschatological not in its final separation but in its *refusal* of separation. It will not even abandon the abandoning transcendence. For all its righteous dichotomies, the trope of transcendence carries an ethic of exodus. This is an ethic that at least within the feminist reaches of theology is beginning to repent of its own patterns of immanent violation.

Might we imagine the overflowing, the transcending, as the unfurling—for which the furls and folds of immanence would be no more a barrier than an embrace, no more an enclosure than a clearing? What self-transcendence would it require, what auto-deconstruction, for transcendence to reinhabit its own body, relations, earth? To accept its wombs and its tombs as the finite media of its very infinition? Could it exercise its transgressive energies of risk without reinscribing its belligerent flight, its wounding subjugation? Would it still be transcending? Movement that does not break away, but that *moves*? That does *not separate, but differs*? Would its infinitely distant divinity *move* within every distance, and so, intimately, with/in us, *Emmanuel—or Shekinah*?[15]

Creatio ex profundis

I hope I have made clear that the gender-inflection of transcendence is not reducible to a dominative masculinity. Nor is masculinity identifiable with the breakaway transcendence. It is rather that the politics, sex and philosophy of this ahistorical "beyond" together constitute a certain theologically readable force, a sovereignty quite originally theological—indeed constitutive of the very master myth of origin, the dogma of *creatio ex nihilo*. Let us remain within the disciplinary borderland of this essay and observe how the dogmatic formula secures the Levinasian ethic of separation. "To affirm *origin from nothing by creation* is to contest the prior community of all things within eternity, from which philosophical thought, guided by ontology, makes things arise as from a common *matrix*" (Levinas, ibid., p. 293, my italics). The God beyond being cannot be a ground or *mater* of being, indeed cannot ground or guarantee ethics. Indeed Levinas has no interest in theological dogma as such—the absolute transcendence of the *ex nihilo* leaves its trace only in human responsibility for the neighbor.[16] "The absolute gap or separation which transcendence implies could not be better expressed than by the term creation, in which the kinship of beings among themselves is affirmed, but at the same time their radical heterogeneity also, their reciprocal exteriority coming from nothingness" (Levinas, ibid., p. 293).

Any ecofeminist theologian could concur that "creation" designates at once the difference and the interrelatedness of all creatures. But here again the *difference* that enables relationship is reduced to *separation*, guaranteed by the original break. So otherness is protected by a void—between creator and creatures and therefore between the creatures, an absolute nothingness, providing an absolute boundary. That sounds like closure. But Levinas intends opening. "One may speak of creation to characterize entities situated in the *transcendence that does not close over into a totality*" (Levinas, ibid., p. 293; cf. Hennessey in *Levinas and Biblical Studies*). Such a self-enclosure of transcendence is what theology might learn (with Levinasian aid) to avoid. But in order to resist totality must we accept any such reinscription—however nondoctrinal the intent—of the orthodox doctrine of creation?

For Christianity it was the *creatio ex nihilo* that created the very idea of a production from sheer, exterior nothingness, empty even of God—*Non de Deo, sed ex nihilo* (Augustine). And yet precisely the *ex nihilo* serves to close the transcendence into a totality—a self-identical aseity, an homogenous *homoousia*. Indeed, contrary to rumor (rumors authorized by Christian, Jewish and Muslim orthodoxies and circulated as common sense[17]), the *creatio ex nihilo* is held by no text of the Bible; it is an invention of late-second-century Christian onto-theology. I have demonstrated elsewhere that the full logic of the *ex nihilo*, as creation not *from* a formless matter but as the creation *of* matter itself from nothingness, is occasioned by the repudiation of a female. Irenæus produces that logic in a specific passage of *Against the Heretics*, in a spasm of polemical disgust in the *face* of a goddess. She takes the form of a gnostic allegory of the arising of the world's matter from the fluid affects—Irigaray's sensible transcendental?—of the female Achamoth. "They do not enquire whence were supplied to their Mother . . . so great an amount of tears, or perspiration, or sadness, or that which produced the remainder of matter." He lacks all patience with the subtle allegories of the Valentinians: "How can these things fail to be regarded as worthy of contempt, and truly ridiculous?"[18]

With this scornful new logic—call it "ex-nihilist"—the biblical story of a creation from another feminized fluidity, the *tehom* or Deep itself, was at the same textual moment quietly transcended. Genesis lay too close for orthodox

Catherine Keller

comfort to the Platonic *khōra*; and, worse, to the plethora of biblical and pagan
creation myths which recall, whether honoring or defaming, the salt-watery
womb of becoming. They pulled against the rising myth of a sovereign, controlling He-god who creates all from nothing. He creates and is created from
the onto-theological hybrid of a Platonic *apatheia* alien to scripture and an *ex
nihilo* alien to Plato. Orthodox Christianity installed a doctrine of creation
from nothing at the site of a prior ambiguity, where beginning was not exclusive origin, where transcendence was not mere exteriority. Rather, the transcendence moves within and beyond a bottomless and boundless that is both
other and same. That bottomlessness is neither a thing nor a nothing; and it is
signified in the Hebrew of Genesis 1.2 as *tehom*, the deep. But might the deep
itself signify a relation of transcendence—precisely as infinity? Or does it signify merely the briny Other, the residual immanence of matter, to be produced, ordered and *transcended by* Logos?[19]

Immanations

In pursuit of this conference's fleeting topic, I fell like Alice down the rabbit
hole through a Levinasian footnote, onto Jean Wahl's neologism, *"transascendence."*[20] Levinas omits its twin term—*transdescendence*. Gesturing toward
D. H. Lawrence's "dark god," the grounds—*les bases*—of being, and the unknown God, Wahl's own contribution remains tantalizingly brief. He suggests
that transdescendence is *the movement of transcendence toward immanence.*
"Perhaps the greatest transcendence is that which consists in transcending
transcendence—*lorsque la transcendance se transcende elle-même*—that is, of
falling back into immanence."[21] If I presumed that to transcend transcendence
poses a tautology that is helpless to rescue the desolated immanence, does the
reflexivity of his formulation perhaps adjust the meaning? Is it possible that
"when transcendence transcends *itself*" the *movement* surpasses the *state* of
transcendence, and thus also overcomes the tautology? Reflecting on "the
second immanence" that then appears after the shattered transcendence (*la
transcendance détruite*), Wahl suggests the following:

> But this destructive idea, if it must be destroyed in its turn, is never com-
> pletely destroyed, never completely transcended, and rests in the back-
> ground of the spirit, like the idea of a lost paradise, of which the hoped-for
> and mourned-for presence, and the loss, comprise the value of our attach-
> ment to the here-below. (*Existence humaine et transcendance*, p. 38)

The here-now. So a certain ghost and loss characterize the trace of transcendence that lingers—after the auto-de(con)struction of transcendence. One
thinks of Kristeva, of Irigaray, on the sex of the lost paradise, the abject mother,
the lost object. This spectral transcendence delivers, as a work of mourning,
the value of our fragile creaturely connections. The pillar of salt trembles in
recognition.

Might this double or self-negating transcendence (its existential voice in originative conversation with Beauvoir and Levinas) help to articulate the work of feminism within theology? It moves "beyond" the breakaway transcendence, beyond the transcendence that petrifies into an onto-theology as sexed and static as the immanence it dooms. Concretely: When in classical theology "the transcendence of God" functions as a one-way genitive (I did not say "genital"), it hardens into the ontology that Jean-Luc Marion, like Levinas, exposes as idolatry. But will not these iconoclasms harden in turn, if they do not unlock their own gender codes? John Caputo has deployed "the beautiful distinction between icon and idol" in Marion to ask a crucial question:

> if we insist upon the masculinity of . . . God, is that to get back to the original or is it to stop with an idol and substitute—something human, something obviously, conspicuously male, and a human-all-too-human structure, masculine-all-too-masculine, socio-politico-sexual power structure, an historical contingency? Is it God's transcendence we have in view? Or do we fall down before the oldest, most phallocentric idol one can imagine?[22]

This reverberation of a "more radical hermeneutics" with feminist theology destabilizes any claim upon a revelation transcending creaturely limitation. Such claims themselves reveal the divinization of human—and in theology that has meant almost exclusively male—limitation. "If God is a male then the male is God."[23] The phallocentric projection would represent the dominant form of separative transcendence, of motion hardened and so permanently blocking any possible *self*-transcendence. Only an unbecoming God remains onto-theologically conceivable. So let me suggest that the self-transcending transcendence offers a cure for idolatry.[24]

What then of Wahl's "second immanence"? Who on the postmodern scene, privileging as it does the signifiers of transcendence—alterity, impossibility, apophasis, absolute gift, promise, messianicity—has spoken for this immanence? This would be first of all Deleuze, who with Guattari deploys immanence against transcendence as vehemently as Levinas deploys transcendence against immanence. "So modern philosophical attempts to rediscover the transcendent within immanence, or to reconcile them (like Jaspers's 'encompassing') are no more than 'a reservoir for eruptions of transcendence'." These attempts continue what they characterize, not wrongly, as the history of Christianity. "Religious authority wants immanence to be tolerated only locally or at an intermediary level, a little like a terraced fountain where water can briefly immanate on each level but on condition that it comes from a higher source and falls lower down (transascendence and transdescendence, as Wahl said)."[25] Another Wahl-sighting! Wahl however was not advocating any such hierarchy, but hinting at a radical—presumably irreversible—fall into immanence, and so anticipating the Deleuzean trajectory. Likewise the postmodern immanence would not be immanent *to* something else, which would thereby transcend it.

Catherine Keller

One does not break out of the bounds of this immanence. For it is not a bounded space but a relation to the boundless. "Transcendence enters as soon as the movement of the infinite is stopped" (Deleuze and Guattari, *What Is Philosophy?*, p. 47). This protest against transcendence forms a mirror opposite to the deconstruction of immanence. Boiling out of a common intellectual matrix, this opposition forms a fluid postmodern chiasmus. What Levinas finds in *transcendence*—the *overflowing infinite*—Deleuze and Guattari find in *immanence*. Yet for the former, the infinite is produced in the ethical relation, as a negation of totality; while for the latter it signifies the ecstatic plenum, the dimensionality making possible all dimensions, the *omnitudo* that resembles what mythologically and now scientifically is called chaos.[26] Thus, "the plane of immanence which we lay out in thought 'reconstitutes' a sort of chaos"; it "slices through the chaos"; so "every plane is not only interleaved but holed, letting through the fogs that surround it" (ibid., p. 51). This anarchic language, lacking any ordering origin, Other, or Order—may send the fainthearted running for transcendent cover. Nonetheless there is something that theology needs from the Deleuzean immanence. It would be a gift akin to that of Vattimo's kenotic Christian translation of the "death of God" into the "dissolution of divine transcendence." *Not* of the divine.[27]

In passing, Deleuze produces a device that will let immanence resist its own petrifaction—a verb. To **immanate**. For if immanence *moves*, then it cannot be held captive within boundaries defined by an abstract transcendence. And it might, paradoxically, thaw out the immobilized transcendence. That would not be the Deleuzean intention. But at least to ecofeminist ears, the Deleuzean nomadology of escapes and captures—his "war machines," his lines of flight and "infinite speeds"—threatens to accelerate the ancient desert mobilities to a velocity matching that of the breakaway transcendence. Might immanence be more sustainably mobilized by an internal, if ironic, relation to its own *theological* potentiality—its divine *immanation*?

Deleuze and Guattari often invoke the great neologism of *Finnegan's Wake*, the "chaosmos." Neither disorder nor order, it implies a hermeneutic of creation paradoxically more true to Genesis than to the Levinasian *ex nihilo*. Not coincidentally, it is under the sign of the chaosmos that Deleuze advocates the theistic philosophy of A. N. Whitehead.[28] Whitehead lets Deleuze distinguish his own *nomadology* from a Leibnizian *monadology*.[29] The "actual occasion" as "event," with its prehensive relations of immanence to every other event, lets Deleuze open the monad into a spatiotemporality of flows, a universe of infinite unfoldings. These prehensions are the action of immanence—they can be said to *immanate* from the other, as the other, into the subject, before the subject has quite become. Indeed the prehensive relation is a flowing implantation in the other, and of the other in the self—not a confusion, as heterogeneity rather than fusion is the aim. The becoming-concrete of a subject here/now is in Whitehead a "concrescence" of these relations of immanence.

Yet in Whitehead each event also *transcends* the others. Indeed he never repudiates divine transcendence, only its imperial ontology of dominance: "The church gave unto God the attributes which belonged exclusively to Caesar."[30] The culminating aporetic antitheses of Whitehead belong within the present volume: "It is as true to say that God transcends the world as that the world transcends God. It is as true to say that God is immanent to the world as that the world is immanent to God." The world is in every here/now an embodiment of the divine, which always and everywhere exceeds any particular creation. "It is as true to say that God creates the world, as that the world creates God."[31]

This theologic suggests not a transcending of transcendence that would cancel transcendence *out*; it implies rather the self-transcendence of transcendence, in a perichoresis rhythmically but not perspectivally coincidental with immanence. The divinity, precisely in its alterity, would be at any moment transcended, interpreted, exceeded—by the world. The world at once embodies and resists divinity. Such a God does not in the classical sense create and control the world; the world affects, indeed surprises divinity—but from *within*. More than any other resource for theology, Whitehead and his school (a seedbed of U.S. feminism and ecotheology), enables the deconstruction of the *ex nihilo* dogma. We may spread a new rumor—of genesis from *tehom*, the matrix or *khōra* of a chaosmic creativity. *That transcendence itself immanates, and only so transcends. That immanence itself transcends, and only so immanates.*

The oscillating rhythm of divine-cosmic relations recalls the panentheism (rather than pantheism) of Nicholas of Cusa, with his *explicatio-implicatio* pattern. Deleuze has from early in his thought absorbed this pattern, via Bruno, into his own unorthodox trinity. "The trinity complication-explication-implication accounts," claims Deleuze, early in his thought, for a world or a text:

> The chaos which contains all, the divergent series which lead out and back in, and the differenciator which relates them one to another. Each series explicates or develops itself, but in its difference from the other series which it implicates and which implicate it, which it envelops and which envelop it; in this chaos which complicates everything.[32]

We might make a perversely theological use of this trinity, not quite translatable into father, son and ghost of a (feminine) spirit. Let me close with a brief constructive tehomic displacement of the trinitarian personae. I address these three as "capacities" rather than "persons."

A Trinity of Folds

The First Capacity. We might invoke the *complicatio* as the *tehom* of *genesis* itself, the text of the primal chaos of all beginnings. We might inscribe its darkness, as Eckhart did, as the darkness of our own unknowing, Cusa's *docta ignorantia*, and so also as the negativity of in/finity, its *Gottheit*—Godhead, or better, *Godness*—a divinity that is never quite god, not yet or no longer god. Here the creative spirit pulses rhythmically upon the face of the waters (*mayim*). Of the deep. *Tehom* appears only upon its own surface, upon—the face. And Levinas, though not thinking here of Gen. 1, puts such a relation exquisitely: "The idea of infinity, the infinitely more contained in the less, is concretely produced in the form of a relation with the face" (Levinas, *Totality and Infinity*, p. 196). But the face of the deep does not confront us from a mere exterior. All the more strange by virtue of its familiarity, or all the more familiar for its strangeness, its alterity appears at once infinitely distant and infinitesimally intimate—"closer to us than we are to ourselves." This godness is no more a person than Schelling's or Tillich's "divine abyss," yet contains, indeed *capacitates*, all the pasts and all the possibilities of personhood. This first capacity of the divine would be *transcendent* as *apophasis*, by which it infinitely exceeds and precedes each finitude of self, body, word—but only by way of a *bottomless kenosis*, its transdescendence. In other words the *complicatio* capacitates both the *implicatio* and the *explicatio*, the immanating and the transcending capacities.

The Second Capacity. It is always *difference* that transcendence seeks to *explicate*. I have argued that transcendence, seeking to protect difference, actually *threatens* it, when it encircles it with a void, and tops it with a changeless omnipotence. Then it is that transcendence stops the motion of the infinite. The unfinished creativity gets trapped in the mirror of a finished creation. The movement of transcendence becomes stasis, it becomes state. The *basileia* becomes the empire. The mover, unmoved, becomes the preemptive power of domination. But we need no longer hear the speech-act of creation—the *let there be*—as an imperial command. "Let it *be*," sings forth invitation. This difference saves—and is saved by—certain ancient names of God.[33] In this divine capacity, this persona, we personally call upon (personal) names—*dabar*, Sophia, Elohim, Christ, Logos, *Verbum*. This verb in its transcending motion may interrupt, disrupt, even as it calls forth and distinguishes. But its great distances do not metaphysically separate anything from anything, with nothing between. Its breaks are not clean; they require, like the kabbalistic "breaking of the vessels," future redemptions. Only by a feat of utmost abstraction do we construct a nothingness void even of potentiality for new creation. As the unfolding, the *explicatio*, of the plane or face of immanence, it moves *beyond*— but *always in relation to*—whatever already is. In other words—as the word of the other and the otherness of the word—it makes a difference. A world.

The impersonal godhead may expand infinitely, in an indifferent beyond or beneath. Yet the metaphor or name of God calls forth and is called in *difference*. It explicates an unfolding of history at its edge, eschaton, not on either side of a barrier. So the explicate unfolds the implicate—in its irreducible complication.

The Third Capacity. What transcends also *immanates.* Before any word speaks or any difference takes place, its breath is pulsing on the waters, synching with the ebb and flow. The *implicatio,* the "infolding," would be the primal inhalation, the curling in of the wave—like the motion of *ruach,* wind, whirlwind, or waterbird vibrating upon the chaos, echoing, repeating, *tōhû wā bōhû,* a rhyme preceding its reason. Never repeating the same—as a repetition, it is already different from what it repeats.[34] For Caputo, "repetition starts at the beginning, not at the end."[35] In its rhythmic kinesis in Genesis, the spirit performs no separative transcendence, nor yet a merely subordinate immanence (as something sent down from Him who is really God). The iterations of the spirit pulse through a Sabbath cycle, in which return and rest restore rhythm without circling backwards. "Repetition," Deleuze argues, "is the power of difference."[36] Without his permission, we might recognize this power as spirit. Thus this third capacity is the very implication of the chaosmos in its world, as explicated by its word. The immanence is the relation *between* the negativity of the infinite—and the positivity of its explications. This pneumatic interior of every event, every instant, every subject, is a "within" without walls, itself endlessly unfolding, multiplying and hybridizing. For when the finite creature is bounded by a fold rather than a wall or a cut, even a wound of separation exposes layers of dense relation, laboring to heal.

Fragile Foldings of the Infinite

Transcendence here transdescends—or immanates—within a fluid matrix whose boundaries, like that of the "known" universe, cannot be ascertained. Its boundaries comprise the creation of the infinite itself, the negating of any particular finitude. Its movement would transgress any boundaries that sever inside from out. Or beginning from end. It deconstructs every ethical fundamentalism and so makes space for ethics, indeed for the eschatological of a counter-apocalyptic ethic.[37] This thought is close to that of Levinas, when he says: "Submitting history as a whole to judgment, exterior to the very wars that mark its end, it [the infinite?] restores to each instant its full signification in that very instant" (*Totality and Infinity,* p. 23). Yet in that very judgment and the struggle for its peace, we admit leakage from the exterior. The transcendence always already immanates. How could it not? By the very logic of an infinity that cannot be bounded, it cannot remain outside of anything. The following rendition by Caputo of Levinas suggests a pervasive, if unacknowledged, site of immanence: "From a hermeneutical point of view, the infinity that Levinas describes is *present in us all.*"[38] Present in all of us—yet contained by none, as Irenæus claimed of the cosmic logos. It recapitulates all things in itself. That is how it *saves.* By a *singular repetition.*

If divinity leaves Trinitarian traces, we might call them Infinity, Word and Spirit. Or feminine words invoke the Sophia of the transcending *explicatio,* the *Ruach* of the immanating *implicatio*—and certainly the womb of the complicating *Tehom*. I have not proposed a new sex-gender binary. Nor have I suggested a dialectical opposition or complementarity of transcendence and immanence; or the sublation of one by the other. To Augustine's *non de Deo, sed ex nihilo*, we may counter: *Si de Deo, sed ex profundis*.[39]

This becoming-theology offers at the very least a parable for ethics. For every exterior unfolds another—indeed an Other's—interior; every interior is a fold of its own boundless exteriority. Liberation might require escape into the exterior space of exodus—but that desert will invariably prove to be already replete with immanent life, whole populations, which like Jericho, can be treated to the transcendent breakthrough by which the walls of immanence come tumbling down. Holy massacre. Then the separative power will construct new walls, partitioning itself off from the resentment and the resistance of the subjugated immanence. It will call upon a preemptive omnipotence to "liberate" or to "defend" it. As an alternative, those populations (only some of whom are human) might be recognized as fragile folds of the chaosmos, trembling with otherness and repetition. Sometimes they can face us in conversation.

In the meantime neither sameness nor separation will save us from the others. Our difference inflicts upon us all distance and interdependence. Our speech will settle into the dumb silence of a state—or it will explicate a movement beyond war, beyond empire, within the infinitely unfinished complications of our finitude. These incarnate complications always exceed the ethic that lets them unfold. If they exhibit their sex in new ways, it is because the clear boundaries of gender—not its differences—are breaking up. We cannot bring Lot's wife back to life or name. But we may find as we come back round through the desert, fleeing new apocalypses, that she serves as signpost. What does she point *beyond*? Beyond that transcendence—be it God, Man, politics or science—that cuts its bonds to whatever precedes or exceeds it? That bleaches out the traces of the immanent? Beyond the beyond of a separative transcendence, what would be *coming*? The sea itself? The last wave of the primal flood, coming to incapacitate us? Or only the next, offering the pneumatic crest of its difference, here, now? What a bottomlessly implicating project confronts us with its possibility—that of a genesis collective, a planetarity *capax dei*, and so, rumor has it, hospitable to all these mutually immanating, mutually transcending creatures.

NOTES

1. The term "ecofeminism" seems to have been coined by Mary Daly as part of "Gyn/ecology," and Rosemary Radford Ruether and Sallie McFague are its primary Christian exponents. I consider most of my work to fall within its semantic field. But the term may seem to subdivide theology rather than, as it intended, to insist upon the terrestrial immensity of our embodied relations.

2. Emmanuel Levinas, *Totality and Infinity: An Essay on Exteriority*, trans. A. Lingus (Pittsburgh: Duquesne University Press, 1969), p. 73.

3. Gilles Deleuze and Felix Guattari, *What Is Philosophy?*, trans. H. Tomlinson and G. Burchell (New York: Columbia University Press, 1994), p. 45.

4. "Look, I have two daughters who have not known a man. Let me bring them out to you, and you may do to them as you please; but do not do anything to these men, since they have come under the shelter of my roof" (Genesis 19:8, JPS *Hebrew-English Tanakh*, 2nd ed.).

5. Cf. Elizabeth Johnson's correlation of the medieval *via negativa* and the apophatic critique of idolatry, with contemporary Christian deconstruction of the exclusive masculinity of God-talk in *She Who Is: The Mystery of God in Feminist Theological Discourse* (New York: Crossroad, 1992).

6. Genesis 18:16–33.

7. Simone de Beauvoir, *The Second Sex*, trans. H. M. Parshley (New York: Vintage, 1952), p. xxxiii, my italics. Cf. my analysis of Beauvoir's separative transcendence in Catherine Keller, *From a Broken Web: Separation, Sexism and Self* (Boston: Beacon, 1986), chap. 1.

8. Cf. Mary Daly, *The Church and the Second Sex* (Boston: Beacon, 1986). Its application of Beauvoir to the still-promising scene of Catholicism after the Second Vatican Council is as good a candidate as any for founding work of feminist theology.

9. Cf. the perfectly titled, "Love Your Neighbor as Another: Reflections on Levinas's Ethics and the Hebrew Bible," Tamara Cohn Eskenazi, in *Levinas and Biblical Studies*, ed. T. C. Eskenazi, Gary A. Phillips and David Jobling (Atlanta: Society of Biblical Literature, 2002), p. 149.

10. Emmanuel Levinas, *Totality and Infinity: An Essay on Exteriority*, trans. A. Lingus (Pittsburgh: Duquesne University Press, 1969), p. 109ff. Of course this separation, and its "absolute," subserve the ethical relation and are not meant as a transcendence of relationality itself. It indicates a "psychism" and an interiority that "maintain the distance that separates the metaphysician from the metaphysical, and their resistance to totalization." Thus Tamara Cohn Eskenazi can argue:

Levinas dethrones logocentrism in philosophical discourse and replaces it with relation. He constitutes a subject—a self—on the model of connectivity, rather than the dominant patriarchal, separatist object/subject self. He opposes the fusing self of normative Western tradition with one that does not merge/assimilate the other into oneself, but remains, instead, in relation of responsibility. (*Levinas and Biblical Studies*, p. 149)

I cannot "separate" myself from this interpretation—though I offer it in contrast to my own argument—as the very terms are avowedly "connected" to my early distinction between the "separative," "soluble" (fusing) and "connective" selves. Cf. Catherine Keller, *From a Broken Web: Separation, Sexism and Self* (Boston: Beacon, 1986).

11. "The notion of a transcendent alterity—one that opens time—is at first sought starting with an *alterity-content*—that is, starting with femininity" (Emmanuel Levinas, *Time and the Other*, trans. Richard Cohen, Pittsburgh: Duquesne University Press, 1989). So in his own terms, one cannot identify femininity with immanence—au contraire, it is in a certain sense transcendence itself. The feminine is not just a difference—nor even just a radical (Irigarayan) difference—but "the very quality of difference." Earlier, he writes: "The feminine is described as the *of itself other*, as the origin of the very concept of alterity" (cit. Eskenazi, *Levinas and Biblical Studies*,

p. 152). This transcendent alterity seems to transcend the woman—in her difference as woman and in her specific differences as this particular woman—almost absolutely.

12. Emmanuel Levinas, *Nine Talmudic Readings*, trans. Annette Aronowicz (Bloomington: Indiana University Press, 1990), p. 173. The borderline between his own position and that of the traditional commentators remains ambiguous.

13. Cf. Susan E. Shapiro's incisive critique, "'And God Created Woman': Reading the Bible Otherwise":

> I would suggest that Levinas's ideological blind spot about Woman and the feminine keeps him from realizing that his instituting of gender hierarchy—even into eschatology—reinscribes the injustices of both totality and Eleatic metaphysics . . . In reading Genesis solely in ontological terms[!]—and in terms in which being-for-the-other cannot include Woman as such as this Other—Levinas undercuts his understanding elsewhere of both ethics and eschatology. (*Levinas and Biblical Studies*, p. 193)

Yet feminists also defend him in the difficult effort, as Eskenazi writes, to construct "an ethical system in which the fragility of our commitment to the other as other can be protected in the face of the engulfing attraction to the same" (*Levinas and Biblical Studies*, p. 157).

14. Luce Irigaray, *Forgetting of Air in Martin Heidegger*, trans. Mary Beth Mader (Austin: University of Texas Press, 1999), p. 106. See also "Questions to Emmanuel Levinas," in *The Irigaray Reader*, ed. Margaret Whitford (Oxford: Blackwell, 1991).

15. I hope it is evident that I do not find Christianity to be more conducive than Judaism to feminist transformation: Monotheistic patriarchy represents on of the great common denominators of the Abrahamist faiths, and none of these possesses a monolithic position. It is interesting that Levinas more or less accuses Martin Buber—whose relationalism more closely approximates that of much feminist theology, including that of the present endeavor—of effeminacy: "The I-Thou in which Buber sees the category of interhuman relationship is the relation not with the interlocutor but with feminine alterity" (*Totality and Infinity*, p. 155).

16. Yet for the present reading of philosophical texts as parables of a theological struggle, the power of the creation symbol within Levinas's non-dogmatic ethics testifies to the foundational force of the dogma. For an affirmative assessment of the links of ethics to the ex nihilo doctrine, cf. Scott Hennessey's elucidation of the *creatio ex nihilo* as response to the chaos of the Shoah, "Creation, Chaos and the Shoah: A Theological Reading of the Il Y A" (in *Levinas and Biblical Studies*, ed. T. C. Eskenazi, Gary A. Phillips and David Jobling, Atlanta: Society of Biblical Literature, 2002, p. 49ff.). I have elsewhere, in an analysis of Karl Barth's repudiation of any creation from chaos, asked why such a phenomenon as National Socialism, like other forms of totalizing power, should be in theological retrospect associated more with "chaos" than with "order"; see Catherine Keller, *Face of the Deep: A Theology of Becoming* (London: Routledge, 2003), pp. 84–99.

17. A new, popular version of the rumor: In *Angels and Demons* (New York: Pocket Star, 2000) author Dan Brown (of *The Da Vinci Code*) blithely identifies Genesis 1 with the possibility that a God created the universe "from nothing"; and thus, a priest-scientist has worked to "prove Genesis was possible."—"Prove Genesis? Langdon wondered. Let there be light? Matter from nothing?" (p. 71).

18. Irenæus, *Against the Heretics*; discussed in Keller, *Face of the Deep*, chap. 3.

19. I have raised these questions with the help of Derrida's *khōra* and the bottomless sur/face, in Keller, *Face of the Deep*, pp. 157–171.

20. Emmanuel Levinas, *Totality and Infinity: An Essay on Exteriority*, trans. A. Lingus (Pittsburgh: Duquesne University Press, 1969), p. 35, n. 2; and indeed, Levinas dedicates this volume to the Wahls.

21. Jean Wahl, *Existence humaine et transcendance*, Neuchâtel, 1944.

22. John D. Caputo, *More Radical Hermeneutics: On Not Knowing Who We Are* (Bloomington: Indiana University Press, 2000), p. 212.

23. Mary Daly's mantic maxim, in *Beyond God the Father: Toward a Philosophy of Women's Liberation* (Boston: Beacon, 1993).

24. This *immanent* therapy sympathizes with the dilemma of a transcendence frozen in a dissociative gesture of great original dynamism, a transcendence intended to protect difference, to prevent the collapse of the creator into the creaturely. The self-transcending transcendence allows a fresh feminist appreciation of theological arguments for the political ethics of transcendence made, for instance, by Kathryn Tanner. Cf. esp. Kathryn Tanner, *The Politics of God: Christian Theologies and Social Justice* (Minneapolis: Fortress, 1992); and *God and Creation in Christian Theology: Tyranny or Empowerment?* (Oxford: Blackwell, 1988).

25. Gilles Deleuze and Felix Guattari, *What Is Philosophy?*, trans. H. Tomlinson and G. Burchell (New York: Columbia University Press, 1994), p. 45.

26. Edith Wyschogrod cannily exposes the "fault line" within postmodernism itself, between an ecstacism of the plenum and the ethics of difference: "On the one side the stress on alterity, temporal and spatial diffraction in the work of Derrida, Levinas, Blanchot and others; on the other Deleuze and Guattari's reversed plenum with its substitution of lines of flight for lack and difference" (*Saints and Postmodernism: Revisioning Moral Philosophy*, Chicago: University of Chicago Press, 1990, p. 229). I do not want to erase this line, but rather, by reading it as a chiasm, signal a difference between the boundless chaosmos of radical immanence and the bounded totality imputed to it by an absolute transcendence.

27. The "death of God" looks by now like a hand-me-down of the avant-garde. But theologies that evade its test will only continue to dry up, trapped in a desert whose temptations they have failed to face directly. And such theologies will continue to appear impotent against the fundamentalist resurgence. Limp transcendence, timid immanence. See Gianni Vattimo, *After Christianity*, trans. Luca D'Isanto (New York: Columbia University Press, 2002).

28. Rather startlingly, Wahl already was introducing Whitehead to the continent; cf. his comparison of Whitehead and Heidegger in *Existence humaine et transcendence* (Neuchâtel, 1944). And indeed—Wahl, Deleuze and the Deleuzean philosopher of science Isabelle Stengers comprise the major francophone reception of Whitehead.

29. Gilles Deleuze, *The Fold: Leibniz and the Baroque*, trans. T. Conley (Minneapolis: University of Minnesota Press, 1993), pp. 76–84, 137. For an alternative map of the relations key to the present essay, see Roland Faber, "De-Ontologizing God: Levinas, Deleuze and Whitehead," in *Process and Difference: Between Cosmological and Poststructuralist Postmodernisms*, ed. Catherine Keller and Anne Daniell (Albany: SUNY, 2002), pp. 209–234.

30. Alfred North Whitehead, *Process and Reality: An Essay in Cosmology*, corrected ed., ed. David Ray Griffin and D. W. Sherburne (New York: Free Press, 1978), p. 343.

31. Ibid., p. 348.

32. Gilles Deleuze, *Difference and Repetition*, trans. P. Patton (New York: Columbia University Press, 1994), pp. 123–124.

33. Of course, Derrida's "Sauf le Nom," in *On the Name*, ed. Thomas Dutoit (Stanford: Stanford University Press, 1995), in which he links apophasis with justice and with *khōra*, by way of Silesius, is immanent within and transcendent to the present meditation. I have needed to leave Derrida an *ineffable* in the present exercise—in resistance to his gravitational force; in honor of his (im)mortal effects.

34. In *Repetition and Difference*, Deleuze draws from the idea of repetition in Nietzsche and Kierkegaard something very like what Caputo has found more recently, and more theologically—"the courage for the flux . . . the wavering and fluctuating . . . the fear and trembling . . . not therefore a sheer novelty wholly discontinuous with the past." As Caputo cites Kierkegaard: "Genuine repetition is recollected forward."

35. John D. Caputo, *Radical Hermeneutics: Repetition, Deconstruction, and the Hermeneutic Project* (Bloomington: Indiana University Press, 1987), p. 15.

36. Indeed, Deleuze recognizes hints of immanence in the Kierkegaardian repetition—despite the transcendent absolute of the Other. Deleuze, *Difference and Repetition*, p. 220.

37. Catherine Keller, *Apocalypse Now and Then: A Feminist Guide to the End of the World* (Boston: Beacon), 1996. The counter-apocalypse emerges as a third genre. Beyond both the retro-apocalyptic proclivities of every fundamentalism, and the anti-apocalyptic animus of much secular, feminist and postmodern thought, the counter-apocalyptic acknowledges the eschatological edge of emergenc(y) as an infinite process, not a terminal annihilation.

38. John D. Caputo, *More Radical Hermeneutics: On Not Knowing Who We Are* (Bloomington: Indiana University Press, 2000), p. 253.

39. "Not from God, but from nothing?"—Yes from God. But from the deep. This argument, including its Trinitarian traces, comprises the tehomic hermeneutics (or *hermenautics*).

Intimations of Transcendence

Praise and Compassion

Sallie McFague

I would like to make a modest suggestion: That we look at two characteristic activities of religious people—their habit of praising God and their attempts to love others—as hints or traces of transcendence. Postmodernism has privileged the second of these activities, the ethical, and in fact has helped to return much of western theology to its primacy. This is a great gift. To a lesser extent, postmodern hermeneutics has also encouraged the other characteristic activity of religious people—praise. However, it has done so in a somewhat parsimonious, minimalist way; I suggest praise should be exuberant and exorbitant. Compassion and praise are related, I believe, for it is the aesthetic appreciation for the Other—God and our neighbors—that prompts the ethical response. We look and say: "It is good"; we can then (sometimes) act in love toward the Other. I have found that one fruitful way to bring these two activities—the aesthetic and the ethical—together is to imagine the world as God's body. Attempting to live within this model allows us to see the beauty of God through the bodies of creation and to realize that the greatest need of these lovely bodies is to be fed. Thus beauty and need, aesthetics and ethics, God and the world, join at the place where people praise God and serve the basic needs of others.

Praising God and Loving Neighbor

Humility is the only permitted form of self-love. Praise for God, compassion for creatures, humility for oneself.

—Simone Weil[1]

And now faith, hope, and love abide, these three; and the greatest of these is love.

—1 Corinthians 13:13

The two most distinctive activities of religious people are gratitude toward God and compassion toward others. The most prevalent religious emotion does not appear to be fear, but thanksgiving. A sense of gratitude seems to well up in us, even in those who are not "religious." We nod in agreement when Annie Dillard writes: "I go my way, and my left foot says 'Glory,' and my right foot says 'Amen' "; or when Rilke exclaims, "Being here is magnificent."[2] Indeed it is. It is also horrible and horrifying beyond all our imaginings, from the reckless waste and bloody violence of nature's ways to the even more shocking perversion of human greed and hatred. We live in a terrifying, wonderful world and in the midst of it some people, many people, end up full of praise, feeling blessed and wanting to bless. People as various as Job and Francis of Assisi do; so do the writer of Psalm 104 ("I will sing to the Lord as long as I live") and Gerard Manley Hopkins ("The world is charged with the grandeur of God"); as well as two non-believing biologists, E. O. Wilson, who wrote that "biophilia" was a natural human emotion, and Stephen Jay Gould, who used a gloss on the Capra film *It's a Wonderful Life* for the title of his book on evolution.[3] Dillard puts it this way: "The canary . . . sings on the skull."[4]

It seems that in all religious traditions and outside them as well, gratitude and delight emerge from human beings, spilling out from us in exorbitant words of praise. Is this phenomenon an intimation of transcendence? I do not know, but all this language cannot simply be ignored or rejected. Both Jean-Luc Marion and Jacques Derrida acknowledge this language in their discussions of the "gift" as the impossible possibility—what we most desire—but can never have short of idolatry.[5] They acknowledge it, however, in a minimalist way (and for good reason, as they have argued). But is this sufficient to account for the depth and breadth of the language of exorbitant praise? Whether one looks at the writings of mystics of all traditions, the Islamic poets, the Hindu sacred scriptures, the psalms of the Hebrew scriptures, the religious ceremonies of First Nations peoples—and even the theologies of such Christians as Irenæus, Augustine, Thomas Aquinas, Teilhard de Chardin, and Elizabeth Johnson—we find a huge discourse of thanksgiving. Even many so-called non-believers who are aware that they did not create themselves and are grateful to whatever did, use such language. One way of describing this discourse is with the ancient term *via positiva*, the way of affirmation, but that is not entirely accurate. This language is not intended to describe God as much as it is meant to express a sense of trust—what Paul calls "faith" and what Weil calls "praise." It is the acknowledgment of a way of being in the world, one in which gratitude and humility seem like the most appropriate stance, regardless of "belief in God."

Hence, the first thing I want to suggest is that we take this language seriously. Here one should not be minimalist, but let all the stops out: There is no praise too great, no language too extravagant for expressing our Yes to the gift of life, in spite of the shocking negativities and evils it involves. It is a gesture, a "thank you," that wells up from human beings in the most likely and unlikely places, from moments of exquisite joy (the birth of a child) to times of excruciating pain (the death of a child). Is it an intimation of transcendence?

Another place where transcendence may be found is in compassion, the practice of love. We should note in the Corinthian passage that God does not have faith or hope, but God *does* love. Is the Augustinian conversion of "God is love" into "Love is God" suggesting that love of neighbor and not praise to God is primary?[6] Is love for the other, particularly the other in lowercase, the heart of religion as well as the *primary* intimation of transcendence? It may well be. It is interesting to note that there is not a single religion in the world that has as its commandment: "Blessed are the greedy." In fact, there is almost universal agreement concerning the importance of self-limitation and self-abnegation so that others may live and prosper. The language of doing, of love, certainly is taken seriously by deconstruction. Both Derrida and Levinas—as is true also of the Hebrew scriptures and of Judaism—focus on the good deed. This is a welcome direction after centuries of Christian and especially Protestant obsession with belief in God as the primary issue. The deconstructionists are correct, I think, in claiming that as John Caputo puts it, "the name of God is the name of a deed."[7] By so doing, the central project of religion is centered in ethics, not in theology. Issues of the existence and nature of God, which have been the focus of western Christianity, now become secondary, as do ontology and metaphysics. The distinctive activity of religious people is not agony over the existence or non-existence of God. This seems to be a peculiar activity, a special concern, of western Christian theologians who are, after all, a minor voice relative to the approximately six billion people who belong to one of the world's ten thousand or so religions. Most of these people spend more time thanking God and trying to live as God wishes than they do worrying about God's existence.[8] Moreover, need transcendence mean "God's existence"—a being or being-itself that exists apart from the world and is in control of the world? Might intimations of divine transcendence be hidden within human praise and compassion—those strange countercultural activities of religious (and other) people; those activities of thankfulness, even when the world is a thankless place; and of love for others, even when such deeds are contrary to the market-capitalist ethic of self-fulfillment?

Now, of course, I have no firm evidence for these outrageous suggestions. They ring true in terms of my own experience and I notice them elsewhere in saints and ordinary people in my own religious tradition and in others. But they are merely anecdotal. With no pretense of proving them, I would at least like to play with their possibility for a while. More specifically, I would like to play with the model of the world as God's body, as a way of filling out how praise and compassion might be intimations of transcendence for Christians. The model of the world as God's body grounds Christian praise and doing in the ordinary, physical world. It suggests that the conventional meaning of transcendence as other than this world, beyond and separate from this world, is subverted into transcendence as radical immanence. It dares to make this move on the basis of the Christian assertion that the Word was made flesh, that God is incarnate in the world. It radicalizes the orthodox belief that Jesus of Nazareth alone is the Word made flesh, to imagine the world—all of creation— as God's body. Incarnationalism means that transcendence becomes radical immanence. Christians are invited to imagine the entire universe—all matter and energy in all its billions of differentiated forms—as God with us, or more accurately, as the body, the matrix, in which we live and move and have our being. With a sharp turn from the Barthian notion of transcendence wherein God relates to the world only as a tangent touches a circle, the model of the world as God's body suggests that God is the *milieu* in which we exist—exist at all levels and in all ways, but in ways that begin and end with the *body*. This model asks us to play with the possibility that Christianity is not about two worlds—the transcendent, heavenly one where we really belong (and where God abides), and the immanent, earthly one where we work out our salvation in sin and sorrow (and from which God is absent). Rather, the world as God's body suggests that there is *one* world, one reality; and that this world, this reality, is divine. The divine is physical (as well as spiritual) as we—all of us— are. There is no absolute line dividing matter and spirit, body and soul, nature and humanity, or the world and God: Contemporary science tells us this, but it is also the heart of incarnational, immanental thinking. The model of the world as God's body suggests a creation theology of praise to God and compassion for the world, in contrast to Christian theologies of redemption that focus on sin and on escape from the world.[9]

How, more specifically, is the model of the world as God's body a way of speaking of transcendence in Christian terms? How are praise and compassion, when focused on the world's body, intimations of transcendence? Two central issues are posed here. First, what is the status of metaphorical language for God-talk? What kind of assertions does it make? Is it a form of onto-theology? Does it limit itself to appropriate human humility and minimalism? Are metaphorical statements different from analogical and symbolic ones? Second, what kind of transcendence is suggested by body language? How can what is radically immanent (the body) be the place of transcendence? How would we praise God and serve our neighbor differently if we were to do so within the model of the world as God's body?

We will, therefore, be attending to two issues—the status of metaphor as a way to speak of transcendence, and the ways in which praise and compassion are intimations of transcendence when practiced within the model of the world as God's body. To state my thesis in its bare bones, I turn to Exodus 33: "And you shall see my back, but my face shall not be seen" (v. 23b). We do not know God or see God. What we know and see is what Moses saw—the "back" of God, the body of God which is the world. Through this mediation of God via the world, we praise God *using the world*, since we have no other means to do so. Likewise, we care for and have compassion for our world, God's body, in all its needs, especially the most physical ones like food, water, home, and health. A thoroughly immanental—or "backside"—theology accepts the limitations of our earthly, bodily existence, finding intimations of transcendence *in and through* the world, intimations that at times cause us to say "thank you" and to mean it. At other times, they impel us to pay attention to others, to their most basic needs—their bodily needs. Such intimations of transcendence are small and modest. Moreover, they are by no means the only intimations—just bodily ones. By encouraging us to look through the filter of physicality in looking for God, they highlight the sensuous, bodily, physical, basic aspects of life, while blocking out many others. The body metaphor is one important one; it is by no means the only one, and must be complemented by others. Finally, functioning within metaphor, this theology can make few pretensions to metaphysical assertions. As Derrida and many others have pointed out, metaphor lies between nonsense and truth.[10] Indeed it does. Metaphor says that the world is/*is-not* God's body. All it asks is that we entertain the nonsense for a while, in order to see if there is any truth in it.

Metaphor and Model as the Language of Transcendence

In his essay on metaphor, Derrida makes a distinction between how a philosopher and a theologian judge the status of metaphor. For the philosopher, he says, metaphor is a poor medium, always effacing the presence it seeks to illumine, subverting its own attempt at metaphysics by a "white mythology."[11] But he allows that "a theologian could be content with metaphor. And metaphor must be left to the theologian."[12] Good. I accept metaphor; it is all the theologian, I believe, needs. Metaphysical language—the language of certainty, of the absolute—claims to know God. But metaphor does not; it is modest. It makes a claim, but only with "assertorial lightness" or "soft focus," undercutting it immediately with the "is not."[13] The world is/is-not the body of God. Analogy and symbol both make much bolder assertions: Analogy rests on likeness between the Cause and its effect (Thomas Aquinas), while symbols participate in the reality to which they point (Paul Tillich). But metaphor is more a heuristic fiction than it is a metaphysical claim. It invites us to imagine, to live as-if, to entertain a novel possibility, which initially both shocks and intrigues. The world is God's body? Surely not—and yet . . .

Metaphor is an "in-between strategy," avoiding the presumption of the *via positiva* and the silence of the *via negativa*. It respects deconstruction's fear of idolatry, essentialism, and fundamentalism, but claims that this fear need not reduce us to silence or near-silence. In fact, it takes an entirely different strategy—piling on the language, going crazy like the psalmists and mystics do. It says: Admit our language about God says little (if anything) about God, but rather than parsimonious humility that can scarcely mumble the word "God," let us count on outrageous audacity to be its own negative, its own critique. Two strategies are possible in order to underscore the inadequacy, the non-sense, the falsity of God-talk. One advises us to say little or nothing, secure in the knowledge that if we say nothing, we will not be wrong. The other calls us to play with metaphors, many metaphors, sucking the juice out of them and throwing them away (as the Hebrew psalmists did), using everything and any-thing the world provides for talking about God. Metaphorical theology avoids dead metaphors that can pass as descriptions (God is king), preferring outland-ish suggestions (God is mother) which no one takes as literal. Nonetheless, even with its absurd metaphors (God as mother, the world as God's body), it calls us to imagine ourselves *within* the world that these shocking metaphors imply. Metaphor is a trickster, trying its chance, seducing us to give it a chance—the chance of seeing *differently* and perhaps of saying Yes to a dif-ferent way of being in the world.

As we dig more deeply into the potential of metaphor for God-talk, let us dwell on the following comment by Merold Westphal: "The critique of onto-theology . . . is directed not at *what* we say about God but *how* we say it, to what purpose, in the service of what project?"[14] He goes on to add, "We go to church in order to sing, and theology is secondary."[15] If this is so, if language about God is mainly praise (and not metaphysical assertions), then all sorts of lan-guage might be permissible—whatever language helps us to praise God more fully, more appropriately. Would Derrida object to this use of metaphor? I think not. What he does object to is metaphysics, which he defines as "con-cepts that have forgotten their metaphorical, sensuous base."[16] I object to that also. Hegel believed that there was a hierarchy of images and concepts, and we leave the former behind when we climb the ladder of truth. This view claims that the concepts of metaphysics do not need the concrete, sensuous base of metaphor; concepts rise above metaphor and release themselves from their earthly, relative beginnings with its built-in negation. But what if we did not forget the metaphoric base of all God-talk? Suppose that what Hegel calls the language of children, primitives, and women—the language of images—is the only language we have to speak of God, and that we stay with it?[17] What if we also always remember the "is-not" of metaphor, so that it does not mutate into symbol or analogy? What if we take as a watchword Derrida's claim that "Metaphor . . . always has its own death within it"?[18] Were we to surround metaphor with these qualifications, could we then dare to let metaphor try its chance—be a detour between nonsense and truth?

It is necessary to underscore the difference between metaphor, symbol, and analogy (not to mention simile, allegory, story, etc.). Unlike these other forms of imagery, metaphor does not result in organic, systematic works. It does not stress the similarity, the participation, the secret wisdom, the narrative coherence, the sense of beginnings and endings, the relation between cause and effect that these others do. In fact, metaphor is closer to parable than to any of the above images.[19] It has the same disorienting shock and sense of novel recognition/insight as Jesus' parables. David Tracy suggests something similar when he says that the genre needed in our time is the metaphor of "fragment": Not narrative, analogy, or dialectic, but something similar to Kafka's fragmentary parables, which do not make the strong claim of symbols, but rather a slight one—"some hint of redemption, even if that redemption is neither understood . . . nor even fully experienced."[20] Metaphors are fragments, even the metaphors that become models, though well-established models of God—for instance, God as king or father—resist such designation. The world as God's body, a model with considerable explanatory potential for interpreting the God-world relationship, sin and salvation, and Christian discipleship is also only a fragment.[21] Metaphors "say a lot"—good ones are rich with hermeneutical possibilities for making sense of things—but they do not "mean much." As Tracy writes, "If only Hegel had written the words 'A Thought Experiment' at the beginning of all his books, then Kierkegaard would be the first, he says, to honor Hegel as the greatest of all philosophers. But of course Hegel did not."[22] Yet, theologians are (or should be) content with metaphor, with thought experiments, as Derrida reminds us. This, I believe, is what all theology is; it never "advances" to concepts, to metaphysics, to certain or absolute claims. It is always just metaphor.

After all, as Aristotle first set down, metaphor is saying something about one thing using language that belongs somewhere else. It is not, like symbol or other images, based on likeness, stressing similarity; rather, it takes all the richness, detail, and concreteness of things we know something about to try to give a glimmer of something we do not know much (if anything) about. Hence, "love is a rose" can provoke endless talk of roses—of their smell, variety, texture, decay, and so on—in order to say something about enigmatic "love." Likewise, "the world is God's body" gives us lots of language—the language of bodies, earth, flesh, food, beauty, health and sickness—as a way of speaking abut the transcendence and immanence of God, of divine presence. The world/body becomes a stand-in for what we do not know. Does all this rich language come to anything? Is it true? There is no way to know. Does this language help us to praise God? Yes, I think so. Does it also give direction as to how we should love our neighbors? Yes, I think it does. Metaphorical language is not principally about "truth"; rather, it is about gratitude for the gift of life and our attempts to show that gratitude.

The Sacramental and the Prophetic

We will shortly flesh out these two projects of metaphorical theology, but before leaving metaphors and models, let us put the issue of metaphorical language within the classic Christian dialectic of the sacramental and the prophetic. This is one of the oldest and most fruitful conversations. The sacramental sees continuity between God and the world; the prophetic, discontinuity.[23] The first has been characterized as the Catholic sensibility (Thomas Aquinas), the second as the Protestant sensibility (Karl Barth). The sacramental allows for the two books of revelation—nature and Scripture—while the prophetic insists on *sola scriptura*. The first sees the entire universe as the image of God, for nothing less could begin to reflect God's glory (Irenæus, Augustine, Aquinas, G. M. Hopkins, Teilhard de Chardin); the second is terrified lest any visible, present thing claim to *be* the invisible presence of the divine. The first presses the iconic, advocating deification, the transparency of the world to its source, while the second fears idolatry, admonishing humility due to the opaqueness of all things before the wholly other. John Caputo suggests a similar dialectic with his notion of "historical association" and "messianic dissociation," the human need to concretize transcendence and the caution against doing so.[24] Another characterization is, of course, that of the kataphatic and the apophatic. Both of these impulses rise from deep in the imagination of all religious traditions—the desire, indeed, the need to speak of God; and the fear, the terror, of doing so. Which impulse is greater, the need or the fear, determines whether people veer toward one or the other extreme— fundamentalism (we have the truth in these words); or agnosticism (we have no truth in any words).

What I see as characteristic of many of the papers from the Villanova conference, is a desire to do something else—what Caputo calls "a happy minimalism."[25] This is excellent advice. It means that all our versions, our interpretations, are always provisional and revisable: "Whatever was constructed in the first place is deconstructible."[26] This means, as he insists, that *we* must be responsible for our theologies; they are constructed, not given. We have only signs and traces, not the things themselves. I agree completely. He advises us (in good Thomistic fashion) to start "from below, in medias res, in the midst of the tumult, amidst supplements and signs, mediations and substitutes, without a heavenly hook to bail us out, doing the best we can. It is a question of beginning where one is, as Derrida tells us—not where God is, we may add."[27]

This makes eminent sense, except for Caputo's addition, "not where God is." Is there anywhere where God is not? Does the Thomistic rule of starting with the senses, with where we are, prohibit God from being here/there also?

Augustine would surely say it does not; and so also the Jewish and Christian traditions which insist that God is Emmanuel, whether as the One who accompanied the Hebrews through all their earthly trials, or the One who is incarnate in the flesh, in the world. The prophetic impulse does not negate the sacramental. And here we come to a crucial point in the subject of the present volume—"transcendence and beyond." Need transcendence always mean what is *not* mundane? This seems to be an assumption suggested by the following statement by Caputo, in which he is speaks of determining "what is transcendent and what is mundane, what is original and what is copy, what is part and parcel of the calming reassurance and continuity of the same or immanence, and what belongs to the shock of the divine, the jolt and trauma of something different, of something—*grâce a Dieu*—divine and discontinuous."[28] There appears to be a predilection in deconstruction to privilege the wholly other, the *tout autre*, what cannot be said, the prophetic, silence, the sterile Protestant sensibility, the nonmundane, the invisible, as "transcendence." On the other hand, what is said, the sacramental, the words of praise, the fertile Catholic sensibility, the earthly and earthy, what is historical and concrete, is merely "immanent"—and perhaps suspiciously idolatrous? Could it be that the elliptical, "and beyond," in the volume's title suggests that we look once again at these meanings of transcendence and immanence to see if they are as inimical as commonly supposed? I am, for example, intrigued by a comment by Simone Weil: "That God is good is a certainty. It is a definition. And it is even more certain that God—in some way that I do not understand— is reality."[29] The certainty and incomprehensibility that God is reality forms the background to the intimations of transcendence, praise and love, to which we now turn.

Living within the World as God's Body

We begin these reflections with a reminder of the opening quotation from Simone Weil: "Humility is the only permitted form of self-love. Praise for God, compassion for creatures, humility for oneself."[30] Weil goes on to define humility as "attentive patience" and elsewhere writes that "attention animated by desire is the whole foundation of religious practices."[31] Paying attention is also at the center of a theology of the world as God's body. Weil says: We should look, not "eat." We seldom do this. Human love is usually "cannibalistic," wanting to use God and others for our own benefit, to fill up our own emptiness.[32] But the two distinctive intimations of transcendence we are considering —praising God and loving the neighbor—are characterized by an aesthetic distance, the ability to look but not devour, not possess. Love is the recognition of the other as other, whether it be God (the other as beauty) or the neighbor (the other as needy). The intimations of transcendence that come to us through the model of the world as God's body are ordinary—they arise from attentive patience to the actual, concrete, everyday world in which we live. To praise God through the glories of creation involves patient attention to small things—looking into the heart of a daffodil, hearing the splash of a frog in a pond, feeling the touch of another's hand. At certain times when we really pay attention to something outside ourselves—to the immensely complex beauty of the world—we want to repeat what God says in Genesis after creating the water and the land, the sun and the moon, the plants and the animals, including human beings: "It is good. It is very good." God does not say, creation is good for "me" or for human beings, but simply that it is good. To love the neighbor within the model of the world as God's body is also an ordinary everyday event. It involves attention to the needs, primarily the bodily, physical, mundane needs of other human beings and other life-forms. It means feeding and clothing others; trying to alleviate their pain and the oppressions they suffer; doing what is necessary so they may flourish. It involves, among other thing, *knowing* what makes others flourish—"ecological literacy."

Intimations of transcendence within the context of the world as God's body means being satisfied with *mediated* experiences of divine transcendence. "Backside" theology finds the glory of God in the beauty of the earth and in service to the neighbor. It means finding transcendence in the earth, in the flesh, in the ordinary, in the daily round. This is an odd suggestion, but one I believe is at the heart of Christian faith, that "transcendence beyond transcendence" is radical immanence. Using the model of the world as God's body as a thought experiment for "transcendence beyond transcendence," we arrive at the place *where we are*. We meet God in and through the world, if we are ever to meet God. God is not out there or back there or yet to be, but hidden in the most ordinary things of our ordinary lives. If we cannot find the transcendent *in* the world, in its beauty and its suffering, then for us bodily, earthy creatures it is probably not to be found at all. Finding transcendence in and the through the earth means paying attention to others: The ethical rests on the aesthetic, which is the prior moment of realizing that something outside of oneself is real. Only then is one capable of the kenotic action, the retreat of one's relentless ego, to allow the glory of God and the need of the neighbor to fill oneself. The aesthetic is the recognition of otherness; the ethical is the practice of self-denial necessary so that others—God and neighbor—may be praised and served. Thus, with the thought experiment of the world as God's body, we can affirm with Simone Weil that "God is reality": The body of the world, the ordinary reality of our lives, is where we meet God. "God is reality": Intimations of transcendence are found by rejoicing in the beauty of the real world and by serving the real needs of people and other life-forms. We conduct our ordinary lives within the divine milieu. All is divine, even this earth and its creatures, in ways we do not understand but of which we can become increasingly certain.

And how does one become certain? Not by thinking or even believing, but by living within the world *as if it were the body of God*. It involves the practice of paying attention to the world, to its beauty and its need. As the Catholic, sacramental sensibility has always insisted, this world is the only reality available to us and in and through it we find God. Teilhard de Chardin expresses this sensibility when he says that from the time he was a child, he had two passions—a passion for the world and a passion for God—and he could not imagine giving up one for the other.[33] In this sensibility, visibility and physicality are not shunned because of fear of idolatry; rather, as Francis Schüssler Fiorenza has said, "A theology that makes the fear of idols central may be a theology that ends up having room for neither icons of the divine, or the divine."[34] Or as Richard Kearney claims, "There is more to God than being. Granted. But to pass beyond being you have to pass through it."[35] And Weil notes, "How can Christianity call itself catholic if the universe itself is left out?"[36] Look and love, she says: Look at the world and be astounded by its beauty. "Of all the attributes of God, only one is incarnated in the universe, in the body of the Word; it is beauty."[37] An incarnational, immanental theology gives us permission to love the body of the world, and through the world's beauty to find intimations of God. An incarnational, immanental theology is suspicious of deconstruction's privileging of words over body, text over nature, interpretation over experience. While it is certainly not true that deconstruction claims "there is nothing outside the text" (as some simplistically believe), the physical world, both its beauty and its needs, is not often the focus of deconstruction. While we do indeed "construct" nature with our words, nature also constructs us with its beauty and its needs.[38] It confronts us with beauty that commands our attention (the "it is good" of Genesis). Nature also constructs us by confronting us with its inexorable and unavoidable laws and limits, its vulnerability and finitude, when faced with insatiable human greed. We too must eat—all of us—and no human construction of nature can erase nature's limitations as the one and only provider. Living within the model of the world as God's body awakens delight in each and every thing that makes up this body, but also an awareness of the needs of the body, its deprivations and sufferings.

What is this body that we are to praise and love? It is the universe, all matter/energy that constitutes physical reality since the Big Bang billions of years ago. It is not any one body and certainly not the human body (the model is not anthropomorphic or anthropocentric). The body of God is all of creation, all of nature, all that "is," all that exists. To imagine the world this way—as being in and of God—and to imagine God this way—as being the matrix of all that is—means that sharp lines between the world and God are erased.[39] The dualism of deism and theism are gone; we are in the realm of panentheism, and perhaps pantheism. In order to underscore the immanence of God in the world this model prefers the threat of pantheism, to the tradition's lapse into deism. Since our theologies will always be "wrong," is it better to err on the side of the presence or the absence of God? An incarnational, immanental theology opts for presence, with all the caveats, qualifications, and negations that metaphor necessitates. The model, however, defends itself against pantheism with two subsidiary metaphors: First, as we are to our bodies, so God is to the world (the body infused, enlivened by, mind/soul/spirit); and second, the world is in God as a baby is in the womb.[40] These metaphorical "fragments" by no means give us an organic system of the relations of God and the world. All they do is make some analogical suggestions for thinking about the implications of the model.

Look and Love: Feeding the Body

I would prefer to dwell on the beauty of the world rather than its needs; most of us would. But they are related, as Dorothee Sölle suggests when she writes of those who side with the oppressed: "The resistance of Saint Francis or . . . of Martin Luther King grew out of the perception of beauty. And the long-lasting and most dangerous resistance is the one born of beauty."[41] We were created to desire God, to love God through the beauty of the earth. It is not fear that prompts us to pay attention to the world's needs, but delight and joy—Rilke's "Being here is magnificent." Indeed it is—agonizingly magnificent. Our daily thoughts of death are but the other side of our appreciation of the world's magnificence. We want simply "to be here" in the glory that we see in a child's smile, in fresh rain, or the smell of an orange.

When Augustine's "God is love" is transposed into "Love is God," we are, says John Caputo, deflected from knowing God and toward loving the neighbor, from the joy of simply being here to doing something. "The *deflection* of God is the translation of God into a deed: Lord, when did we see You thirsty and give You a drink?"[42] Or as Edith Wyschogrod writes: "The saint's supreme *moral* principle is the *material* condition of the Other."[43] The intimation of transcendence at the heart of Christian faith is the awakening to the needs and sufferings of others. Loving God means feeding the suffering body of the world. Loving God is not a mystical immersion, but a mundane task—a "female" nurturing, caring task. It is lowly and basic, having to do *first of all* with physical needs (food, water, housing) and physical pain (suffering, deterioration, destruction). Living within the model of the world as God's body means focusing on these material, bodily matters. It does not mean that there are no other needs (mental, spiritual, emotional ones, etc.), but a metaphorical, incarnational theology privileges the lowly (and universal) physical ones. *All* must eat and *all* can suffer; hence, this model encourages us to find intimations of transcendence in and through the material conditions of others.

We prepare ourselves to do this by paying attention—by, as Weil puts it, looking, not eating: "The only people who have any hope of salvation are those who occasionally stop and look for a time, instead of eating."[44] Our tendency, says Weil, is to love others because of *our* needs, not theirs. Our fat, relentless egos want more, more, more; the insatiable greed of Adam Smith's economic man (*sic*) is but a contemporary version of original sin—the devouring, violent ego that wills to possess all. A first step in "salvation" is to stop and look, and say with God, "It is good," and let it be. Educating the loving eye, the eye that pays attention to the other as other (in contrast to the arrogant eye that objectifies and uses others) involves a dis-possession of the ego.[45]

John Woolman, a remarkable eighteenth-century American Quaker and abolitionist, saw the connection between possessions and sin in slavery: An increasing desire for goods resulted in the oppression of others in order to meet those desires. "Every degree of luxury hath some connection with evil," he wrote.[46] In order to keep the self out of the center, the eye must be kept "single," that is, able to see the needs of others clearly. This singleness of sight can be achieved only by dispossessing the self of possessions. Otherwise, he claims we always see double: The other will be seen only *through* the lens of the self's desires. At the close of his life Woolman had a dream in which he heard a voice saying, "John Woolman is dead."[47] He interpreted this to mean the death of his own will, that he was so mixed up with the mass of human beings that henceforth he could not consider himself a distinct being. His credo of universal love ended with his disappearance as a separate individual.

Likewise, Francis of Assisi's dispossession of the self in order to love others involved total poverty at both material and spiritual levels. Money and the ego, he believed, are the root of violence and exclusion; to live differently, one must renounce all possessions. Obedience is a kenotic movement, "a therapy for the liberation of desires," exemplified in the beggar archetype.[48] To be so liberated, one must give up not only money but authority, power, envy, self-glorification. One must become empty; in fact, one must become like a corpse: "This is true obedience: not to ask why you are moved, not to care where you are placed, not to insist on being somewhere else."[49]

This dispossession has been called many things—purification, conversion, purgation, repentance, de-creation. It is a process of kenosis, of self-emptying, that allows the other *to be seen*, for a place to be made for the other (not unlike divine kenosis in creation and incarnation, which "makes room" for creatures and the world). Pulling back, self-limitation, sacrifice, asceticism, simplification: All of this language, so typical of many religious traditions, is nothing more than making space so others can be, can live. It is not easy to do this. In fact, for people like us, who take up a lot of space—most of the space on the planet, given our level of consumption—it is probably the hardest thing we can imagine. Can we empty ourselves of the self so that the Other—the transcendent in the body of a hungry person or a clear-cut forest or an endangered species—might have room? Looking but not eating, kenosis, the single eye: These are not mere recommendations for our spiritual growth; rather, for us well-off North Americans, they are an intimation of transcendence—the command to let others live. Within the model of the world as God's body, this is as close to an absolute as one gets. Feed the body, not the self; look and love—do not devour.

An insatiable appetite is the mark of global market capitalism; it is also a definition of sin within the model as the world as God's body. "Salvation is consenting to die," writes Weil.[50] Excessive? Extreme? Not for us well-off human beings within a Christian incarnational context: If we pay attention to others, if their material condition becomes our central concern, we must decrease, retreat, and sacrifice that others may be. Sölle writes: "Eventually the great majority of humankind hangs on the cross of empire and, in an extended mystical understanding of suffering, with her species and elements our mother earth, too, hangs on the cross of industrialism."[51] This implies that we meet God not face to face, but by way of God's "backside"—by way of the world in its sickly, deteriorating, suffering condition. It is a prophetic cry to attend to a dimension of the divine, the world, that desperately needs our total attention and energies. As Wyschogrod puts it, "The term Other can be a collective sense as referring to the wretched of the earth." She goes on to say that "the saintly response to the Other entails putting his/her body and material goods at the disposal of the Other."[52] Wyschogrod calls this "carnal generality"—a disinterested saintly love expressed in one's entire corporeal being.[53] In other words, attention to other bodies (the material needs of others) demands doing so with one's own body (the material goods one possesses). Meeting God through the needs of other bodies by putting one's own body on the line—this is an intimation of transcendence as *radical immanence*. We meet God in and through other bodies, by laying down our own body for them. This theology of the cross is not a one-time atonement by God for humans; rather, it is a prophetic call for all to live differently *at the bodily level*. It is a call to attend first and foremost to the physical needs and health of planet earth and its inhabitants. Body theology is basic theology: Feed the hungry.

But we do not want to hear this or see this. The model of the world as God's body is repulsive to us not because most of us are shocked by linking God and bodies (though some may be), but because we cannot imagine putting our own bodies and material goods at the disposal of the Other. In a society where consumerism has become religion, where the insatiable individual is encouraged, the model is repugnant. It would mean looking at all the wretched of the earth—the teeming millions of the poor, the oppressed, the sick and dying—and making room for them. It would mean giving up some of our space, our place, our food so that others might live and eat. It is unimaginable to most of us. But its very offensiveness convinces me that it is perhaps an intimation of transcendence for our time and for people like us.

To focus on bodies, to dwell upon them, to pay attention to them: What might that bring about? Might it make us saints? Not likely, but it might mean a shift in our accepted anthropology—that is, in who we think we are in the scheme of things. It might make us realize that attending to the basic needs of creation's life-forms, human and nonhuman, is our job, our vocation, who we are in the scheme of things. Weil has a chilling passage in which a soul indicts God for allowing a hungry person to suffer: Why have you forsaken him, the soul asks? And in the silence that follows, the soul hears God's reply: Why did *you* not feed him?[54] This small anecdote contains the answer to the theodicy questions for the twenty-first century: God does not cause others to suffer; *we* do. One reason why the world as God's body is an intimation of transcendence for us is that *we know this*. We know that much that has been blamed on God (the world's evils) are the results of our sin—our insatiable appetites which cause the growing gap between the rich and the poor and the deterioration of the planet. It is not God that does this; we do. Therefore, the body, the material condition of bodies, the basics that all creatures need to live—this is our intimation of transcendence, this is our call from God: Look and love; feed my world.

Let me close with a few personal comments. I know very little of what I am talking about. Only sometimes do I praise God through the beauty of the earth, and even fewer times do I try to renounce my ego and possessions so as to attend to the material condition of others. While both of these intimations of transcendence are only that—intimations—I believe, I trust, that they are so. I have found that my miserable attempts to live as if the world is God's body have brought about a few changes. I dare now to find God in the world (which is shocking for a former Barthian to admit), in and through everything in the world. I have become outrageously sacramental; I feel comfortable with language about God that is maternal, immanental, spirit-laden, oceanic, all-embracing. I happily say with Augustine:

> Since I do indeed exist and yet would not exist unless you were in me, why do I ask you to come to me? . . . Therefore, my God, I would not exist at all, unless you were in me; or rather, I would not exist unless I were in you 'from whom and by whom all things exist' . . . To what place do I call to you to come, since I am in you? Or from what place are you to come to me? Where can I go beyond the bounds of heaven and earth, that my God may come to me, for he has said: 'I fill heaven and earth'?[55]

I feel as if I live within the divine milieu and can worship God in the intricacies, specialness, and particularity of each thing. I am not even afraid of pantheism; the line between God and the world is fuzzy. As for the other, related intimation of transcendence—dispossessing myself that others might live—that is much harder. The most I can say is that I am certain it is true. I believe that is why we are here; it is who we are in the scheme of things—we are the agents, the mediators, who can work to help the rest of creation flourish. We are that part of the body of God that has become conscious of our proper role—to work with the incarnate God for the wellbeing of the earth. For us well-off human beings, however, the cost of doing this work will be enormous.

Finally, let us recall two important points about metaphors: Many are needed, and they do not make large claims. The limits of the body model are obvious; no one model can function alone, lest it become hegemonic, become "descriptive," become the way things are. Erich Heller reminds us: "Be careful how you interpret the world. It *is* like that."[56] I have suggested that the body model is especially relevant as a way to interpret Christianity in our time, but other models are needed. Moreover, metaphors and models say a lot, but mean little. The imaginative, as-if world they paint is rich and detailed, but the ontological assertion is slight. The "certainty" of metaphorical theology is not in its assertions, but in the opportunity it provides to live differently. It allows "the world as God's body" to try its chance as serving as our way of being in the world. It is bold in filling-out what life would be like within such a model, but modest in its pretensions to truth. It is, at best, a faith, a hope, a possibility. Can people live committed, meaningful lives simply on faith and hope? Perhaps it is the best we can do. But it may be enough. The gracious words of 1 Corinthians tell us that faith, hope, and even love "abide"—become our dwelling place, our abode.

NOTES

1. Simone Weil, *First and Last Notebooks*, trans. Richard Rees (London: Oxford University Press, 1970), p. 104.

2. Annie Dillard, *Pilgrim at Tinker Creek: A Mystical Excursion into the Natural World* (New York: Bantam, 1975), p. 279; as quoted by Dorothee Sölle in *The Silent Cry: Mysticism and Resistance*, trans. Barbara Rumscheidt and Martin Rumscheidt (Minneapolis: Fortress, 2001), p. 91.

3. *Poems and Prose of Gerard Manley Hopkins* (London: Penguin, 1953), p. 27; E. O. Wilson, *Biophilia* (Cambridge, Mass.: Harvard University Press, 1984); Stephen Jay Gould, *Wonderful Life: The Burgess Shale and the Nature of History* (New York: W.W. Norton, 1989).

4. Dillard, *Pilgrim at Tinker Creek*, p. 8.

5. See *God, the Gift, and Postmodernism*, ed. John D. Caputo and Michael J. Scanlon (Bloomington: Indiana University Press, 1999), intro., chaps. 1 and 2.

6. See Michael J. Scanlon, "A Deconstruction of Religion: On Derrida and Rahner," in *God, the Gift, and Postmodernism*, p. 228.

7. John D. Caputo, *On Religion* (New York: Routledge, 2001), p. 115.

8. For an interesting discussion on this issue of onto-theology versus praise, see Merold Westphal, "Overcoming Onto-theology," in *God, the Gift, and Postmodernism*, pp. 150, 164.

9. Catherine Keller writes: "Might the 'in' of panentheism begin to designate *creation as incarnation?*" (*Face of the Deep: A Theology of Becoming*, New York: Routledge, 2003), p. 219. While Keller's perspective is more clearly Whiteheadian than mine, there are nonetheless many points of overlap between her understanding of "apophatic panentheism" and my view of the world as God's body. Both perspectives ask, as Keller asks: "If the incarnation is co-extensive with the body of creation, then might not all matter—and not only the baby's skin, the lover's eye, the winter sunrise—exude an incandescence of the deep?" (*Face of the Deep*, p. 221).

10. Jacques Derrida, "White Mythology: Metaphor in the Text of Philosophy," *New Literary History* 6 (1974): 6–73; see particularly pp. 41–42.

11. Ibid., p. 11.

12. Ibid., p. 70.

13. See Philip Wheelwright, *The Burning Fountain: A Study in the Language of Symbolism* (Bloomington: Indiana University Press, 1968), p. 86.

14. Merold Westphal, "Overcoming Onto-theology," in *God, the Gift, and Post-modernism*, ed. John D. Caputo and Michael J. Scanlon (Bloomington: Indiana University Press, 1999), p. 150.

15. Ibid., 164.

16. Derrida, "White Mythology," p. 11.

17. See Thomas A. Carlson's statement on the subordination of religious (imagistic) to philosophical (conceptual) thought in Hegel:

> The annulment of time, the death of death, and the correlative conception of love in terms of infinite self-consciousness—all occur within a framework that subordinates religious to philosophical thought. From the Hegelian perspective, that subordination is necessitated by the inadequacy of the religious, or representational, form of thought with regard to the philosophical, or wholly conceptual, form. (*Indiscretion: Finitude and the Naming of God*, Chicago: University of Chicago Press, 1999, p. 241)

18. Ibid., p. 74.

19. See Sallie McFague, *Speaking in Parables: A Study in Metaphor and Theology* (Philadelphia: Fortress, 1975).

20. David Tracy, "Fragments: The Spiritual Situation of Our Times," in *God, the Gift, and Post-modernism*, p. 179.

21. See Sallie McFague, *The Body of God: An Ecological Theology* (Minneapolis: Fortress, 1993).

22. Tracy, "Fragments," p. 172.

23. See, e.g., David Tracy, *The Analogical Imagination: Christian Theology and the Culture of Pluralism* (New York: Crossroad, 1981).

24. John D. Caputo, "What Do I Love When I Love My God? Deconstruction and Radical Orthodoxy," in *Questioning God*, ed. John D. Caputo, Mark Dooley and Michael J. Scanlon (Bloomington: Indiana University Press, 2001), p. 304.

25. John D. Caputo, *More Radical Hermeneutics: On Not Knowing Who We Are* (Bloomington: Indiana University Press, 2000), p. 7.

26. Ibid., p. 200.

27. Ibid., p. 207.

28. Ibid., p. 213.

29. Simone Weil, *First and Last Notebooks*, trans. Richard Rees (London: Oxford University Press, 1970), p. 307.

30. Ibid., p. 104.

31. Ibid., p. 111; Simone Weil, *Waiting for God*, trans. Emma Crauford (New York: Harper & Row, 1973), p. 197.

32. Weil, *First and Last Notebooks*, p. 284.

33. See Pierre Teilhard de Chardin, *How I Believe*, trans. Rene Hague (New York: Harper & Row), 1969.

34. Francis Schüssler Fiorenza, "Being, Subjectivity, Otherness: The Idols of God," *Questioning God*, ed. John D. Caputo, Mark Dooley and Michael J. Scanlon (Bloomington: Indiana University Press, 2001), p. 352.

35. Richard Kearney, "The God Who May Be," *Questioning God*, p. 169.

36. Weil, *Waiting on God*, p. 161.

37. Weil, *First and Last Notebooks*, p. 83.

38. See Sallie McFague, *Super, Natural Christians: How We Should Love Nature* (Minneapolis: Fortress, 1997), chap. 3.

39. The model of the world as God's body is an old and widely prevalent one; see Sallie McFague, *The Body of God: An Ecological Theology* (Minneapolis: Fortress, 1993),

chaps. 2 and 3.

40. See, e.g., A. R. Peacocke's discussion of female birth imagery as a metaphor for divine creation:

> Mammalian females . . . create within themselves and the growing embryo resides within the female body and this is a proper corrective to the masculine picture—it is an analogy of God creating the world within herself . . . God creates a world that is, in principle and in origin, other than him/herself but creates it, the world, within him/herself. (*Creation and the World of Science*, Oxford: Clarendon, 1979, p. 142)

41. Dorothee Sölle, *The Silent Cry: Mysticism and Resistance*, trans. Barbara Rumscheidt and Martin Rumscheidt (Minneapolis: Fortress, 2001), p. 302.

42. John D. Caputo, *On Religion* (New York: Routledge, 2001), p. 137.

43. Edith Wyschogrod, *Saints and Postmodernism: Revisioning Moral Philosophy* (Chicago: University of Chicago Press, 1990), p. 72.

44. Simone Weil, *First and Last Notebooks*, trans. Richard Rees (London: Oxford University Press, 1970), p. 286.

45. See my discussion of the loving and the arrogant eye in Sallie McFague, *Super, Natural Christians: How We Should Love Nature* (Minneapolis: Fortress, 1997), chaps. 4 and 5.

46. John Woolman, *The Journal and A Plea for the Poor* (New York: Corinth, 1961), p. 43.

47. Ibid., p. 214.

48. Paul Lachance, "Mysticism and Social Transformation According to the Franciscan Way," in *Mysticism and Social Transformation*, ed. Janet K. Ruffing (Syracuse, N.Y.: Syracuse University Press, 2001), p. 69.

49. As quoted in Murray Bodo, *The Way of St. Francis: The Challenge of Franciscan Spirituality for Everyone* (New York: Doubleday, 1985), p. 51.

50. Weil, *First and Last Notebooks*, p. 212.

51. Dorothee Sölle, *The Silent Cry: Mysticism and Resistance*, trans. Barbara Rumscheidt and Martin Rumscheidt (Minneapolis: Fortress, 2001), p. 141.

52. Edith Wyschogrod, *Saints and Postmodernism: Revisioning Moral Philosophy* (Chicago: University of Chicago Press, 1990), p. xxii.

53. Ibid., pp. 50–52.

54. See Weil, *First and Last Notebooks*, pp. 94, 312.

55. *The Confessions of St. Augustine*, bks. 1–10, trans. F. J. Sheed (New York: Sheed & Ward, 1942), bk. 1, sec. 2.

56. Erich Heller, *The Disinherited Mind: Essays in Modern German Literature and Thought* (Cleveland: World, 1961), p. 211.

nine
Topologies of Transcendence

David Wood

By way of orientation, I list seven key moments in thinking and rethinking transcendence, so that readers can see where I am coming from, and where we are and are not on the same page:

- Kant's distinction between two senses of transcendence—outside within the world, outside the world.
- Kierkegaard's account of faith, and of my being grounded transparently in the Power that constituted me.
- Nietzsche's announcement of the death of God.
- Wittgenstein's remark on human dependency, and "that on which we depend, we may call God."
- Heidegger's astonishment that people should still want proofs of the existence of the external world.
- Derrida on the gift and on infinite responsibility.
- And lastly, not so much a moment, but a set of references to try to hold on to—Feuerbach on God, Bataille and Foucault on transgression, Marion on the pure gift, Levinas on the Other (Woman as other, animal others, and so on).

Perhaps I may be permitted also to lay out some of the key issues that concern me here:

- What is the relation between the epistemological and ethical senses of transcendence?
- What is the relation/distinction between the ethical and the religious/metaphysical senses of transcendence?
- How far is transcendence in some or all of its manifestations an artefact of an original conceptual or schematizing failure? (Here Heidegger's critique of the "self in the box" would be exemplary.)
- As a corollary—should we worry if people want to refer to all kinds of imaginary beings? Is that not just one of many ways of talking? Who are we to legislate?
- What methodological virtues should inform our reflections here? (If we are phenomenologists—what is phenomenology? See the debate between Jean-Luc Marion and Dominique Janicaud.)

I brush up against most of these questions, though, needless to say, I do not completely resolve all of them. The core of this paper centers on two final questions:

- Is our thinking of transcendence any more than an unconscious way of being caught up in certain hard-to-shake spatializing and/or representational schemas?
- How far can we interpret/translate the various phenomena of transcendence in terms of modal transformations of the quality of our response to the world and to others, setting aside any and all onto-theological constructions referring to a beyond?

Deconstruction / Genealogies of Transcendence

Three observations to begin with.

1. The title of the present volume, *Transcendence and Beyond*, nicely highlights what we might call the productivity of the idea of transcendence—that transcendence arises wherever we construct a bounded space. The constructivism of transcendence, as I shall call it, would have as its task and challenge tracing back the various modes of transcendence to the acts or the circumstances that led to the original framing. Every beyond is a beyond of something. It would be a traditional move to try to distinguish these modes or moments of transcendence that are chosen, and in some sense optional, from those tied up with who or what we already are. Or is this very reliance on choice something we need to move beyond?

2. There is something seductive, compelling, and yet disturbing about the spatiality with which we are tempted to think transcendence. The photograph of Heaven I once saw on the front page of the *National Inquirer* is only an

extreme instance of a broader temptation to think of the beyond of transcendence in spatial, or at least topological terms—that it represents a different terrain or dimension or level,[1] a space beyond. And even when the literalness of this way of thinking is set aside, we still fall back on the logic of a certain naïveté about spatial relation, as if topology did not already offer us other more complex ways of constituting and regulating relations between different dimensions.

3. Connected to this spatializing temptation is a representational and objectifying temptation—a temptation to treat the transcendent as *something* that transcends. And if we do not understand this transcendent a literal "thing," we are content to identify it in its abstract unity—as freedom, love, the other.

Let me now rework these three issues in a little more detail.

1. Turning back from a direct focus on the Beyond to a certain scrutiny of the construction of the boundary that provokes its appearance is, perhaps, a continuation of that Copernican displacement by which Kant characterized his own project. Kant himself contributed greatly to this very attempt to think transcendence (and the transcendental is part of his answer). What we today are more likely, more emboldened, to ask is—what interests, theoretical and practical—are served by this or that schematic arrangement? What does it facilitate, or block? We do not need to be reductive to acknowledge that theoretical frameworks are not innocent. And it is precisely by their structural invisibility that they exercise their power. I am not exactly saying that transcendence ends in politics (see Lacoue-Labarthe), but I am saying that a genealogical tracing of the boundaries of our thinking itself opens certain lines of questioning.

2. As we have said, the spatiality of our understanding of transcendence is rarely as crude as imagining "another place" (or another time) where transcendence happens. But we should never underestimate the power of the most vulgar models. And if we were to take the *reversion* to simple spatial models seriously, we might consider whether anything could be done, "at that level," to prevent such models regenerating and fuelling the imagination with simplistic schemas. I am thinking particularly here of how such ideas as inside/outside, self/other, us/them, friend/enemy—and hence immanent/transcendent— operate as exclusive binary oppositions. Obviously this simplification can be addressed by complementing our "spatial" understanding with a "temporal" one. But even then, the models of time that we deploy can be as simplistic as the models of space they are intended to supplement or complete. It is no accident that, as Derrida has shown, long before deconstruction many thinkers stumbled upon what we could call the irreducible complexity of the boundary —and hence of the logic of any beyond, and any extra or supplement that might (need to) be added on.[2] We can attempt to articulate these paradoxical logics— the supplement that completes, makes whole, what was already complete. We can even attempt imaginatively to deploy the opportunities for topological reworking made available by such figures as Kline bottles, and Möbius strips,

which allow us to transfigure our fundamental dimensional schematizations. But the question remains, whether we are addressing ourselves to saving a topology of transcendence that might need to be jettisoned altogether.

3. Transcendence has many names—freedom, love, God, and so on. I am not proposing that these are synonyms. But what they share is the idea that transcendence can be named, or at least successfully indicated, by a word. The word transcendence itself makes the same claim. Or perhaps we could say that it raises the question as to whether language, or a certain referential use of language, is adequate to the task of capturing whatever it is that leads us to posit a certain beyond. A more radical question—perhaps more of a suspicion, one we could trace to Nietzsche—would be whether, far from referential language being only problematically up to the task, it is precisely this grammatical imperative that lies at the root of the idea of transcendence. Naming and referring are primitive linguistic accomplishments that importantly, perhaps essentially, outstrip what is immediately available to us—"transcend" the present, where finger-pointing would otherwise do.

These considerations—the transcendence of language, objective and subjective genitive—point in the two different directions carried by the expression "transcendence": Language (or a privileged moment of language) as transcendence; and language as the limit that needs transcending. First Nietzsche, and then Kierkegaard, perhaps.

Heidegger's Contribution to Thinking Transcendence

I know there are some who would like to put Heidegger in a box and move on, but when it comes to the question of transcendence that would be a mistake. As Heidegger himself says, we need to take a deep breath in pursuing this topic. I would like to review the treatment he provides of this problem in his *Metaphysical Foundations of Logic*, which genuinely advances the problem. First Heidegger distinguishes two senses of transcendence, caught up as it is in two different binary oppositions—the first opposes transcendence to immanence, and the second to contingency. He claims that the transcendence/immanence distinction reflects a model of an enclosed consciousness groping toward a problematic "outside," while the transcendent/contingent model addresses the sense of our relation to something unconditioned, a beyond with a higher degree of Being. And he quickly identifies the locus of our confused entanglement of both problems of transcendence. "This tangle of partially and falsely posed problems is continually confused in ontological philosophy and systematic theology; the tangle gets passed along from hand to hand and the state of entanglement gets further confused by receiving a new name."[3] Kant he says felt the "urgent impulse" to free himself from these shackles, with only partial success. Obviously Heidegger's diagnosis of these two senses of transcendence is indebted to Kant's distinction in the first *Critique* (A373), between two senses of the expression "outside us." We must go deeper. Heidegger claims, "The whole of Kant's *Critique of Pure Reason* is circling around the problem of transcendence—which in its most primordial sense is not an episte-mological problem but the problem of freedom." Heidegger's response to this situation is to set aside both the epistemological and theological senses of transcendence by attempting to rethink transcendence as a "crossing over" in terms of the basic comportment of Dasein. Dasein, he writes, "is itself the passage across." Dasein's freedom consists in a surpassing of nature. Dasein surpasses things in encountering them within a world. In short, transcendence is Dasein's being-in-the-world. Of course, he admits, it is difficult to pose the problem of transcendence clearly when there is really no inside![4]

Now we would really miss the importance of Heidegger's understanding of transcendence in terms of "world" if we moved too quickly here. Heidegger offers us a tour through the history of philosophy (and onto-theology) insofar as it has thematized "world." At times (for example, in Paul) the worldly has been contrasted with the divine; and more broadly the phenomenon of world has often been confused with things in the world. Heidegger, however, pushes the idea that world is the space of the for-the-sake-of-which, in which Dasein lives, moves and has its being. It refers to the "how" of our being, even when that is being understood restrictively (e.g., in Augustine). But as I see it, Heidegger is taking his cue from these various discussions that it is indeed the how of orientation, comportment, the way we relate to things and to others, that is captured by "world"—something, we might add, that is invisible. And there is the obvious implication that the reason we think we need to move to some-thing invisible "beyond the world," is that we do not see that "world" in this sense is already the invisible how of our comportment in "it."

No less invisible—and hence no less a candidate for understanding how we may too swiftly pass over the very phenomenon we are seeking, in our quest for a misplaced sense of "beyond"—is time, or as Heidegger puts it "ecstatic temporality." In this discussion of temporality, Heidegger attempts to capture the ways in which—as the phrase itself suggests—human time already lays out dimensions of existential projection and self-transcendence.[5] For Hei-degger, the horizon of temporality is the ultimate condition of possibility of transcendence.

Now we may understand these remarks as ultimately deconstructing only the epistemological sense of transcendence, leaving us still to deal with the metaphysical and/or theological sense of transcendence. I have already sug-gested that Heidegger is at least tacitly proposing that what we could call the recessiveness of the phenomenon of world and temporality may be sufficient to account for the apparent need to go beyond them, to something invisible, when world and temporality are the very invisible we are looking for. But I would add a supplement to his account of ecstatic temporality here—namely, his account of being-toward-death in *Being and Time*.

Already in discussing the transcendence implicit in being in a world, Heidegger speaks of Dasein "surpassing itself as a being." He continues:

> More exactly, this surpassing makes it possible that Dasein can be some-
> thing like itself. In first surpassing itself, the abyss [*Abgrund*] is opened with
> Dasein, in each case, is for itself. This abyss can be covered over and
> obscured, only because the abyss of being-a-self is opened up by and in
> transcendence.[6]

I understand this passage to capture the spirit of Heidegger's reflections on
being-toward-death in *Being and Time*, and in each case—ecstatic temporality, and being-toward-death—these are prime candidates for capturing
at least something of the impulse so easily misdirected into metaphysical
transcendence.

Temporality and Transcendence

What does Heidegger mean by ecstatic temporality? He essentially means that
our possibilities and potentialities of selfhood are projected onto and worked
through temporal horizons—past, present and especially future. The ecstatic
horizonality of time supplies what we could call constitutive transcendence,
and also metaphysical transcendence. Constitutively, the horizons of temporality provide the planes of beyondness which are needed for my thinking,
my actions—indeed, for my being to have any significance. In writing this
paper I imagined the future conference at Villanova—I imagined reading
these words, and I imagined relaxing when the paper was over. I tried to make
the paper worth the time spent writing it, the time my colleagues would spend
listening to it, and so on—perhaps even a paper that reflects something of my
experience of finitude. In these last considerations, we approach what Heidegger would call being-toward-death, or what I would call *mortal intensification*
—the impact of my grasp of the beyond on my "temporal" existence.

Being-toward-death is a many-layered phenomenon. The beyond of death
is, very precisely, not representable. It is not a spatial beyond.[7] Heidegger
understands death as the ultimate horizon of my possibilities of selfhood—a
limit that, in being anticipated as such, can be responded to. We may suppose,
as Sartre does, that in this way Heidegger domesticates death, but this is an
uncharitable reading. As I see it, to acknowledge our own mortality is not to
internalize it; quite the opposite. It is (or can be) to find a way to acknowledge
the impossibility of that kind of closure. If I am right, Heidegger's being-
toward-death is the exemplary structure of irrecuperable intensity, of the limit
as lived. Being-toward-death does not prescribe any specific content to a response. Rather it reflects the most powerful possibility we have of standing
"outside" of ourselves as a whole in the imagination, and translating that finite
glance back into our temporal engagement. The content is temporal; the
aboutness happens in a certain reflective imagination; and the resoluteness
that results is a folding back of the liminal vision into this life.

The same movement can be found in Kierkegaard's account of the movement from infinite resignation to faith. Infinite resignation is something like a stoic detachment from the time of the world, from everyday concerns, from that unhappy space of unfulfilled desire. The knight of infinite resignation as Kierkegaard describes him, however, translates his grasp of his constitutive relation to God into a basis for "bringing the infinite back into the finite." Faith sets aside the movement of detachment from the world, and transforms it into a new way of inhabiting this world.

For Heidegger, as we have seen, the primary source of transcendence is to be found in our being-in-the-world. Dasein, he says, *is* transcendence. And if, as he says, "authenticity is nothing but a modification of our everydayness"—a modification brought about by a certain confrontation with the abyss of self-hood—we have, again, a transformation of an apparent opposition (authen-ticity/everydayness) into a new mode of transcendence. If I am right, Heideg-ger's account of authenticity, of being toward death, and Kierkegaard's account of infinite resignation or of faith, are ways of performing that transcendence—ways that preserve Heidegger's deconstruction of any other beyond.

I contend that Heidegger productively occupies the center of the chess-board when we are trying to think about transcendence. He allows us to think of human existence as essentially reaching out toward its various projected possibilities of Being; and that reaching-out can take on determinations result-ing from further limit encounters. Indeed, we know that the evolution from the early to the later Heidegger was marked by the possibility of a sustained, and sustaining, openness to the givenness of Being—to the "*es gibt.*" It is important to realize, as Heidegger stresses repeatedly, that Being is something of a cipher for him. "*Es gibt sein*" is part of an attempt to think Being as givenness, as gift, which in turn suggests that the question of Being and what we are thinking of as transcendence, are one and the same. This is not to reduce transcendence to Being in a way that would frighten Levinas, say, or Marion. It is instead to suggest that Being is precisely the unnamable site for the performance of transcendence, a site that gets renegotiated as the search-lights shift their focus.

The thrust of this paper is to show, time after time, that transcendence is tied to the experience of limits—limits which are inseparable from our self-constitution. I claim that the significance of transcendence is always to be found in the character of our response to these various limits, and is always betrayed by understanding transcendence literally.

Extending Heidegger

Here I would like to reflect, as I have elsewhere, on the methodological presuppositions I am making here, which have a bearing on the extent to which philosophy can be harnessed for theological ends. At the heart of my position is a kind of deconstructive genealogy which, when it sees a finger pointing into the beyond, cannot help looking at the finger as well as the direction in which it is pointing. Every beyond requires some positing that is being exceeded, and if these positions are mere artefacts, so too will be the transcendence that escapes them. I am enough of a phenomenologist to think we must begin with experience, while we cannot accept it uncritically.

It is helpful here to consider Heidegger's discussion of how we should best approach the work of another thinker, which he couches in terms of "going to the other's encounter,"[8] which can, I believe, be taken quite generally as a recipe for our relation to the other. We should recall that the point of the apparent focus on selfhood in Dasein is not to focus on *my* self, but on any selfhood, any "mineness." And it offers a basis for any encounter with the other, which is to try to encounter in terms of his (or her) "encounter with Being." If we understand this "encounter with Being" as an engagement with the modes of givenness (of things), we can connect it to the idea that things are what they are in terms of their relation to their own boundaries and limits—the horizon of their identity, selfhood, and so on. If rocks and trees and cats have different modes of being, it is because their possibilities of self-relation, and other-relation, are quite different. To relate to any other adequately we need to relate not just to their self-enclosed self-understanding, but to their "encounter with Being"—that is with the other, with the constitutive and regulative boundaries of self—with their groundedness, and with the character of their own grasp of otherness. And it is important to say, if it is not obvious, that this brings into play the material and economic conditions of others, quite as much as the states of their souls.

The genealogical/deconstructive dimension of our dealings with transcendence has to do with the constitution of the "space" exceeded by this or that "beyond." For Heidegger the problem of the external world is an artefact of the epistemological model of selfhood that generates it. In this case, the impetus for deconstruction comes from the intractability of that problem. We do not actually doubt the "external world"; we even think calling it "transcendent" is quaint, and we need to unpack how such thought arose.

But a similar set of variables can present itself with a very different weighting. Here I want to acknowledge—in a deliberately schematic way—the question of sexual difference. If the question of the other is one of the contemporary names for the question of transcendence, then the question of sexual difference requires our attention. If, as Drucilla Cornell puts it, "it is the Lacanian law that women must be denied the otherness of her being for 'men' to be 'men'," it is deconstruction's task and privilege to question "the Lacanian law that ultimately denies the beyond of the 'real' other." The argument is this— that we enter the symbolic order only by assenting to the law of the father, which subordinates woman to the role appropriate in traditional heterosexual domination. On this account the "reality" of woman—woman as truly other— is veiled by the co-opted otherness that women are asked to perform within patriarchy. Woman's true otherness can only appear when she is free from this specific construal of her otherness as a reflection of men's needs and desires. We need to find ways of opening up to a plurality of sexualities . . .

This diagnosis looks as if it takes us in the opposite direction to those moves by which I have tried to understand the transcendent as an impetus to reexamine the closure it purports to exceed. Here, instead, it would seem we are being told there is indeed something "outside the box," "outside the text"; or at least, to play with Richard Kearney's formulation a little, "the woman who may be," possibilities of "being a woman" (and in consequence, of being a man) independent of a binary patriarchal economy. In fact, of course, there never was any question that women were there, were real in some sense. The question was whether that "reality" could be thought outside a patriarchal discourse, and could be allowed to prosper. And the answer is surely to be found in the recognition of relationships, discourses, and ways of inhabiting the space of sexual difference that are not subordinate to such discourse.

We have here what one could call a *Transcendenzstreit*, a struggle over transcendence. Men have often thought of women as transcendent, as "beyond" in all kinds of ways, some seemingly honorific—woman as the exotic, as comforter, as earth-mother, as sublime object of desire. The deconstruction of the economy that generates these images and values would allow women to affirm themselves as other than this other. What is especially challenging, especially for men, is to do the work necessary to make visible the ways in which our dominant discourses do generate these forms of mirror otherness.

An analogous point can be made about various other ways in which we recognize otherness in such a way as to block our response to the true alterity of the other. Animal others, for example, suffer precisely this fate.[9] We recognize their being unlike us, their being as nonhuman animals. We call "them" animals, sometimes creatures, even brutes. We say they are "without a world" (*Weltlos*) or "poor in world" (*Weltarm*). But the schema within which that otherness is acknowledged, is one with us humans, and indeed a particular construal of us humans, in the center. It may be that we could understand Heidegger's *Gelassenheit*, "letting beings be," as a first stab at releasing animals from this constrained alterity. The transcendence of the animal is nothing mystical; it is rather the withholding of our preemptive assignation of otherness. D. H. Lawrence's poem "Snake" is a classic here. He records throwing a stick at a snake drinking at a water hole, and immediately regretting it. "I despised myself and the voices of my accursed human education." And as if describing these two senses of otherness, he writes,

> For he seemed to me again like a king,
> Like a king in exile, uncrowned in the underworld,
> Now due to be crowned again.

Lawrence records the shift from seeing the snake in his world, to seeing the snake as reigning over its own world, "crowned again"—as "one of the lords of life."

The Erotic

We could see the experience of being loved (human and divine), and of the erotic in the same way. Suppose we understand ourselves as autonomous, "independent" willful beings, for whom the world is "out there," my oyster. Suppose, for the most part, we manage the boundaries of self in these terms— protecting our health, our powers, our security. On this model, the "outside" is part grist to my mill, material for my plans and projects, and part obstacle, even threat. There is nothing in this model that acknowledges our fundamental dependency on the world and on others. Indeed such dependency is often abruptly dismissed.[10] For a being so organized, the most powerful experience of an "outside," of something transcendent—where the experience in question is that of the recognition of one's dependency on what one *cannot* acknowledge dependency—will precisely take the form of the revelation of the cosmos as gift, of the love of God (or Jesus), or of the other person. Erotic love just has to be the celebration of the danger and pleasures of the transgression of boundaries—being-held in a letting-go—that can only be temporary, that affirms as much as it breaches these boundaries, and that plays with the fact that there is no one boundary of the flesh, but many laminated layers. In this theater, for example, the horizons of birth and death, generation and mortality, are brought into play. Not to mention chance and purposiveness, truth and illusion, compulsion and consent, control and abandonment, pleasure and ecstasy. The erotic, if you like, is the ultimate theater of transcendence. It is not merely that it takes us out of ourselves, nor that it reflects on the boundaries it opens and crosses, but because it performs and explores the investments in each boundary, each limit. It is tempting to say that this exploration is mutual, which it is. But even this mutuality is in play. "*C'est mieux avec deux*," as Levinas says. We may experience orgasm as an essentially private experience in the presence of the other. Or we may experience synchronized climax as at least a temporary breach of physiological discreteness, as if Empedocles and I were to jump enthusiastically hand-in-hand into the volcano.

On this account, the erotic is a theater of transcendence in that it does not merely transport us into another space (as, for example, in Sartre's account of the caress, which turns my body to flesh), but it opens up what we might call a metaspace—a place in which we can renegotiate boundaries that are normally constitutive. These possibilities are extended or redoubled in fecundity. This makes the erotic very much into a space of elastic depth, one with real implications for our understanding of transcendence more generally. A good lover learns to attend to, and work with and through all the limits and horizons that are in play, including those we might think of as "illusions"—acknowledging indeed the power of "illusion" of every stripe. The comparison between the erotic and the Socratic was made long ago by Socrates himself. We will shortly take the opportunity of reflecting more broadly on what lessons this account of the erotic has for our broader philosophical practice.[11]

Language

The question of our broader philosophical practice takes us inexorably to questions of method, of the role of experience in thinking transcendence, and here I want to address the specific question: How far does our understanding of language help or hinder this concern with experience?

This is perhaps the challenge presented by any phenomenology that would have some sort of transcendence (e.g., the gift, freedom, love) as its content. For if these are not to be mere words, we would need access (or exposure) to experiences which suggest or require positing such shapes of transcendence. It is of particular interest, then, that these ideas are often described as impressing themselves on us by a "call"—which could be said to be "outside" language understood as a content, and yet inseparable from language understood in a different way.

Consider, for example, the "call" that Abraham received from God, in which God spoke to him and told him to sacrifice his son Isaac (Genesis 22:1–2). We could consider this call in terms of its content or "message." But—and if this case is typical, something very strange is happening—it soon becomes apparent that the so-called content of the call replicates the very *structure* of the call. The very first word of God, "Abraham," is already the reminder of a previous call (Genesis 17:1–5), one in which Abram was renamed Abraham, and marked thereby with the sign of his new identity, and its associated mission (to father the tribe of Israel). Isaac is the visible sign of Abraham's faith that God would give him a son (required to complete his mission). This new call (actually a command, "sacrifice Isaac") reactivates the space of the call (Abraham's calling) that Abraham is already living.

Compare this scene to Lacan's account of the child's entry into the symbolic. The child discovers that he has a name—what he is called by others—and acquiesces in this new identity even as it involves acceptance of the other's power over him, because of the other advantages of being a language-user. The moment of the original call, we might say, is the cusp of an identity transformation, the space of a madness resolved by taking on the gift or burden of the name. Abraham's previous call, in which his name is changed, could be said to reenact the original identity trauma of naming with, this time, Abraham being given an identity whose fulfillment depends on him becoming a father, generating a line. The call to sacrifice Isaac on Mt. Moriah is, if you like, a re-call, a performative reenactment of Abraham's already essentially extended and dependent identity.

Kant famously takes Abraham to task for believing it was God's voice at all. For Kant the typical call would take the form of being reminded of one's duty.

David Wood

That a voice would ask what Abraham was asked is evidence of its not being the voice of God at all. But we might respond that in this call, in this re-call, what is being dramatically reenacted is the madness of the name—of Abraham—and even of God himself.

The Abraham/Isaac story would then be a theater of transcendence, one in which the name is already the site of the call "of language." For in the name something is inaugurated—my being outside myself, as Hegel would put it, my being-in-relation to a possibility of myself—in which it is not possible to separate the other as language-community from the other as divine. Such an other supplies the intrinsic possibility of self-relation. The madness of the name marks an original gift/loss, through which the very language of transcendence can appear. The call, on this account, would appear as the call of language, the *Auseinandersetzung* of the name, and at the same time appear in the call of those others who first called me something by christening me. The two cannot be separated because while those who call me by name are indeed other people, they themselves, in doing this, are already drawing on the power of language; they do not invent the name game. Of course, it may be said—it should be said—that when we speak of language here, we are not speaking of a mere collection of words, but also a social practice. To call someone (by name) is both to recognize and to demand acknowledgement. Understanding the call in this way is not to reduce the call to a social or linguistic transition. For it is just as much an event of interruption whose structure gives such transitions the significance they may have.

Pursuing transcendence in this way, through one aspect of the transcendence of language, we have done two things—first, we have located transcendence as the economy of a complex boundary, one that cannot properly be reduced to any of the terms current in the surrounding territory. And in doing this, we have also begun to see what could be meant by such classic refusals of any "outside" or "beyond," as Derrida's "*il n'y a pas de hors-texte.*" Strictly speaking there is no inside either, because the topological naïveté of this inside/outside model has been exploded. Economies that plot transformations across boundaries and so on, do not themselves project a simple space, nor do they license thinking of ourselves as moving from one space to another. The language of economy is the death of the representability of the beyond.[12]

I want to consider here what might be called the problem of projective identification. Wittgenstein variously speaks of God as "the meaning of life," and again as the name "we may give" to "that on which we depend," or "the world independent of our will." "God," he writes "does not reveal himself in the world." Here Wittgenstein gives voice to various modalities of transcendence, none of which are happily identified as representations, and none of which can be encountered *in* the world.

Here we have a limit, it would seem, to any project of reducing transcendence to immanence, if that would mean having God appear *in* the world. But what would it be to appear *in* the world?

1. God would turn up, make an optional appearance—as a voice (for example, to Abraham), as a person (such as Jesus), or in the works of special individuals (like saints).
2. "God" would be a synonym for "true generosity," or "love." On this account when we say "God is love," it would be like explaining a strange term to a child or a Martian. There would be no immediate suggestion that the various instances of love or generosity had a common source. And yet it would not be inappropriate to suppose that people might come to "love" or to "generosity" for good reasons—not just "random acts of kindness"—but after having seen its importance or significance. For example, we may act "generously" in part because we want symbolically to anticipate, perhaps even facilitate, the kind of society in which such acts would be common, because it seems obvious how much better a place we would be in. To act out of a sense of the rightness of an idea is to believe in a value (generosity, love, etc.). To believe in it is not to say it is "real"—that it has some eccentric mode of existence. It is, as we said, to avow the value of a form of life in which it would be a typical way of carrying on. Giving is the gift that keeps on giving. Smile and the whole world smiles with you. We may try to define "love" or "giving" but whether we do or not, we seem to have developed an "idea"—one we can value. So far, we have no trace of metaphysics, theology, or onto-theology. But at this point,
   a) we may ask ourselves whether such a value actually operates in human life, or in the cosmos;
   b) we may have a special experience (revelation, mystical vision) in which it seems clear that such a principle is operating;
   c) we may conclude that human life/the cosmos may actually, or could conceivably be driven by such a principle;
   d) we may conclude that there are a number of competing principles (good, evil) in the cosmos.

On *b*, *c* and *d* we may conclude that if such a principle is operating, initially independently of us, it may require, for its full actualization, an appreciative response on our part. Or, at the very least, we may conclude that our own special efforts to embody such an attitude in our own times, both in itself, and for its exemplary value, would help promote this value.

There is no doubt that one can come to see the cosmos and or human history or community, as the manifestation of a positive principle—the good, love, freedom. And *one can come to see oneself as addressed by the experience* in which this becomes apparent. The address could be described as the dramatization of the *logic* of the experience. If you see the cosmos as operatively exemplifying the power of generosity, creativity—especially if this takes the form of a new discovery, a recrystallization—it is not difficult for this experience to be linked to the reflexive question: And how do *you* fit into this? My

David Wood

sense is that such experiences rarely if ever leave a subject untouched. It would be difficult to experience the cosmic power of love as having nothing to do with me! Or not especially applying to me, not asking anything of me. I call it a dramatization of the logic of the experience because even if the experience does not take the form "imagine if we all acted like this," to the extent that it is a revelation, a new grasp of the meaning and direction of the whole, then it already challenges the view (or lack of vision) that it displaces—senseless dispersal, conflict, and so on. And in the difference between the two ways of seeing there is an affective moment, one in which I am addressed. If things are, are predominantly, or could be, or could be seen, to be this way—where do you stand? Are you part of the problem or part of the solution?

My claim is that on any of these accounts—from mystical rapture, to hearing voices, to simply seeing the world differently—it is hard not to feel one is being addressed. But the logic of such experiences is identical, whether or not one hears a voice. The logic is that a transformation of one's effective grasp of life as a whole has obvious consequences for how one conducts oneself in the sight of such a transformation. The idea that one is being addressed by some actual other, or even something without being, may seem natural if you "hear a voice"; but otherwise it is a superfluous supposition.

We may be tempted to think here of Heidegger's call of conscience, or Kant's sense of the divine as a regulative idea, because the other on this account is not being given any true independence. But is this fair?

Method

Let us return to Lawrence's poem, "Snake." Lawrence here records an experience, an experience he undergoes and reflects on. And this perhaps offers a way of approaching an obvious methodological problem that faces those of us who approach the question of transcendence from a broadly phenomenological point of view. There are some (such as Marion) who think we can discover a pure form of transcendence (the pure gift) as the pinnacle of a series of reductions. Others (Janicaud) see this as a misuse of phenomenology for theological ends. When we run out of intuitions, what is to stop us simply grafting onto phenomenology the results we would like to see it validate? It would be like dropping fish from the market into the fishermen's nets as they haul them in.

Perhaps I could reprise here comments I have made elsewhere on what I called the "return of experience."[13] Certainly with the post-phenomenological French philosophy of the sixties and seventies (Derrida, Foucault), the word "experience" seemed largely absent. The reason for this was a distrust of what we could call the seemingly self-validating presumptiveness of "experience."

Foucault, for example, declares a tolerance for various philosophical methodologies, except phenomenology; and Derrida, more indebted to phenomenology that one might suppose, clearly associates it with a systematic privileging of presence. In each case, appeals to experience would legitimate an undeconstructed subject of experience, and we would be back to square one. How do we explain then the resurgence of experience in Derrida, in Levinas, in Blanchot and in Nancy? What I believe comes to each of these instances, is what we could call a negative (or liminal, or aporetic) experience, an experience of interruption, or (as Wittgenstein called it) a coming-up against limits. Heidegger, for example, had described *Angst* as the experience of the "slipping-away of the world as a whole": It is an experience that can only happen to a being constitutively bound up in a world. And if such an interruption does not in a flash light up everything it puts in question, it does open up a path of reflection, one aimed at interpreting such an experience.

Marion offers us a three-step reduction: In Husserl we find a reduction to a transcendental subject; in Heidegger to an existential subject; and in Marion himself we move "beyond Being" to the gift of an unconditioned givenness. For Marion, Heidegger's existential subject is another form of self-possession—the self answering only to itself—which calls for another reduction to allow God to be given. But does this account of the situation adequately exploit the resources available in Heidegger? Might it not be too hasty? Heidegger precisely contests the claim that he is reinstating autarchy. Instead we may see him as building a certain productive destabilization, a problematic relation to the limit, into Dasein.

In section 11 of the *Metaphysical Foundations of Logic*, Heidegger addresses the very question of whether he is just giving the same old subjectivity an existential twist. His argument is that certainly any identification of his position with some sort of individualistic egoism is sheer delusion, and a failure to make fundamental methodological distinctions. Ontological claims just do not translate ontically. Heidegger insists that the I/Thou relation, for example, can only be understood if the selfhood of both I and Thou are first grasped in terms of their transcendence and freedom:

> [That] it belongs to the essence of Dasein that its own being resides in its 'for-the-sake-of,' does not exclude humans from being in fact concerned about the being of others; this ontological statement, moreover, supplies the metaphysical ground for the possibility for anything like Dasein to be able to be with others, for them and through them.[14]

Here we can see Heidegger as reworking (via being-toward-death) what Kierkegaard calls the transparent grounding of the self in the power that constituted it (in *Sickness unto Death*). And the later Heidegger's development of his thought with respect to our relation to the "open region" takes this thought further. Does Marion's radical givenness not curiously reinstate the subject as opposed to or by the other? And why *unconditional* givenness? Why speak of the *pure form* of the call, when everything points to its impurity? Perhaps the theological move here is nothing but the formal purification (opening the way to the use of the name) of the multiple experiences of interruption.

How different is this from Kant's presentation of God as the rational pre-supposition of a certain order and unity of moral experience, one which would cease to be motivated if we dropped this demand for unity (which was Nietzsche's point).

Janicaud accuses Marion of turning phenomenology into a vehicle of vacuous mysticism, though as John Caputo notes, "Janicaud is careful to grant that phenomenology must come to grips with a certain alterity and excess of experience, a certain 'invisibility'."[15] Is this a proprietary argument about the scope of phenomenology, about what can be "given" within phenomenology; or a broader argument about the boundary between philosophy and theology? Caputo reminds us that Marion concedes that "with the saturated phenomenology we reach the limits of phenomenology, and experience the need for faith to take another step forward and give words to our experience."[16] Can we decide, asks Caputo, what kind of "confusion" (as Marion calls it) we have here? Could it be as Dominique Janicaud suggests, vacuity?[17] More generally, these doubts raise the question of a critical phenomenology, one which would try to address, for example: What is at stake when we try to "give words" to our experience? Are the words we choose necessitated? required? plausibly indicated? How satisfactory is it to begin with a model for which one then attempts to locate a plausible point of fixture or berth? It is one thing to start with the question: How can we provide a phenomenological legitimation of God? And it is quite another to ask humbly and patiently how to interpret certain experiences. A couple of examples of a critical phenomenology? Think of Kant (in *Contest of the Faculties*) when he asks why Abraham did not question whether it was God speaking to him (given what the voice commanded!). Or again, look at John Milbank's questioning of Marion's (and Derrida's) account of self-sacrifice and the unconditional gift as the form of our proper relation to the other. Milbank argues, instead, for the kind of asymmetrical reciprocity that one finds in conviviality. (An example which has its own problems: Who is excluded from the fun?)[18] I would add here that a refusal to open oneself to the gift of the other person, even couched as modest reciprocity, would be an uncharitable denial to the other of the opportunity for generosity.

It is tempting to say that any account of God as pure form (love, gift, etc.) must itself be interrupted. For those who see the transcendent in the flesh that exceeds representation, the earth that invisibly sustains us, the sun from which all energy flows, the unnecessary act of generosity or patience, the opening of the erotic, the eyes of a destitute man—these manifold dimensions of excess, invisibility, transcendence—could all be called God. Or we could cherry-pick only those that exhibit the structure of the gift. Or we could say that God is the principle—of gift, generosity, love, creativity, interruption, the impossible, (some or all of these)—that works through these phenomena.

A humble thinker would not shy away from this multiplicity. He or she would not be afraid of noticing different modes of transcendence—ways in which the boundaries of self are sometimes transgressed to be reaffirmed, sometimes imaginatively set aside, sometimes blown away. And such a humble thinker would think of phenomenology as a moveable feast rather than a party to be gate-crashed.

We suggested earlier that Derrida might be more indebted to phenomenology than was apparent. But is he a philosopher of transcendence? The long chain of expressions he has made his own—supplement, *différance*, alterity, responsibility, gift, promise, hospitality, and so on—could be said to reflect a grasp of the constitutive relationality of identity, together with the impossibility of a reductive "economizing" of that relationality. The understanding of metaphysics as philosophy of presence does not in fact imply that certain concepts that seem to embody that commitment to "presence" must be abandoned, but rather that we must be vigilant about the way we use such concepts. And constitutive relationality precisely does not mean that we can calculate the dependencies of identity. Rather, the boundaries of identity, of selfhood, and so on, are the sites of aporetic events and instabilities at which the beyond, and otherness make their incalculable appearance.

Given such a picture, the question of transcendence may be pursued at a number of levels:

1. Transcendence is at each point the symptom of a certain fixing of the subject of transcendence (what/who it is that is being transcended). Think of Heidegger's lambasting of the very problem of the existence of the external world, in *Being and Time*.
2. Transcendence points to dimensions of relationality, dependence and exposure that are easily lost sight of.
3. Transcendence raises fundamental questions about how the recognition of these relations to the beyond can be (and/or should be) enacted/incorporated into our lives (our thinking, our practice, etc.).

If I may be permitted a substitutive reworking of Heidegger's remark about intentionality, in his preface to Husserl's *Phenomenology of Internal Time Consciousness:* Even today, this term "transcendence" is not an explanatory word but one which designates a central problem.[19] A careful typology of modes of transcendence would surely include:

- Transcendence as an opening to a dependency that restores a deficiency.
- Transcendence as transgression (as in Bataille) in which there is a non-positive affirmation of boundaries.
- Teleological transcendence—transcendence as leading to development of latent possibilities. (See John Donne, "The Good Morrow": "I wonder what Thou and I did 'til we loved . . . Were we not weaned 'til then?")
- Optional transcendence—an achievement, a leap, a creative leap. Consider, for example, John Llewelyn's discussion of erotic transcen-

dence and Plato's rejection of Aristophanes' model of restorative completion.[20])

- Transcendence as openness onto an as yet undetermined space of possibilities.
- Transcendence as dehiscent interruption, call, exposure.

Conclusion

Everything I have said about transcendence today points toward the essential eliminability of transcendent objects in the metaphysical or theological sense. When Wittgenstein says that we may give to our dependency the name God, the obvious response is that we may, but we do not need to. And when he himself immediately offers a substitute—Fate—it seems as if the game is up. When he says that God does not appear in the world, this is quite compatible with his other remark that God is the meaning of the world; or with Kant's identification of God with the presumed rational order of the cosmos. Such an order is not a proper part of the world. In other words, if we continue to think of transcendence as something beyond the human, it can be located as a certain understanding of the significance of the world, as Heidegger again confirmed. Such a significance, we might say, occurs at different level from the world understood simply as a collection of things. But this is a logical level; it is not a cause for metaphysical hypostatization.

Alternatively, if we think of transcendence as intimately tied up with the experience of interruption, or transgression, or excess, or openness to the gift, or the erotic, or to the other, then while the finger may point to a beyond, I claim that what is always at stake is the character, the orientation, the mode of being, the response-ability of the subject. I think Heidegger is right to think that this is both a self-relationship and, thereby, a relation to the other.

Each time we recast the purported beyond as a transformed possibility of human comportment, we ride the possibility of taking such formulations as "God is love," "Man is freedom," or "Hell is other people" as exhaustive explications—the low-down on the entire meaning of these otherwise mysterious words. At the same time I commend the continuing task of genealogical deconstruction as a way of exploring the complex economies of transcendence. I have no doubt we will discover that the experience of the beyond is— as Kant said of transcendental illusion, and as Freud said of neurosis, and as Derrida said of metaphysics—not dispelled by being exposed. But if we do have an infinite responsibility, it must surely include the critical deployment of our rational powers.

NOTES

1. The truth about transcendence may reside in the need to maintain different levels; compare Kant, Heidegger, A. F. Möbius.

2. See his treatment of Rousseau in Jacques Derrida, *Of Grammatology*, trans. Gayatri Spivak (Baltimore, Md.: Johns Hopkins University Press, 1976), pt. 2, sec. 2.

3. Martin Heidegger, *The Metaphysical Foundations of Logic*, trans. Michael Heim (Bloomington: Indiana University Press, 1984), p. 161.

4. Ibid., p. 167.

5. Ibid., sec. 12, "Transcendence and Temporality."

6. Ibid., p. 182.

7. Though, according to a 1997 poll, 88 percent of adult Americans believe in heaven, that it is a real place (with sidewalks?) and that they will meet their friends there.

8. See Martin Heidegger, *What Is Called Thinking?*, trans. J. Glenn Gray (New York: Harper & Row, 1968).

9. See *Animal Others: On Ethics, Ontology, and Animal Life*, ed. H. Peter Steeves (Albany: SUNY, 1999).

10. Again, we need to understand this not just as an error, but as the reflection of an "economic" necessity.

11. It is perhaps the charm and the challenge of difficult writers on the threshold of philosophy and literature to pursue these questions in a way that engages both senses of transcendence at the same time. If a certain naïveté about the referential use of language allows transcendence to be identified, located, pointed to, then the problematizing of that referential function can abbreviate the impulse to transcendence. Barthes' essay "Writing an Intransitive Verb," seems to point in that direction. And in a very different way, perhaps also Blanchot's *Writing the Disaster*. Writing is presented as the dramatic space within which the impulse to a certain referential transcendence is overcome, and that overcoming is celebrated or mourned. In each case, of course, we may say that in so doing, writing reappears as transcendence, as a liberation from the demand of referentiality, as creativity, as imagination, etc.

12. This is not quite true. We may need to recognize that representation is itself an "economic" phenomenon. This is close to rethinking Kant's transcendental illusion, with a Nietzschean flavor.

13. See David Wood, *Thinking After Heidegger* (Cambridge: Polity, 2002), chap. 2.

14. Martin Heidegger, *The Metaphysical Foundations of Logic*, trans. Michael Heim (Bloomington: Indiana University Press, 1984), p. 186.

15. John D. Caputo, *On Religion* (New York: Routledge, 2001), p. 11.

16. Ibid., p. 11.

17. At this point I myself have more sympathy with Kevin Hart's position, in which he understands the experience of God in Derridean fashion as "the very experience of the non-relation or . . . the absolute interruption" (Caputo, *On Religion*, p. 160).

18. John Milbank, "The Ethics of Self-sacrifice," in *First Things* 91 (March 1999): 33ff.

19. Martin Heidegger, "Editor's Preface," in Edmund Husserl, *On the Phenomenology of Internal Time Consciousness*, trans. J. S. Churchill, ed. Martin Heidegger (Bloomington: Indiana University Press, 1964), p. 15.

20. See John Llewelyn, *Emmanuel Levinas: The Genealogy of Ethics* (London: Routledge, 1995), p. 121.

Temporal Transcendence

The Very Idea of *à venir* in Derrida

John D. Caputo

What's important in 'democracy to come' is not 'democracy' but 'to come.'
—Jacques Derrida

Works of Time

The word "transcendence," for all its transcendence, is a relative term. It depends upon what is being transcended or gone "beyond." It can mean transcending the subject in order to get to the object, or transcending the self to reach the other; transcending beings to reach Being, or transcending inner-worldly things to reach the horizon of the world itself; or transcending the sensible world in order to attain the supersensible one, which in turn means transcending the spatiotemporal world to occupy a spot outside space and time—the more classical meaning of transcendence.[1] There are also those who would transcend being in order to make their way to what is beyond or without being, which is I suppose about as far as one can go and constitutes the most transcendent sense of transcendence. In the past, whenever the question of time has come up in this regard, time was taken to be something to be transcended, not a way of transcending. But ever since Husserl, Heidegger and Levinas opened up the question of time in new and more radical ways, philosophers have become more and more interested not in the transcending *of* time but in time *as* transcending. In that sense we have a transcendence in reverse, where what one wants to go beyond or transcend is the classical sense of transcendence (= transcending time), in order to backtrack *to* time now taken in a new and more radical way. The essay that follows belongs to this tradition.

Levinas is an interesting case in point in this regard. While the very subtitle of *Totality and Infinity* is *An Essay on Exteriority*, which turns on a spatial metaphor, what Levinas had up his sleeve all along was time, which he regarded as the key to what he called metaphysics, by which he actually meant ethics. It is important to keep in mind that Levinas denounced the spatializing imagination as mythological and looked scornfully upon the fantasy, the story—Catherine Keller would say the "rumor"—of a "world behind the scenes," of which *Hinterwelt* he was as uncompromising a detractor as was Nietzsche himself. Although we are not inclined to highlight this side of Levinas, it is nonetheless the case that on a theological register, Levinasian ethics makes for a death-of-God theology:[2] Immortality, another world, life after death, celestial happiness, some supersensible being beyond sensible beings—these are so many fantasies trapped within being, dreams of replacing this world with another, hoping to exchange a worldly kingdom for a celestial one with the coin of "meritorious works," which is the celestial narcissism of Kierkegaard's ultra-eudaemonistic search for eternal happiness that Levinas dislikes. The very meaning of our being turned *to* God (*à dieu*), for Levinas, is to be deflected or turned *by* God (*à dieu*) to the neighbor. *And nothing more.* The name of God boils down without remainder into our being turned to the neighbor, *tout court*.

What then is accomplished by ethical trans(a)scendence to the other? In one very definite sense, nothing. Ethics is not *for* something; it is a nonprofit enterprise. Ethics is all the transcendence there is. It does not buy us a ticket somewhere else. There is nowhere else to go.[3] Be good, rise up in ethical splendor (ethical transcendence), and then you die. Why? Ethical transcendence is self-validating; it raises you up above the greedy grubbing sphere of self-love. The trans(a)scendence to the other is a self-transforming self-transcendence. Life is justified as an ethical phenomenon; then you die. In Levinasian transcendence, there is nowhere to *go*, no*where* to go, because for Levinas there is no *Hinterwelt*. Ethical transcendence transpires not in space but in time, not "in" time but *as* time. Ethical trans(a)scendence is the work *of* time. If the turn to the neighbor in Kierkegaard takes the form of "works of love," in Levinas it one of the "works of time," where it provides the only true escape (*l'évasion*) from monotonous and monochronous being. But by time Levinas does not mean the subjective flow of onto-phenomenological time-consciousness, which transpires under the regime of consciousness or the understanding of the "present"—in which a future-present flows into the now/present and then is retained in the past-present. He means a more radically breached or interrupted time—one marked both by an "absolute past," a past that was never present (answering a call I never heard), and by an absolute future, one that we cannot foresee.

John D. Caputo

I would be the first to agree that there is a danger in associating Derrida too closely with Levinas. There is no ontological claustrophobia, no thematics of being "trapped in being" in Derrida—no need to "escape," no "nausea" before being. Derrida has nothing to with Levinas's grim ultra-Kantianism— that ultra-ethicism in which everything but ethics is a vanity of vanities—with its terrible neglect of nature and the animal; with its devaluation of art; with its embarrassing patriarchy and embarrassing politics. Of all of this Derrida has been discreetly, respectfully, but expressly critical. But on this precise point of transcendence as time itself, Derrida is close to Levinas. On this precise point, that there is no *Hinterwelt* beyond the temporal world, that the "beyond" that we could agree to call "transcendence"—in order to appease the organizers of this conference—is the work of time, that it *is* time, Derrida has struck a position that, for all its other differences, is close to Levinas.

Just as with Levinas, one finds in Derrida a rhetoric or a discourse, a tropics or a body of tropes, on the "beyond"—"*hyper, ultra, au-delà, über*"— which organize for him a certain "messianic" beyond that draws us out of our (present) selves. He is often drawn to texts, such as Pseudo-Dionysius's and Plato's, which display a certain "hyperbolic" desire for something "beyond," and where "*hyperbole* names the movement of transcendence that carries or transports beyond beings or beingness, *epekeina tes ousias.*" To which Derrida adds: "Its event announces what comes and makes come what will come from now on in all the movements in *hyper, ultra, au-delà, beyond, über,* which will precipitate discourse or, first of all, existence. This precipitation is their passion."[4] For Derrida this passion of the "beyond," of the *hyper* or the *au-delà,* takes the form of the passion for "going where you cannot," which is, he says, a "passion of, for the place,"[5] a passion for the impossible, for the impossible place of the beyond. Transcendence is a more classical term for what Derrida would call the passion for the impossible—which is also, please note, the passion for existence.

But remember that for Derrida, just as for Levinas, this hyperbolic passion for the place (the beyond) gets fired up without biting on the myth or the rumor of another world; remember that it has a *temporal* meaning and that there is no other place to go.[6] The passion for the impossible is for something that breaks up and breaks into the world that otherwise tends constantly to settle in place all around us; it means something that extends us, that draws us out of ourselves beyond ourselves. This would also be the passion of existence—the spark that drives existence past itself and ignites a certain self-transforming. That for Derrida is what time is, what time does. The burden of making good on this claim falls to what Derrida calls the "event," by which he means a radical and constitutive unforeseeability, a radically unprogrammable future. Our lives are pried open by the coming of the other (*l'invention de l'autre*), by something "coming" to us from beyond the horizon of foresee-ability, something that destabilizes us even as it constitutes us as wounded or destabilized, as cut or circum-cut subjects.

That wounding, destabilizing, circum-cutting, eye-opening yet blinding exposure to the event takes place in virtue of what Derrida calls the "to-come" (à venir). The "event" (événement, from venir) is a function of the to-come; it occurs by reason of the very idea of the to-come. Hence the closest analogue to "transcendence" is to be found in the affirmation of the coming of the event. This is a vital affirmation, not an idle reverie about a utopic or ideal form that we never quite realize. It is not to be thought of, I hope to show, as a work of *idealization* of a definite but distant form, but rather as a work of infinite qualitative *intensification* of an immediate and pressing demand. I will argue in what follows that transcendence, if there is such a thing in Derrida—if this were ever a word we could have enticed him into using in his own name by repeatedly inviting him to the Villanova conferences—is a function of the *à venir*. In Derrida, a certain quasi-transcendence, or analogue or successor-form or side-effect of transcendence, some transcendence without transcendence, unfolding under the different circumstances and transferred dynamics of deconstruction, would refer then to an infinite qualitative temporal intensification, an infinite self-transformation of our temporal lives, which we might also describe as the passion of existence.

In what follows I will track the dynamics—or the tropics—of the beyond in Derrida as a radically temporal movement or temporalizing event, as a work of time or, to give it a high spin, a qualitative intensification of temporality; I will do so by taking what Derrida calls the "democracy to come" as my point of departure.

Democracy Is a Lousy Word

Let us begin by recalling the aporia of time posed by Aristotle, who said that it seems that time does not exist or that it barely exists because its parts do not exist (*Physics* 218a1–5). That seems like a serious problem for something—to be missing its parts, like a conference at which none of the speakers show up. But the aporia that besets the "democracy to come" is quite analogous to this and it is at least as serious. The "democracy to come" is a fine idea, one of Derrida's finest, but for the fact that in virtue of the very idea of the "to come": (1) the democracy to come could hardly be expected to be or be called "democracy," and (2) it could hardly be expected to ever show up. So it seems that the very idea of the democracy to come is impossible, because its parts—both the "democracy" and the "to come"—are impossible.

To be sure, for us hardy deconstructionists, raised on the difficulty of life, who thrive on aporias, the impossible is not bad news. Indeed, *the* impossible is what we love, what drives our passion, and the more impossible the better. It is precisely the impossible that drives things to a fever pitch, a pitch of passion and absolute intensity, without which we would all be mediocre fellows. So instead of saying that the very idea of the democracy to come is "beset" with this aporia, as if this were an affliction to be warded off, let us say that this idea

John D. Caputo

is joyously and incontestably constituted by this aporia, that it is nourished by it, that what does not kill the *à venir* makes it stronger. To this end, let us pursue the impossibility of each part of this aporia and see (savor) just how impossible it is. *O quam suaviter:* Taste and see how sweet is—the impossible.

If the democracy to come belongs to the sphere of the absolute future, and if the absolute future is absolutely unforeseeable—if it will come from beyond the horizon of expectation, like a thief in the night—then how do we know that the democracy to come is or will be a "democracy"? Might not what is coming turn out to be quite different from or other than democracy? Let us be more bold: Is it not *necessarily* the case that the democracy to come must certainly be *other than* democracy? As an "event" is not the democracy to come *tout autre*? Accordingly, is not the very idea of a wholly other democracy to come necessarily wholly other than democracy? In order to be what it is or can be or ever will be, the democracy to come cannot possibly be "democracy," not what we today call "democracy," which would not be wholly other.

"Democracy," Derrida confesses, is a "lousy" word.[7] Some of the worst and most undemocratic things are done in the name of democracy, including proposing the self-congratulatory idea that the world divides between nations that are democratic ("ours") and those that are not, the latter belonging to the "evil empire." (When George Bush was asked to name his favorite political philosopher he said, "Jesus Christ." He would have better concealed the narrowness of his readings in political philosophy by naming George Lucas.) It is in the name of the basic freedoms provided for and protected by democracy— the freedom, for example, to speak one's mind and spend one's money as one sees fit—that democracy is corrupted through and through. It is in the name of supporting the so-called friends of democracy and opposing its enemies, that the American democracy in particular has propped up the bloodiest and most undemocratic regimes. Still, even while "democracy" is a lousy word, things could be worse; the virtue of the word is that it is the least lousy, all the alternatives being even lousier. Were we to say that we are dreaming of an oligarchy or a monarchy to come, or even of a dictatorship to come, that would be even lousier.[8] The best we can say is that "democracy" is the *least* bad word we have now for what is to come; for something which could be named otherwise, for example, as a "republic" to come (as in the distinction that Hannah Arendt makes between a constitutional "republic" and "democracy" as mere majoritarian rule).[9] When the time comes, if it does, we may very well have another word that is not as bad or just as good, which we might signify by calling it a democracy + *n*.

Then what is the advantage of the word "democracy" now? Why is it not as bad as all the other words? Is it because of some "essential nature" of democracy in virtue of which there would be an essential similarity between the democracy at present and some future present democratic condition that would arise under the impulse of the democracy to come? Not if *différance* does what it says it does—not if it constitutes meaning as an effect rather than expressing preconstituted meanings. The deeply anti-essentialist drift in *différance* blocks the way to essential similarities. We might do better to say that there is what Wittgenstein calls a "family resemblance" between the two. On that model, we can say that *a* looks like *b* and *b* looks like *c*, but *a* need not look like *c*. That is a more promising avenue to the *à venir* of democracy. I am speaking of future-present democracies or post-democracies that would arise "under the impulse" of the democracy to come, because it belongs to the very idea of the democracy *à venir*, while it will itself never exist (as we will see below), to provoke a series of transformations, to set a certain seriality in motion, leading who knows where, somewhere into an open-ended future. This democracy to come may solicit, call, or provoke; or it may lure, tempt, or seduce; but it does not exist, not if it is "to come," not according to the very idea of the to-come. Thus, given what *différance* means, or rather what it does, and given what *à venir* means; then between the democracy at present and some future condition that would arise under the impulse of the democracy to come, there would not be a community of essence but only a seriality—an historical, narratival or genealogical link—not an essential continuity but only a narratival sequence. "Democracy" does not have a meaning; it has a history. Democracy is not an essence but an ongoing historical narrative; the word "democracy" is but the word we use today to mark the present slice or cut (or *epoché*) in that series.

To the extent that we do favor the word democracy it is because it would be easier to imagine a series of historical shifts or transitions—sometimes gradual, sometimes abrupt—starting out from what is today called democracy, that would pass through several subsequent successor-states or conditions that would come to be known as something, I know not what, some kind of democracy + n. Now since we cannot even be sure that what that is will be called "democracy," let us formalize this even further as $x + n$. One could imagine that this process would go on indefinitely; in fact, I cannot imagine how it would not. That would mean that a future historian of political affairs would be able to show us how what at various times in the future is called $x + n$ could be traced back to a series of predecessor conditions that lead back to what we today call, with an almost perfect blindness, "democracy" (nothing is perfect). This history would have its ups and downs, so that we are not committed to saying that in this history we are approaching asymptotically some ideal or normative state. We are just coping with a shifting historical tide and trying not to get drowned. Nothing is safe or guaranteed; it is just that if we wanted to enter into that process (and how would you avoid it?) it would be the better bet to start out from what is today called democracy than from any other presently available option. And then hope for the best.

But why does democracy today enjoy this privilege of being the least lousy place to start out from? Because democracy is or should be the form of life that is the most self-correcting and least resistant to change and transition; the least closed-off and homogeneous, the least given to calculating everything according to a rule; the place that is most open to movement and transformation, thereby providing the setting that is most susceptible to setting off just such a seriality or narratival sequence. The very idea of a democracy ought to be that by respecting singularity it thereby cultivates polyvalence and polymorphism, anomalous and innumerable differences. The very idea is to make room for the exotic growths of singularity that spring up in the cracks of regularity, to provide just the sort of thing to allow for paradigm shifts, for unforesee-able innovations and transformations that a too-rigid and regular system pre-cludes and excludes. So the very idea of a "democracy to come" is "openness" to the "to come." Viewed in that light, the expression the democracy to come enjoys a joyous and glorious tautological redundancy, its very terms fitting together like pre-fitted pieces. For if democracy means openness, and if open-ness means letting something come, then the very idea of the "democracy to come" means the coming of what is to come, letting what is coming come. The "democracy to come" means the "coming to come." We would get the same result if we analyzed the democracy to come as the event to come, in which case it turns out to mean the *à venir* of the *événement*, like the tautology about the *ereignen* of the *Ereignis* that makes glad the hearts of Heideggerians.

To be sure, this tautology does not relieve but only intensifies the aporia, inasmuch as the coming of the democracy to come is precisely the coming of what will *never* come, the democracy to come that is *not* going to come, so that this tautology is also very heterologous.

Some words are more promising than others and the word democracy is the most promising word we have today, which means the least bad word we have now for keeping us mindful of a certain political "promise" that is in-scribed in this word.[10] But who is promising what to whom? That is hard to say, but at least this much is clear: A promise stirs within this word even as this promise exceeds the word, since no existing or present democracy would ever meet the demands that are laid upon it by this word; no present or future present democracy could ever be absolutely loyal to this promise. The word "democracy" contains a promise that it cannot contain; the promise of the word is uncontainable. Containing what you cannot contain, by the way, which is not a bad way to describe being pregnant, is also not a bad way to describe deconstruction or an auto-deconstructive process—"in a nutshell" (one that is bound to burst).[11] On my analysis this means that there is a twofold movement at work within powerful, prestigious and promising historical words like "democracy" (there are numerous other examples of such words). The first moment I would describe as one of *historical association*, for this word be-longs to a prestigious tradition, or a complex of interwoven but heterogeneous traditions, which we have inherited, into which we have been "thrown," as Heidegger would say, but with which we also freely associate ourselves. For to have a tradition is to make certain decisions about what that tradition means and what elements within it we accentuate. To receive or inherit the word "democracy" is not a passive process but a matter of taking one's stand within, and assuming a debt to, a long line or series that stretches from the Greeks to the present. Traditions thrive and survive not because they are fed from within by a deep well of essential *Wahrheit*, as Gadamer and Hegel would maintain, but because they make great promises; they live and prosper on promissory notes, on relatively empty intentions that intend the infinite but always deliver the finite, on unfulfilled pledges that we nevertheless trust and love and believe.

But having a tradition also involves a movement of *deconstructive dissociation*, a movement of distrust and discontent—*inquietum est cor nostrum*—of recognizing and affirming the distance between the finitude of the present and the infinite promise that is embedded in the word. So to inherit or receive the word "democracy" is to be given a promise that has not been kept. We stick with this word because we fall for its unkept promise; we are suckers for its empty but good intentions; we succumb to the power of the promise and the pledge that democracy does not and cannot keep. We keep the word because of its very inadequacy, its very powerlessness, its inability to be what it says and to say what it is, which is the power of its powerlessness. The promise of the democracy to come is an open-ended intention—we do not know where it is leading us—but it is not free-floating. We have inherited it and we have some idea of where it came from. We know a little of its provenance but little of its e-venance, its eventiveness. It is heading who knows where but it does not come from nowhere. The real punch or power of the word is not the actuality it has realized but the possibility that it has not, the *peut-être* that stirs within it, the possibility that reaches out all the way to the impossible, to this necessary but impossible future, this unforeseeable possibility of needing to go where you cannot go.

Without this moment of open-ended dissociation, the word "democracy" would become an idol—that is, a finite contraction of the unfinished promise of democracy to a particular figure or construction of democracy, especially to its present form, to the one at hand, right here, wherever you are, say, the United States at the beginning of the third millennium. Without this deconstructive, dissociative moment, it would be impossible for "democracy" to function as an icon—as open-ended promise of something coming, something, I know not what. Without this moment, all the power of temporal transcendence that is harbored by the "to-come" would be blocked off.

Another way to say all this is to say, as Derrida does, that in the expression "democracy to come," and in every expression of the same form (the *x* to come), say, the "justice to come" or the "friendship to come"—in formulations of this same form that we cannot presently even imagine and are still to come—what is important is not the "democracy" or the "justice" but the "to come." The "to come" matters more than the "democracy," the word democracy being just a way to mark a promise, just a way of keeping the future open, the most promising foothold we can get in the present on the promise of the future.[12]

John D. Caputo

It Will Never Come

But the problem is that whatever we call this something (we know not what) that is coming, whatever this unknown something may be for which we are "hoping sighing dreaming" (*à esperer soupirer rêver*),[13] the one thing we can be sure of is that it is *not* going to come. That brings us to the second part of this aporia: Not only will the democracy to come not be called democracy, but also, and in virtue of the very idea of the *à venir*, it will never come. Like Aristotelian time, the expression "democracy to come" experiences distress in each of its parts.

The very idea of the to come is the idea of what does *not* come—of what is coming but never comes. It never actually and indeed shows up, as in the old rabbinic idea mentioned by Blanchot, of the Messiah who never arrives.[14] In this version of the messianic tradition, the very idea of the Messiah is to *not* arrive, his arrival always being much awaited—something "*ausstehendes*," as Heidegger said, "impending" or still outstanding,[15] which is the very structure of expectation and historical time, of hope and promise, of faith and the future. Were the Messiah ever actually to arrive, that would be like death, like the end of time and history. That is why even where it is believed that the Messiah has arrived, we are forced to ask him to please come *again*, which is—in a nutshell—the story of Christianity, the history of which is opened by *différance*, by the deferral of the coming *again*. The earliest Christians were surprised to find that they were to live on and so to have a "history." A "second" coming is necessary in virtue of the very idea of the to come, for otherwise, if the Messiah ever showed up in the flesh, were he ever *leibhaft gegeben* in some final and definitive form, that would spell death and the end of everything. The very idea of the messianic is to keep the future open, which is possible only with the deferral of his appearance. Like the alter ego in Husserl's Fifth Meditation, the very phenomenality of the Messiah depends on his *not* appearing; that is what the phenomenon of the Messiah is or means or does. For otherwise, what would there be to sigh and hope for? What would there be to dream of and desire? What would there be to pray and weep for? If the Messiah ever appeared, the curtains of time and history would draw closed. The Messiah, the messianic figure, is a figure of the very work of time.[16]

The Very Idea of *à venir*

The non-arrival of the Messiah makes clear that the "to-come" is not the name of some future-present moment or condition that we are eventually going to reach after the passing of a certain amount of time and trial and difficulty, if only we can last it out; but rather of our *being-toward* (*sein-zu*) the future and of the future's *being-ahead* of us, to use a little Heideggerianese. It is not a notion that requires our patience but our passion. That is, the to-come is not the name of an occurrence that will transpire at some distant era in the future, which requires our patience, but rather of a structural relationship with the future that is always in place no matter what time it is, no matter what actually transpires in time, and that fires our passion. The to-come is not some happening that occurs *in* time; rather it has to do with the very structure *of* time. But what does it mean to have *being-toward* something that is *always ahead* but never comes? The answer to this question has two sides, the first having to do with our being-toward, and the second with time itself and the structure of the being-ahead.

1. The only thing that is truly "to come" for Derrida is what we do not and cannot see coming. If one can see something coming and anticipate it—if is perfectly "possible" in this sense[17]—then to a certain extent it is already present and it has already happened and we have compromised its coming. But the movement of what I am calling Derrida's "being-toward" is structured by the law of the *sans*, since the only way to be radically "toward" something, to "anticipate" or prepare for it on Derrida's terms, is to be radically unprepared, *sans voir, sans avoir, sans savoir, sans s'avoir*.[18] Derridean being-toward is thus the very opposite of the hermeneutic fore-structures of Heideggerian *sein-zu*, which is constituted by fore-seeing (*Vorsicht*), fore-having (*Vorhabe*) and fore-conceiving (*Vorgriff*), all of which can only lead to a "future-present" as opposed to the "absolute future." But if the relationship to the future cannot be one of seeing or knowledge, then it is strictly a matter of faith and non-knowing. So true is this that "knowledge" would actually compromise being toward the to-come and weaken our faith. To the extent that we know or fore-know what we want or expect or hope for, to the extent that we are guided in advance by implicit, anticipatory clues of something vaguely and pre-ontologically foreseen, fore-known, and fore-conceived, then our "faith" becomes just that much more assured, more determinate, more content-ful, more "credible"—and so much less a "pure" faith. The oligopistologists, the ones of little faith (Matthew 6:30), are the hermeneuts who want to (fore)see and (fore)know and (fore)have what is coming. But Derrida takes the notion of faith and hope very far, even farther really than the confessional faiths, where the object of faith is relatively determinate. In that sense, the circumfessional faith of a "religion without religion" is actually more religious, more faith-filled, more filled with fear and trembling, than the confessional faiths, which enjoy the comfort of a community, of a body of canonical texts, of a tradition and common teaching, which is what Kierkegaard called the comforts of the universal, as opposed to the lonely labyrinth of singularity *coram deo*.

2. Being-toward for Derrida means preparing for something that is *always ahead*, preparing for something that will *never be*, not because we will not have enough time to get to it but because it is not something *in* time at all but the very structure *of* time, the structure of the to-come itself. What Derrida calls the "to-come" is thus not merely temporal, but time itself. It is not in time; it is time. *À venir* enjoys an "infinitival" structure that can never be reduced to a

finite form. Looking more like *être* than an *étant*, the to-come never "is" although it would be true that *il y a de l'à venir*. We might say "it calls" but we will never say "it is." The to-come constitutes the formal structure of time in virtue of which something is always and irreducibly still outstanding, still ahead. Without the to-come, time would implode, collapse in upon itself, contract to a suffocating and unliveable now in which there would be no room to breathe, no space of time, no *Zeitspielraum*, no time at all. But the to-come is not merely a formal mathematical function in virtue of which any time n would be followed by a time $n + 1$, which would constitute nothing more than a simple temporal sequence of now points. The to-come is the time of desire, of expectation and hope in a promise, the time of a prayer; it is not simply a formal, calculable, programmable or mathematical *avenir* but an incalculable messianic *à venir*. The *à venir* is the subject of a *viens*, of an invocation, a call, indeed an interplay of calls, inasmuch as the future calls to us and solicits us to come forth every bit as much as we call to the future, asking it to come to us. The future bids us come forward, provoking us, calling us—and here Derrida can use Neoplatonic tropics—"beyond being and presence," even as we call upon it and invoke the future with tears beyond being, asking it to come. That, I would say, is why being-toward what is always ahead in Derrida is intertwined with "prayer," with what I have called the "prayers and tears" of Jacques Derrida, following Derrida who is himself describing the prayers and tears of St. Augustine, the firstborn in this long line of sons of tears, of these siblings of tears beyond being.[19] That is the religious side of Derrida that I like to emphasize, to the discomfort of his secularizing admirers. But this religion has nothing to do with going to heaven. The very idea of the to-come is the very idea of life in time, of hope and expectation, of prayers and tears, of being toward a future that does not and will not arrive.

Intensification not Idealization

But if being-toward what never arrives is to avoid the void, if it is to avoid falling into despair, must it not mean being toward an "ideal" or an Idea in the Kantian sense, which lifts our spirits by making the present a baseline and providing us with a goal toward which we continually approximate, slowly and asymptotically? *But that is just what it is not.* The "to-come" has no determinate content, no core and invariant semantic content to be approximated, for that would only contract and narrow it to a species or an essence. The "to-come" is more open-ended than any ideal, more indeterminate than any horizon of expectation, more absolutely futural than any foreseeable future present. The "to-come" is not so much a core meaning as a function, not so much a semantic content as an operation that multiplies a given determinate x to infinity, and in so doing multiplies it to the point of impossibility, which means also to the point of nonapparition and nonphenomenality, which is why it never appears. The "to-come" is an infinitival infinitizing operation that cannot be contracted to the finite and specific content of democracy, or friend-ship, or anything else.

(That raises a question: When we affirm the democracy to come, the gift to come, the justice to come, the hospitality to come, and so on, are we in the end affirming the same thing? Are these affirmations of something uncondi-tional and unlimited "convertible" like so many medieval (quasi-)transcen-dentals? Are they "convertible," converging at some *focus imaginarius* "in" the future? Do the several affirmations of the to-come come together in one point? If not, how would they differ? If their content dissipates into an I-know-not-what-to-come, what would make them different? On the other hand, what would make them the same?)

The only "content" of the to-come is the content of hope in a promise, of expectation of a coming, of faith in the future—like a prayer for the coming of the Messiah, like a movement of desire that extends any given content infi-nitely forward, not in the mode of making *infinite progress toward an Ideal* but in the mode of an *infinite intensification of hope.* The infinity in this infinitive *à venir* is not quantitative or progressive but qualitative or intensive. Being-toward the *à venir* is a movement of infinite intensification and not of idealiza-tion. From the point of view of the *à venir* a Kantian Ideal is finite because what it extends to completion beyond any possible empirical confirmation is a definable and determinate concept. As an operation of idealization, this corre-sponds politically to imagining a utopian ideal within the finite framework defined and circumscribed by the concept of democracy. But being-toward the *à venir* does not mean idealizing a determinate empirical content, thereby bringing it to its essential fulfillment. The affirmation of the *à venir* intensifies what it affirms infinitely, and this shatters the empirical figure—of democracy, hospitality, or anything else—rather than extending it to ideal completion. Idealization perfects what it idealizes rather than shattering it. If anything, being-toward the *à venir* is a *counter*-idealization, which takes the view that there is no Infinite Ideal, no *eidos*, for that would always be finite relative to the infinite intensity unleashed by the *à venir.* The to-come is not a future *eidos* up ahead toward which we making gradual progress, but an intense and merciless "white light" under which the present is made to pass. It is not a datable future time but a demand, an expectation, a hope, a desire—so much fuel for the passion for the impossible. The affirmation of the *à venir* will never be ap-peased by anything, not because it despairs but because it always demands and hopes for more. The infinite intensity of the "to-come" means that it submits a presently available historical structure—such as any existing democracy—to an absolute demand, an infinite exaction, an impossible requirement, to be what it cannot be, to go where it cannot go. The *à venir* makes a merciless demand for mercy, an implacable insistence on justice.

"Democracy" is an historical and determinate political form, a finite em-pirical structure, a positive system of law aimed at providing equal rights and uniform protections to all; while the democracy *to come,* the democracy that has been infinitely charged by the to-come, demands infinite respect for each and every singularity, requiring that we count every tear and take heed of every hair on the head of the least among us. Thus there is something within the positive political concept of democracy, Derrida says, that "exceeds politics,"[20] namely, an infinite demand that is demanded not by any finite political form but by the implacable demands of the to-come. If we imagine gathering the greatest minds in the history of democratic theorizing in one room and asking them, *per impossibile*, to draft the constitution of the democracy to come, to try to put it in writing, the result would be like a map that is so precise, so sensitive to the singularity of the terrain, that it would be the same size as the region of which it is the map; that is, it would be so perfect as to be useless. Like the idea of the perfect map, the idea of the democracy to come is auto-deconstructing. That is because this idea cannot be brought to the completion of an Ideal; it is not an "idealization" of empirical democracies, nor an ideal form against which empirical democracies can be held up. It is a white light that is directed upon every historical formation—an infinite intensification of a promise that stirs within the word democracy, that mercilessly exposes the defects of any given historical actuality. The democracy to come demands more, demands something different, something *au-delà*, and this because it demands the impossible, something that will not and cannot come. It is not a finite Ideal but an infinite expectation. There is no capitalized Ideal or Idealization-process, only an endless process of self-transformation and auto-deconstruction, a fragile series that is fully exposed to the risk that these transformations will not make progress but make things worse, which is not only not desired but downright dreaded. Once exposed to the harsh demands of the "to-come," the *present* in any order of representation or desire—the order, for example, of what is today called the gift, hospitality, forgiveness, democracy, justice, friendship—becomes absolutely intolerable. The present is radically relativized and opened up vis-à-vis the absolute future of that order—the gift to come, the hospitality to come, and so on, all of which might in the end be the same thing. Or different: Who knows?

Je ne sais quoi

So the democracy to come does not exist because its parts do not exist; it is impossible because its parts are impossible. The democracy to come will not be and could not be *democracy*, and besides it will *never come*. But it is precisely this never-coming of I know not what that keeps us awake through the night, that solicits and provokes our passion, that calls to us from afar and makes us endlessly restless with what in fact has come, constituting the passion or our existence. *Inquietum est cor nostrum*—thus spoke Rabbi Augustinus Judaeus. It is the never-coming of the democracy to come that makes us long and sigh for something impossible that would overtake us like a thief in the night, whenever we sigh and pray, whenever we cry out and say *"viens,"* calling and weeping, listening for the coming of something we know not what. The democracy to come is the least bad name we have for something, I know not what. For something we love with a desire beyond desire, with a hope against hope. For a time that has never been and that also never arrives. The very idea of the democracy to come is not that it was or will ever be, but rather to provoke us to say and pray, *"viens, oui, oui."*[21]

In another time, in another place, in another language, that might have been called a passion and a prayer—for transcendence, *s'il y en a.*

NOTES

Jacques Derrida, "Politics and Friendship," *Negotiations: Interventions and Interviews*, ed. and trans. Elizabeth Rottenberg (Stanford: Stanford University Press, 2002), p. 182; my reflections here on the democracy to come are stimulated by a few remarks Derrida makes in this interview. This paper first appeared in French translation as "L'idée même de l'à venir," trans. Patrick Dimascio, in *La démocratie à venir: autour de Jacques Derrida*, ed. Marie-Louise Mallet (Paris: Galilée, 2004), pp. 295–306, the volume based on the 2002 Cerisy la Salle conference on Derrida's idea of the "democracy to come"; it reappears here, slightly adapted to the purpose of the present volume. Derrida kindly refers to this essay in *Rogues: Two Essays on Reason*, trans. Pascale-Anne Brault and Michael Naas (Stanford: Stanford University Press, 2005), p. 37.

1. The word's most characteristic use in the high Middle Ages was in *transcendentalis*, meaning a property convertible with being (like being, one, true, etc.), where what is crossed over or transcended is one of the ten categories or genera of Aristotle. The word does not acquire its contemporary sense until the eighteenth and nineteenth centuries.

2. See the vividness with which Levinas first poses to himself in 1935 the task of "escaping being" in *On Escape*, trans. Bettina Bergo (Stanford: Stanford University Press, 2003); and see the interesting "Annotations" by Jacques Rolland in *On Escape*, especially no. 10, pp. 89–90, which makes this same point about a Levinasian "death of God."

3. If Levinas says, in speaking of being, that what he seeks is not to be otherwise but otherwise than being; we might say that in contrast, in speaking of time, what he seeks is to temporalize otherwise and not otherwise than time.

4. Jacques Derrida, *On the Name*, ed. Thomas Dutoit (Stanford: Stanford University Press, 1995), p. 64.

5. Ibid., p. 59

6. Spatial figures in Derrida tend to center either around *khōra*, as the primal spacing or differential play "in" which all meanings are forged, or around ethico-political figures of displacement, of the homeless, the exile and the refugee, who have been driven out of their place in the name of (somebody else's) "homeland." Derrida on this account is deeply suspicious of the politics of place, of *Heimat*, and it is this above all that divides him from Heidegger.

7. Jacques Derrida, *Negotiations: Interventions and Interviews*, ed. and trans. Elizabeth Rottenberg (Stanford: Stanford University Press, 2002), p. 181.

8. But I do believe that I could make the case that it is worth dreaming of a "kingdom to come." If we are wary of putting our unconditional trust in any given word,

John D. Caputo

like "democracy," we must also be wary of unconditionally denouncing any given word. (*Lefebure* is not a bad word.) Shocking as it may seem, I could imagine speaking of a "kingdom to come," which would be not at all kingly or monarchical; indeed this kingdom might even be *an*archical, highly hier-an-archical, inasmuch as it would make the singular, the exceptional, the least among us, the *an-archē*, very sacred. So there might be contexts in which we would want to speak of a kingdom to come, in which we would pray "let the kingdom come," for that would be a kingdom *ironice*, a kingdom tongue in cheek, a kingdom of the unkingly, without a purple robe in sight, a kingdom of the unroyal and the powerless, that makes a mockery of what is called a kingdom in politics. That, if I may be permitted a shameless reference, is the point of John D. Caputo, *The Weakness of God: A Theology of the Event* (Bloomington: Indiana University Press, 2006).

9. Hannah Arendt, *On Revolution* (New York: Viking, 1963), pp. 164–166.

10. Derrida, *Negotiations*, p. 180.

11. I have made several attempts to find such nutshells in *Deconstruction in a Nutshell: A Conversation with Jacques Derrida*, ed. with comm. John D. Caputo (New York: Fordham University Press, 1997).

12. All of this means that what we call "democracy" today is an "interim" solution, an interim politics. Democracy is always to come, but in the meantime we need democracy now, today. Democracy is a politics for the time being that is held together by a lick and a promise, a provisional arrangement that has been hastily erected for the moment, thrown together for the time between now and the eschaton, the time of the to-come, something with which we just have to make do in the meantime. The thing is, it is *always* the meantime. The very idea of the *à venir* is that the time to come is never going to turn up; it will never arrive, so there is only ever the meantime, being-toward in the meantime. It is always the time between now and what is to come. We live our lives in the interim, constructing an interim ethics, an interim politics, an interim democracy, one that will see us through the day and, if we are lucky, that will last us through the week, and maybe until the democracy to come arrives. Which will never happen. We are always to do with interim democracies and transitional regimes. Democracy cannot wait. That means: (1) democracy cannot wait to get here, it is eager to make its appearance, if only it can, if only it is permitted to arrive; (2) we cannot wait for democracy, we must have democracy now, in the meantime, even before it comes. It must come before it comes because we cannot wait for it to come. It is impossible but it is needed immediately and urgently. The democracy to come must already be here, today, otherwise we would not know what we are waiting for, even as the democracy to come cannot possibly be here, otherwise we would not be waiting.

13. Jacques Derrida, "Circonfession: cinquante-neuf périodes et périphrases," in *Jacques Derrida*, Geoffrey Bennington and Jacques Derrida (Paris: Éditions du Seuil, 1991), p. 290; "Circumfession: Fifty-nine Periods and Periphrases," in *Jacques Derrida*, Geoffrey Bennington and Jacques Derrida (Chicago: University of Chicago Press, 1993), p. 314.

14. Jacques Derrida, *Politiques de l'amitié* (Paris: Galilée, 1995), p. 55; *Politics of Friendship*, trans. George Collins (London and New York: Verso, 1997), p. 46, n. 14.

15. *Austehehen* also suggests something dreaded, which is likewise a part of messianic expectation.

16. The Messiah is an inherited and historical concretization of very idea of the to-come, which clothes the to-come in the determinate historical garments of a particular

202

(biblical) tradition—rather the way Johannes Climacus clothed his account of the "condition," the "paradox," and the "god" in the *Philosophical Fragments* with the historical name of "Christianity" in the *Postscript*. The other way to look at it—there being no way to decide between these formulations—is to say that the very idea of the to-come is the "formalization" of the concrete idea of the Messiah that we have inherited from the biblical tradition.

17. See Jacques Derrida, *On the Name*, ed. Thomas Dutoit (Stanford: Stanford University Press, 1995), p. 59.

18. See Jacques Derrida, *Parages* (Paris: Galilée, 1986), p. 25; I have added *s'avoir* to Derrida's string here.

19. See John D. Caputo, *The Prayers and Tears of Jacques Derrida: Religion without Religion* (Bloomington: Indiana University Press, 1997).

20. Jacques Derrida, *Negotiations: Interventions and Interviews*, ed. and trans. Elizabeth Rottenberg (Stanford: Stanford University Press, 2002), p. 181.

21. Derrida, *Parages*, p. 116.

eleven

Transcendence and Transversality

Calvin O. Schrag

In this essay I want to approach the topic of the present volume—a topic of both historical and contemporary importance—with some reflections on transcendence as transversal.

The concept of transcendence has been in the vocabularies both of the vulgar and the learned for a very long time. The locutions of everyday language and the discourses of expert knowledge provide testimony that it is difficult to converse about matters either mundane or metaphysically lofty without references, either explicit or oblique, to that which is transcendent. One can hardly make one's way about in the everyday world, to say nothing of navigating the thickets of the conversations and the treatises of the learned, without talking and writing about that which in some manner or another illustrates transcendence.

Entries in both general and discipline-specific dictionaries and encyclopedias indicate a widespread usage of the term. The relevant entry in *Webster's Third New International Dictionary*, for example, is quite straightforward in highlighting the senses of *exceeding* and *surpassing*. That which transcends, we are informed, in some manner or other exceeds or surpasses. It exceeds certain limits and transgresses certain boundaries—and in some cases exceeds and transgresses to the point of surpassing the universe and life on the planet as we know it. This entry does not conceal the complexities that accompany the widespread usage of "transcendence," and the reader proceeds down a series of derivative lexemes, to wit "transcendency," "transcendental," "transcendentalize," and "transcension."

Entries on transcendence in dictionaries and encyclopedias of philosophy and theology also illustrate a polysemy and shades of meaning against the backdrop of an exceeding or going-beyond human comprehension or indeed beyond corporeal existence itself. The new *Cambridge Dictionary of Philosophy* is quite explicit on matters of a notably accentuated sense of transcendence. Transcendence, we are told, has to do with "the property of being, in some way, of a higher order." And we are then presented with an example: "A being such as God, may be said to be transcendent in the sense of being not merely superior, but incomparably superior, to other things, in any sort of perfection."[1] We are here presented with what one might call a rigorous and bold metaphysical take on the meaning of transcendence. In any case, what one quickly learns from the sundry entries in the spectrum of assorted dictionaries and encyclopedias is that "transcendence," like "being" as attested to by Aristotle, is indeed said in many ways.

Quite aware that one can never begin at the beginning in addressing issues of such magnitude, one need nonetheless begin. And when one begins one finds that one is always already begun, situated in medias res as it were. Aware of this situation, we launch our inquiry with the observation that in its multiple senses of exceeding and surpassing, transcendence has to do with that which is *other*. Transcendence and alterity are twin moments of an august event. Such is the case as one moves across the landscapes of perceptual, ethical, aesthetical and religious consciousness. The perceptual object transcends the act of perception. The rose in my garden, as object of perception, is other than the perceptual act that delivers the rose as the meant or intended object. The glare from my desk lamp is distressingly other as it obtrudes upon my perceptual consciousness as a coefficient of adversity. The signifiers in the economy of perception attest of a transcendence of data that solicit our awareness.

Moving from perceptual to ethical consciousness we note similar indications of that which transcends. Ethical consciousness is positioned to make claims for the transcendence of raw desire and inclination by the moral act. The garden variety of ethical theories that have been proposed throughout the history of philosophy in various ways acknowledge features of transcendence. Teleological ethics postulates a transcendent telos as ultimately normative, providing the direction for self and social actualization. Moral duties as required by deontological ethics are rooted in a transcendent ought that resides on the hither side of that which is. Kant, sometimes considered the father of deontological ethics, has clearly instructed us that you cannot get an *ought* from an *is*. Utilitarians, although they tend to be of a much more this-worldly frame of mind than are teleologists and deontologists, nonetheless remain beholden to an envisioned state or condition that defines what is good for both the individual and the greater society. The ethical consciousness, however articulated in its form and function, testifies of a region that transcends the given state of affairs.

The sublime as beheld by the aesthetical consciousness transcends, is other than, the particular instances or cases of the beautiful. One can come upon specific instances and examples of the beautiful as object of aesthetical consciousness. But the vision of the sublime, on the hither side of the sensible and the visible, resists perceptual and conceptual determination in its limitlessness and boundlessness. It is here that the creativity of the aesthetic imagination registers its contribution, intimating and alluding to the intercalation of sublimity and alterity beyond the ken of perceptual apprehension and categorial determination.

God as the proper object of the religious consciousness provides us with another example of transcendence. Defined in the annals of classical theism as *totally other* in His/Her exceeding and surpassing of the finite world of temporal becoming, God is considered to be transcendent in a quite superlative sense. Here it would seem that we have exceeded the stipulations of transcendence as it plays on the landscapes of perceptual, ethical, and aesthetical consciousness, and move to a discourse and wider narrative in which the alterity of transcendence is accentuated in scope and intensity. In any event, a quick review of the dynamics of transcendence across the fields of consciousness, from perception to religious experience, requires that one be attentive to its multiple expressions in the travail of human endeavoring.

As one is able to discern a coupling of transcendence with alterity in the history of its usage, so also one is quickly apprised of a span of tension between transcendence and immanence—a span of tension which at times has led to an abrupt *de*coupling of the intended referents. This decoupling of the transcendent from the immanent received a pronounced expression in the early history of western metaphysics. One is here reminded of Plato's doctrine of universal, eternal, immutable forms as intensities of perfection, providing one with a paradigmatic instance of *metaphysical* transcendence—beyond all economies of the particular, the temporal and the changeable. Hand in glove with the metaphysical transcendence in the grand schemes of Greek philosophy, western theology fashioned a theological construct of God as infinite and eternal being, functioning as an *ens causa sui* of all that is finite and temporal, fleshed out in the religious vocabulary of *ens creator* versus *ens creatum*. The concept of God as conjunct of cause and creator of the universe provided the philosophical foundation for the edifice of a *metaphysics of theism* in which it was believed that the destinies of Athens and Jerusalem had come to an amalgamated fulfillment.

The span of tension between transcendence and immanence, however, has not always been that sharply defined—neither in the annals of philosophy nor in those of theology. Much depends upon the landscapes of the sub-disciplines in which the notions play out their dynamics. Edmund Husserl, for example, in working-out a phenomenological account of the sources and nature of human knowledge, found himself talking of a "transcendence-within-immanence." Within the epistemological economy, the dynamics of transcendence stimulates the commerce within the ego-cogito–cogitatum structure of intentional consciousness. The cogitatum, the object "as meant," in the performance of intentionality transcends the ego-cogito as seat and origin of intentional consciousness. This is the first moment of transcendence in the life of cognition. The second moment, disclosed through the phenomenological *epoché*, is the transcendence of the object "as existing," which has been put into brackets to enable a clear focus on the meaning of that which is presented. Existential claims are suspended so as to clear a path to the source of meaning. The "object as meant," *phenomenon* in its originative significa-tion, is not to be conflated with the "object as existing." Hence, as the "object as meant" transcends the cognitive act, so the "object as existing" transcends the "object as meant."

But these distinctions and differences within the dynamics of transcen-dence, Husserl emphasizes, remain within the folds of immanence. Hence, the grammar of "transcendence-within-immanence." And here we need to confront some additional perplexities. The immanence at issue has to do with the space of the *transcendental*—the field of transcendental subjectivity and transcendental intersubjectivity, forcing us to achieve clarity on the distinc-tion between "transcendent" and "transcendental." Husserl's phenomenology, from its earliest stages to the last, flies under the flag of *transcendental* phenom-enology. Plainly enough, Kant's understanding and use of "transcendental" is in the mix here, although one needs to be wary of simply interchanging Kant's transcendental/empirical doublet and Husserl's transcendental/mundane dis-tinction. But a common denominator informs the philosophical programs of Kant and Husserl alike. The transcendental has to do with the logico-epistemological conditions that render knowledge possible. It does *not* pertain to transcendent objects of experience about which claims for existence can be made. Hence, Husserl remains quite immune to the charge of semantic im-propriety when he talks of a transcendence-within-immanence that is opera-tive within a field of transcendental subjectivity.

But matters become even more complicated in our search for the mean-ing of transcendence as it relates to immanence when we encounter efforts to either exalt the one over the other or simply reduce the one to the other. Illustration of the latter strategy can be found in Gilles Deleuze's doctrine of "pure immanence" as articulated in his small volume by that name. Imma-nence, interchangeably described by Deleuze as "pure" and "absolute," is "in itself; it is not in something, *to* something; it does not depend on an object or belong to a subject."[2]

And with a somewhat unexpected conciseness, Deleuze summarizes his take on the transcendence/immanence problematic as follows: "Although it is always possible to invoke a transcendent that falls outside the plane of immanence, or that attributes immanence to itself, all transcendence is constituted solely in the flow of immanent consciousness that belongs to this plane. Transcendence is always a product of immanence."[3]

Positioned on the other side of the transcendence versus immanence ledger is Deleuze's fellow countryman, Emmanuel Levinas. Levinas, the apostle of a heavily accentuated and robust transcendence, offers a veritable inversion of Deleuze's claim by highlighting the preeminence of transcendence over immanence. And the transcendence of which Levinas speaks is, plainly enough, a transcendence that "exceeds" and "surpasses" in a quite superlative manner. It is not simply the "first other"—the other of an initiating cause or first principle—it is in truth "other than the other, other otherwise, and other with an alterity prior to the alterity of the other, prior to the ethical obligation to the other and different from every neighbor, transcendent to the point of absence."[4] Here we are presented, I submit, with a remarkable and magnificent hyperbole, exceeding our ordinary run-of-the-mill hyperbole in power and majesty!

How is one to manage the veritable *différend* in which Deleuze and Levinas find themselves? Might one somehow be able to attest to the claims of both, possibly through an appeal to the familiar rhetorical strategy of "on the one hand *x* and on the other hand *y*"? But this would require some common ground, and it is difficult to imagine what this common ground might be. Yet, it is unquestionably the case that in the history of philosophy and religion alike there have been voices making claims for the realities of that which is both transcendent and immanent without reduction of the one to the other. Even Plato's celestial forms were understood to ingress into the world of becoming without sacrifice of identity. Such would seem to be the case particularly in the later dialogues, the *Cratylus* and the *Statesman*. The shuttle-maker implants the blueprint of the shuttle into the wood, and the astute statesman will be able to incorporate the ideal state into the political arena to the degree that it is possible for a finite human being. So also the concept of God, as developed particularly in western religion, provides an example of an attempted accommodation of dimensions of transcendence and immanence within the life of the Deity. God is transcendent in His/Her interior being, but in some manner has the power and will to become immanent in a finite and temporal world of which He/She allegedly is in some sense the author.

One of the more interesting efforts to achieve a cosmological balance of the registers of the transcendent and of the immanent, theologically articulated as the relation of the infinite and the eternal to the finite and the temporal, is that found in the teachings of process theology and its doctrine of panentheism—of which the late Charles Hartshorne was the most articulate spokesperson. Panentheism proposes to avoid the Scylla of absolute transcendence and the Charybdis of pure immanence by forging a passage between a theistic supernaturalism that views God as wholly other and a pantheistic naturalism that views God and nature as convertible terms.

Much of the inspiration for Hartshorne's panentheism derives, of course, from Alfred North Whitehead's process philosophy and his distinction between the primordial and the consequent nature of God. The primordial nature, which houses the eternal objects, effects an ingression into the world of becoming as God's consequent nature in such a manner that it enters the life of the procession of actual occasions without loss of identity. That such a position, on the level of metaphysical inquiry, might afford an interesting alternative to the quandaries of metaphysical/cosmological construction could well be the case. But it is precisely the bugbears that travel with the metaphysical/cosmological framework of inquiry that continue to haunt us in our quest for an understanding of the dynamics of transcendence as a problematic for the religious consciousness. And it is for this reason that we wish to offer a thought experiment requiring a linguistic and hermeneutical shift in addressing the issue of transcendence.

Our experiment involves a combined shift of root metaphor and interpretive stance on matters of both transcendence and immanence. The root metaphor that has informed the transcendence/immanence doublet as a metaphysical problem from the time of the ancients to the moderns is the spatial metaphor of verticality versus horizontality. The vertical dimension, whether it provides the backdrop for Platonic forms, an Aristotelian prime mover, the *actus purus* of St. Thomas Aquinas, the supremely perfect being of Descartes, the Infinite Substance of Spinoza, or the Godhead of classical mysticism, is *indicative of*, in some sense *refers to*, in one manner or another *displays*, a being about which existence claims can be made and to which an essence can be assigned with certain characterizing attributes—notably infinitude, eternality, immutability and an unsurpassable degree of perfection. Such a being, in its superlative vertical transcendence, assumes the status of an *ens realissimum* portrayed in St. Anselm's well-known definition of God as "a being than which none greater can be conceived," or the status of an *ens causa sui* as portrayed in St. Thomas Aquinas's ruminations on the nature of the Deity.

The horizontal dimension, on the other hand, indicates, in some sense refers to, or in some manner displays, a region or realm defined as finite, temporal, mutable and subject to imperfection. As the vertical dimension houses a being, positioned along the axis of either height or depth, the highest being or the ground of being; so the horizontal dimension marks out the region of lesser beings subject to a coming to be and passing away. Truth to tell, we are here in the lofty citadel of metaphysics with its peculiar grammar of existence and essence, substance and attribute, eternal and temporal, immutable and changing, perfect and imperfect—all of which stands in service of constructing a metaphysical divide, of varying intensities to be sure, whereby the transcendent and the immanent are set in opposition.

Let us now consider a thought experiment in which we delimit the spa-

Calvin O. Schrag

tial metaphor of verticality versus horizontality with its accompanying meta-physical freight by shifting to another metaphor, that of diagonality, forging a path toward an analysis of transcendence into transversality. It is important to take notice at this juncture that we are not recommending an abandonment of metaphors per se, en route to unencumbered literal descriptions of what in fact is the case, sans interpretation and bereft of competing perspectives. Meta-phors remain within the figures of our discourse as we move about in our projects of making sense together. We continue to think in metaphors, or we do not think at all. From Nietzsche we have all learned that truth is a caravan of metaphors that "trans-port" or "de-liver" (*meta-pherein*) understanding and comprehension.

So we do not *displace* the metaphorical, but rather seek to delimit the metaphysical weight in the metaphorical—and in our current project, delimit the grammar of universal versus particular, eternal versus temporal, and im-mutable versus the changeable—a grammar that has become a fellow traveler with the spatial metaphor of verticality versus horizontality. On this need to delimit the metaphysical weight of the metaphorical, a critical note on Hei-degger's devaluation of the metaphorical is in order. Heidegger almost got it right—but not quite—when in *Satz vom Grund* he tells us that the metaphori-cal resides only in the metaphysical: "*Das Metaphorische gibt es nur innerhalb der Metaphysik.*"⁵ Unfortunately, many times it is the case that the metaphori-cal continues to make purchases on the metaphysical. And such is particularly the case in the history of the metaphysics of theism. But it is not necessary, we would maintain, that these purchases be made.

Simplified to the extreme, our project utilizes the metaphor/concept of diagonality, with its coefficient of extending over and lying across, to facilitate an analysis of transcendence into transversality—in a special sense of "analy-sis," however. What is projected is not *reductive* analysis but rather *interpretive* analysis—an entwinement of hermeneutical understanding and explanatory discernment that enables a setting-forth of the content and measure of tran-scendence in its transversal dynamics. To be sure, the concept of transversality is not a concept of recent date. It has been used across the disciplines for some time now. It has been a staple in topology, functioning as a generalization of orthogonality, punctuating the dynamics of moving across surfaces without coming to rest at any particular point, touching but not coinciding. It is used in particle-theory physics to explain the ratio of accelerating forces by distinguish-ing transverse mass from longitudinal mass. In the field of physiology bodily fibers are defined as transversal in character and function. In the science of anatomy the vertebrate provides a telling example of transversal operation. In linguistics, translation from one language to another can be described as a transversal achievement.

It was Jean-Paul Sartre, however, who called our attention to the philo-sophical capital in the vocabulary of transversality. In his celebrated critique of Husserl's doctrine of the transcendental ego, he used the concept to explicate the unity of consciousness as a transversal performance. The unity of consciousness, Sartre argued, can be accounted for without appeals to a stable and self-identical ego within the interior depths of intentional consciousness, as Husserl had maintained. What is simply required, concludes Sartre, is a re-description that yields a portrait of a "consciousness which unifies itself, concretely, by a play of 'transversal' intentionalities which are concrete and real retentions of past consciousness."[6]

Sartre's fellow countryman, Félix Guattari, has illustrated the workings of transversality in the institutional settings of medical practice, demonstrating its utility for organizational communication—shifting the focus from transversal consciousness to what Guattari names "transversality in the group." As a practicing psychiatrist, Guattari sought to illustrate how the achievement of psychiatric healing involves a transversal communication and ordering in the decision-making that extends across the constitutive parties involved in institutional care. The administrative staff, the medical staff of doctors and nurses, the patients and the families and friends of the patients, with their distinctive expertise and interests and concerns, all quite clearly have a stake in the decision-making process. And this is a process that according to Guattari must not fall victim to a vertical, hegemonic seat of authority that rules top-down. But it also needs to avoid the indecision and breakdown of communication in a horizontal dimension of diverging interests and concerns. In short, what the situation requires, summarizes Guattari, is the dynamics of transversality as "a dimension that tries to overcome both the impasse of pure verticality and that of mere horizontality."[7]

In all of the above illustrations, exemplified in the different fields of human learning and endeavor as we move across the assorted disciplines, we can observe the play of transversality as a convergence without coincidence, a congruence without identity, and an interaction without assimilation—undercutting in one fell swoop as it were the ideology of a transcendence of pure verticality and the ideology of an immanence of pure horizontality. It is of particular interest to us that in each of these illustrations of the grammar of transversality there is an acknowledgment of the impingement and role of that which is other—other surfaces, other fibers, other vertebrae, other linguistic regimens, other moments of consciousness, other interested parties in pursuit of medical wellness. Alterity is an intrinsic component of transversality, *but it is not an alterity that is vertically super-imposed, hierarchically over-arching, hegemonic and heteronomous.* In short, it is not the alterity within the requirements of a classical vertical transcendence, neither of an epistemological or metaphysical sort. Nor, however, is it the evanescent alterity of a random juxtaposition and serial succession on a horizontal plane of pure immanence—which, it would appear, is the only kind of alterity that Deleuze's concept of pure immanence will allow. In a quite peculiar manner the alterity of transversality splits the difference between the metaphysical postulates of vertically elevated transcendence and horizontally demarcated immanence.

There is admittedly a measure of semantic meandering in our shift away from an understanding of transcendence against the backdrop of a grammar of verticality versus horizontality, toward an understanding of transcendence along the lineaments of a play with the grammar of diagonality and transversality. It would appear that diagonality makes sense only against the backdrop of the vertical/horizontal opposition. And clearly one needs to recognize that there is a sense in which this is the case, and further one needs to acknowledge the inability to fully extricate oneself from that which one seeks to negate. We always think and speak from the sedimentations of a tradition. But we are not condemned to remain imprisoned within these sedimentations—in this case the sedimentations of a vertical versus horizontal matrix of opposition. Such a matrix of thought can be at once *delimited* and *de-metaphysicalized.* It cannot be entirely displaced as a figure of discourse in the background, but it can be refigured in the search for new perspectives.

It may be helpful at this juncture to recall Derrida's two strategies of deconstruction. On the one hand there is the strategy of "a deconstruction without changing the terrain, by repeating what is implicit in the founding concepts and the original problematic," and on the other hand a deconstruction that makes an effort "to change terrain, in a discontinuous and irruptive fashion, by brutally placing oneself outside, and by affirming an absolute break and difference."[8] And as Derrida himself is quick to acknowledge, any choice of the one or other strategy of deconstruction remains shot through with ambiguity. Any change of terrain when dealing with figures of discourse and modes of thought can never be final and definitive. We need to work with the concepts and metaphors that have been delivered to us, and the task of critical inquiry is to use them against themselves in an effort to articulate new landscapes for thought and action. The lesson to be learned from this is that the truth of deconstruction resides in the recognition that no complete deconstruction is possible.

Truth to tell, there clearly are ambiguities that travel with every effort to think *beyond* a tradition whilst thinking *from* a tradition. Such would seem to be particularly the case when the matter of transcendence is at issue. And here we have much to learn from Gianni Vattimo's characterization of contemporary philosophico-religious reflection on "the Other" as a "discontinuity in the horizontal course of history." The problem with such a description according to Vattimo, is that

> this discontinuity and irruption is too often understood . . . as a pure and 'apocalyptic' negation of historicity, as an absolute new beginning that renounces every link with the past and establishes a purely vertical relation with transcendence, regarded in turn as the pure metaphysical plentitude of the eternal foundation.[9]

Here we encounter the disquieting bugbear—vertical transcendence standing in for "the pure metaphysical plentitude of the eternal foundation"!

The play of transversality, splitting the difference between the purity of a vertical metaphysical transcendence on the right and the purity of a horizontal metaphysical immanence on the left, receives different expressions as one moves along the continuum of perceptual apprehension, cognitive judgment, creative imagination, aesthetic evaluation, moral obligation and religious experience. What Max Weber and Jürgen Habermas dubbed the three "culture-spheres of modernity"—science, morality and art—suffer the imprint of transversality, albeit it in different ways. Weber and Habermas credited Kant for providing the backdrop for the separation of the cognitive interests in science, morality and art, in the publication of his three celebrated *Critiques*. According to Weber, the three culture-spheres stand in a relation of "stubborn differentiation." Habermas sought a melioration of sorts, taming the stubbornness in the differentiation of validity claims in the spheres of science, morality and art, with a theory of communicative action informed by a communication based notion of rationality that remained friendly to all three spheres.

Inquiry into the three culture-spheres as delineated by Weber and Habermas clearly affords its own rewards. The fact, however, remains that they were mistaken in their count. There are four culture-spheres, not three! They forgot religion as the fourth culture-sphere—as Kant, actually, had himself suggested in *Religion Within the Limits of Reason Alone*. And it is of some import that Weber and Habermas alike were unable to find the markings of religion as a separate domain of inquiry in their invention of the culture-sphere vocabulary. This is particularly regrettable because the working of transversality is given a quite distinctive punctuation in the sphere of religious praxis. And it is this distinctive punctuation in the sphere of religious thought and experience that is our principal concern in the present exercise.

What is the content, measure and dynamics of the alterity that is attested to in the praxis of religious discourse and action? Such would seem to be of a quite different sort than that which one encounters in the economies of the scientific, the aesthetic and the ethico-moral culture-spheres. What resources of discourse are available to enable one to speak of a transcendence that somehow exercises a claim on us, in some manner revealing a divine presence, becoming extant in our wanderings about in the mundane culture-spheres? Or to frame the issue with the help of Levinas's piquant title, what is the content and measure of the transcendence "of God who comes to mind"? In what sense "coming to mind"? In what sense "revealing presence"? In what sense "extant" in the corridors of civil society? These are not questions of recent times, but recent times require that we experiment with new responses to them.

Continuing our thought experiment, let us suppose that the status of transcendence at issue here is not that of a being—not even that of the most elevated being on a vertical chain of being proceeding from the lowest to the highest—not the *ens realissimum* and *ens causa sui* of a metaphysics of theism. Let us further suppose that the transcendence in our God-talk is not that of an *onto-theology* that bounces off the ontological-ontic difference, as this "difference" has been interpreted by certain theologians appropriating the thought of the later Heidegger. After a dissatisfaction with the metaphysical, ontically based portrait of the deity as the highest of beings within a vast celestial hierarchy, there is a temptation to refocus one's philosophical lenses and try somehow to zero in on that which exceeds or surpasses the totality of beings as such. Maybe one should scrounge around for a notion of BEING, inscribed in bold capitals indicating a severance from the ontic, beyond the ken of all categories that define the hierarchy of beings in their causal connections. The possibility of some such move would seem to have already motivated some early fourth and fifth-century proponents of *negative* theology, and most prominently Pseudo-Dionysius the Areopagite, who although he insisted on the indescribability of the nature of the Deity still found himself talking of God as "Superesssential Essence" and "Superexisting Deity." Proponents of negative theology have difficulty avoiding the semantic predicament of maintaining the ineffability of the Divine while continuing to "effabilize" that which is allegedly ineffable!

Efforts to continue the use of an ontological grammar after a rejection of a metaphysics of theism can also be observed in Paul Tillich's project of "transcending theism" through an appeal to a "God above God." Although Tillich recommends that we be done with the categories of theistic metaphysics, in his three-volume *Systematic Theology* he still finds a utility in the resources of ontology for speaking about the God above God as "Being-itself," "the Ground of Being," and "the Power of Being." The impact of Heidegger's ontological explorations on Paul Tillich's philosophical theology is quite evident and merits more attention than it has currently received in the literature. To be sure, there is more than the Heideggerian influence that provides the backdrop for Tillich's majestic *Systematic Theology*. Tillich draws deeply from many wells, including the theological traditions of St. Augustine, Jacob Boehme, Meister Eckhart and Martin Luther, coupled with recurring references to the philosophical contributions of Kant, Hegel and Schelling. However, it is of some consequence to note that Heidegger's project of fundamental ontology played a not insignificant role in Tillich's semantics of the Deity.

The influence on Tillich by Heidegger, who was Tillich's colleague at Marburg University in the 1920s, was forcefully brought to my attention when I served as Tillich's assistant during a period of my graduate study. During one of our discussions of the philosophy of Heidegger, Tillich told me that after a colloquium address by Heidegger, one of his early articulations of the distinction between "Being" and "beings," he and Heidegger took the usual after-lecture walk, during which he provided Heidegger with a consummate assessment of his presentation: *"Das war ein gute Predigt!"* (That was a good sermon!) Clearly, it would seem that there must be something about transcendence at issue here!

Might it be that Heidegger's notion of Being (*Sein*), dutifully marked off from the concept of beings in their totality (*Seiendes*) as the subject matter of metaphysics, could put us on the path to a viable onto-theology? Plainly enough, Heidegger needs to bear some responsibility for the entertainment of such a move. In his *Letter on Humanism* he invites the reader to consider a rather direct connection between the truth of Being and the question about the meaning of "God." He writes: "Only from the truth of Being can the essence of the holy be thought. Only from the essence of the holy can the essence of divinity be thought. Only in the light of the essence of divinity can it be thought and said what the word 'God' is to signify."[10] Given such a close alignment of the problem of Being and the question about the signifying power of the word "God," one might expect a positive response from Heidegger to Tillich's assessment of his lecture as a "good sermon."

But one needs to tread with some caution at this juncture, given Heidegger's own spin of what was at stake in his reference to God in the *Letter on Humanism*. In "The Conversation with Martin Heidegger; Recorded by Herman Noach," Heidegger attempts to set the record straight.

> With respect to the text referred to from the *Letter on Humanism*, what is being discussed there is the God of the poet, not the revealed God. There is mentioned merely what philosophical thinking is capable of on its own. . . . The Christian faith does not need to consider itself as an "historical destining disclosure of Being," nor does it have need of treating the mystery of the incarnation with concepts such as the "ontological difference" (between "beings" and "Being"). We understand one another better when each speaks in his own language.[11]

Now this resonates nicely with Heidegger's occasional remarks that were he to write a theology the word "Being" would not appear—and apparently not even under the much-celebrated erasure of Being, the "crossing out" (*kreuzeweise Durchstreichung*), in which of course the word "Being" still remains to be seen and read as crossed out! It would appear that at this juncture one is found alluding to that which is quite *otherwise* than Being, beyond not only the constraints of a metaphysics of theism but beyond the sirens of onto-theology as well.[12]

Continuing our thought experiment along these lines, which augers away from both theistic metaphysics and onto-theology, we are inspired by the path opened up in John Caputo's essay "In Search of a Sacred Anarchy," felicitously subtitled "An Experiment in Danish Deconstruction."[13] Let us suppose that talking about the Deity is less like talking about either "a being" or even "the Being of beings" within the vocabulary constraints of the ontic-ontological difference, and more like talking about *différance* as at once disruption and deed, recalling the prophetic role and function of religion as enunciated by the prophets of ancient Israel. The leveraging question posed by Amos, Hosea and Micah was not, "What is the meaning and/or truth of Being?" It was rather the question, "What does the Lord require of you?" Responding to this ques-

Calvin O. Schrag

tion, the prophet Micah consolidates the prophetic requirement: "To do justly, and to love kindness, and to walk humbly with thy God" (Micah 6:8). In the asking of this question, issuing a call to responsible discourse and action, we move to another vocabulary and another grammar, more verb than noun-oriented—recalling Rabbi David Cooper's provocative little volume titled, *God Is a Verb*.[14]

Our experiment, propelling us along the stages of life's way, introduces some additional ingredients for our peculiar laboratory exercise, and these are, following the recommendations of Professor Caputo, of a quite distinctive "Danish" sort. Suppose that our semantic experimentation with *différance*, disruption, deed, call for responsible action, and the preference for verbs over nouns, finds an epiphany of sorts, an unexpected consolidation and illumination, in the trajectory of Søren Kierkegaard's unparalleled *Works of Love*. This would enable us to see that the disruption, deed, and call for responsible action, that stands in for the Deity, culminates in the workings of love, and specifically in response to the commandment that one love one's neighbor as oneself. And this love, as Kierkegaard is quick to underscore, is of a quite extraordinary sort. This is a love that is at once *unconditional* and *encompassing*.

It is unconditional because it expects nothing in return. Unlike the ordinary, mundane, and preferential love that loves only if it is returned in kind, the love of one's neighbor is a love that loves for the sake of loving, without condition that something be given back, devoid of any expectation of return, outside the economy of exchange relations, without desire for reward or recompense. We might be disposed to name such a love *the Gift in the fullness of time*. Such is the content, measure and dynamics of a *genuine* gift—outside any economy of gift-exchange wherein gifts become incursions of debt, soliciting repayment.

This gift of love is not only unconditional; it is also, and therefore, encompassing. It extends, as Kierkegaard is quick to point out, to the rich man, the beggar, the widow, the orphan, the male, the female—and, yes, even to the *enemy*! "Therefore the one who truly loves the neighbor loves also his enemy," avers Kierkegaard. And he continues: "The distinction *friend* or *enemy* is difference in the object of love, but love for the neighbor has the object that is without difference. The neighbor is the utterly unrecognizable dissimilarity between persons or is the eternal equality before God—the enemy, too, has this equality."[15]

The requirement of which Kierkegaard here testifies—that of an unconditional and encompassing love of neighbor—is I suggest a concrete illustration of transcendence as transversality, a convergence without coincidence. Such a love, outside all economies of symbolic exchange relations, inscribing a call to a love that overrides even the distinction between friend and enemy, is truly a love that exceeds and surpasses, transcendent in a quite robust sense, an *other* that is truly other than all the others within the circulation of distribution and exchange that stimulates the economies of the mundane culture-spheres. It is surely such a love that Derrida has in mind when he writes of "the dissymmetry of a gift without exchange" that is "infinitely disproportionate from the vantage point of terrestrial finitude."[16]

Yet, there is something quite peculiar about this infinitely disproportionate love as a gift that solicits no exchange. It intersects our terrestrial finitude at decisive moments. And as such it enables us to solve, with Kierkegaard, "the great riddle of living in eternity and yet hearing the hall clock strike."[17] But in intersecting our terrestrial finitude the infinitely disproportional gift of love for neighbor does not become coincident with our terrestrial strivings. It illustrates a convergence without coincidence, a congruence without identity, an interaction without assimilation. In short, it exhibits the dynamics of transversality.

And this now puts us in position to learn that transversality is older than even *différance*. It was Derrida who taught us that *différance* is "older" than Being—older than the ontic-ontological difference and older than the truth of Being. Being is an "effect" of *différance*, Derrida tells us.[18] Now continuing the conversation with Derrida, let us propose that before *différance* there was transversality, that *différance* is itself an "effect" of transversality—and more precisely a transversality understood as the transport (*meta-pherein*) of the *Word* that takes on flesh and becomes efficacious within the bounds of terrestrial finitude, supplying the dynamics of *différance* with the truth of transcendence.

And it is this dynamics of the truth of transcendence, borne by an analysis of transcendence into transversality, that solicits a fitting response. It calls us to our responsibility of seeking to manifest the gift in the dealings of our daily comings and goings. But the gift retains its alterity—it is always other and prior to our discourse and action. It is the content and measure of our discourse and action on the plane of terrestrial immanence, but it is never assimilated into it. This is the truth of ethico-religious transcendence after the metaphysico-cosmological constructs of transcendence have been disassembled—always exceeding and surpassing, finding its dynamic in a transversality that lies across and operates between the margins of our terrestrial finitude and the infinitely disproportional gift of love.

NOTES

I would like to express my gratitude to Villanova University, and especially professors Caputo and Scanlon, for their resourcefulness in organizing the fourth international colloquium on Religion and Postmodernism, and thereafter in preparing the present volume for publication.

1. *The Cambridge Dictionary of Philosophy*, 2nd ed., gen. ed. Robert Audi (Cambridge: Cambridge University Press, 1999), p. 925.

2. Gilles Deleuze, *Pure Immanence*, trans. Anne Boyman (New York: Zone Books, 2001), p. 26.

3. Ibid., pp. 30–31.

4. Emmanuel Levinas, *Of God Who Comes to Mind,* trans. Bettina Bergo (Stanford: Stanford University Press, 1998), p. 69.

5. Martin Heidegger, *Der Satz vom Grund,* ed. Günther Neske and Emil Kettering (Pfullingen: Neske, 1958), p. 89.

6. Jean-Paul Sartre, *The Transcendence of the Ego: An Existentialist Theory of Consciousness,* trans. Forrest Williams and Robert Kirkpatrick (New York: Noonday, 1957), p. 39.

7. Félix Guattari, *Molecular Revolution: Psychiatry and Politics,* trans. Rosemary Sheed (New York: Penguin, 1984), p. 18.

8. Jacques Derrida, "Ends of Man," in *Margins of Philosophy,* trans. Allan Bass (Chicago: University of Chicago Press, 1982), p. 135.

9. Gianni Vattimo, "The Trace of the Trace," in *Religion,* ed. Jacques Derrida and Gianni Vattimo, trans. David Webb et al. (Stanford: Stanford University Press, 1988), p. 86.

10. Martin Heidegger, "Letter on Humanism," in *Martin Heidegger: Basic Writings,* rev. ed., ed. David Farrel Krell (San Francisco: HarperSanFrancisco, 1993), p. 253.

11. Martin Heidegger, *The Piety of Thinking,* trans. James G. Hart and John C. Maraldo (Bloomington: Indiana University Press, 1976), p. 65.

12. For Heidegger's discussion of the "crossing out" of Being see his *Zur Seinsfrage* (Frankfurt: Vittorio Klostermann, 1956), pp. 30–35. For a timely response to the project of onto-theological construction, see Merold Westphal's collected essays under the title, *Overcoming Onto-Theology: Toward a Postmodern Christian Faith* (New York: Fordham University Press, 2001).

13. John D. Caputo, "In Search of a Sacred Anarchy: An Experiment in Danish Deconstruction," in *Calvin O. Schrag and the Task of Philosophy After Postmodernity,* ed. Martin Beck Matuštík and William L. McBride (Evanston, Ill.: Northwestern University Press, 2002), pp. 226–250.

14. Rabbi David Cooper, *God Is a Verb* (New York: Riverhead, 1997).

15. Søren Kierkegaard, *Works of Love,* trans. Howard V. Hong and Edna H. Hong (Princeton, N.J.: Princeton University Press, 1995), p. 89.

16. Jacques Derrida, *The Politics of Friendship,* trans. George Collins (New York: Verso, 1997), p. 256.

17. Søren Kierkegaard, *Either/Or,* vol. 2, trans. Walter Lowrie (Princeton, N.J.: Princeton University Press, 1949), p. 116.

18. Jacques Derrida, *Speech and Phenomena: And Other Essays on Husserl's Theory of Signs,* trans. David B. Allison and Newton Garver (Evanston, Ill.: Northwestern University Press, 1973), pp. 153–154.

Transcendence and Beyond

A Concluding Roundtable

Moderated by John D. Caputo

John D. Caputo: Let me say at the start that I have learned a great deal this weekend, both from the gifted speakers we have heard, and from Hurricane Isabel, which roared up the northeastern coast on Thursday and nearly put an end to our program. I have learned something about the transcendence of nature. And I have learned to never again speak in praise of the unprogrammable disruption, the interruption, the incoming of the wholly other or the unforeseeable event. From here on in, I plan to advocate uninterrupted continuity and the absolutely programmable! Kierkegaard has Johannes Climacus say somewhere that the idea of contingency among the philosophers is such an abstract and empty term for them that the only thing that would make them understand it is an earthquake—to which I would add a hurricane. So I suppose we should all consider ourselves well instructed on this matter of contingency!

We have posed the question of "transcendence and beyond" precisely in order to signify the way in which this concept can be rethought or redescribed in a postmodern and deeply pluralistic context. In the course of these three days we have seen this "beyond" take on many meanings, from Marion's powerful beginning on Thursday evening through the radical demythologizing approaches taken to this idea in the work of Vattimo and David Wood to the redescription of transcendence from feminist and ecological perspectives in Catherine Keller and Sallie McFague. We have heard a succession of distinctly important essays, each of which requires considerable study. In this final session, we will see if we can put some of it together by coming back to several questions that were raised in the course of the past few days. I begin by going back to the opening essay of Jean-Luc Marion (chap. 1), a tantalizing and complex argument for a radical or ultra-transcendence, beyond the classical metaphysical transcendence which is not transcendent enough for Marion. I know that David Wood has some questions about Marion's essay, so I want to open the discussion by inviting David to share his concerns with us.

David Wood: I am very excited to be here. This is the strongest brush with theology that I've had since high school, when I won the Hooke theology prize for an essay on the necessity of atheism. I have to say I feel like a poor man at a table groaning with delicious food. I'm hungry but this food is exceedingly rich and I can only pick at it a little bit at a time. I did make some critical remarks about Marion in my own essay (chap. 9) on the basis of what I had read of his work before I came here. I have not wholly digested the essay that he gave us, but it is fair to say that that essay represents almost everything that I find problematic about how he understands transcendence.

I have three basic problems that I would like to share with you. As far as I have grasped the scaffolding of his thought in general—a God beyond being, a God of the impossible, a God of love—it rests on a serious and repeated misreading of Heidegger's struggle with the question of Being. Of course, if you read Heidegger as a traditional ontologist he needs leaping over. But both Levinas and Marion really do not understand the way in which Being for Heidegger is a space of transformation for our being-in-the-world, both our self-relation and our relations with others and with the Other. This is both a technical issue about reading Heidegger and also addresses what we have to do to be able to think the sort of things that are worth thinking. It is just when we start considering how to reshape our being-in-the-world that something like love really comes in. Love, that is, in all its fragility, complexity and vulnerability. Marion's understanding of God's love seems to me removed from the very contingency that makes human love so precious. I suppose my question would be, can a God without a body—who is not mortal, who cannot fear or hate—can such a God love at all? I am not asking: Can his (or her) love be infinite, but does love make any sense without those mortal conditions? That's my first question.

As a second general observation, I find the argument about God's possibility deriving from the impossibility of his impossibility really wholly unconvincing as an argument. I really liked what I would describe as the rational drive in the second half of Marion's essay, but I did not think this argument worked. I'm really quite suspicious of arguments that proceed by multiplying possibilities, and this one reeked of a new scholasticism, whereas we should be all moving in exactly the opposite direction. I much prefer what I take to be Derrida's position. To mix Derrida with Wittgenstein, this possibility of impossibility is something that *we may call God*—we might call God—but in such formulations there would be a certain modesty, hesitation, tentativeness about the very use of that word. I didn't find any of that caution in Marion's essay. That is my second reservation.

My last concern runs along similar lines. I worry about saying that all sins are sins against God. This may be uncontentious within certain forms of Christianity, but it is, for all that, deeply problematic. The idea that only God can forgive is an appalling claim to make—it is both metaphysically spurious and deeply misguided from an ethical standpoint. The impossibility of complete forgiveness means that we must never underestimate how difficult it is, *not* that only a big muscular God can do this impossibly heavy lifting. We do not need a hypostatized perfection to be able to work with and fight against our own imperfection. In short, Marion seems to me to be engaged in an evacuation of the ethical from the space of the human, capitalizing it in the shape of God's infinite love. I think this is a tragically mistaken direction.

Caputo: Richard, do you think that this argument about the impossibility of impossibility is a persuasive argument in Marion?

Richard Kearney: I feel a little uneasy answering the question. But it's a good question in the sense that David has put three very strong, trenchant and brutally honest objections—as is the wont of the British—to Jean-Luc Marion. It's not really my place to try to answer for Jean-Luc Marion. In fact, I have to say while I wouldn't be quite as contentious as David, I tend to concur with some of his thinking, but with this slight inflection of difference. I think the talk of the possibility and impossibility of God as a logical conceptual exercise which operates at the level of modal logic is given too much latitude, time and energy in Jean-Luc's essay. I do not want to turn this into a "Jean-Luc is wrong and I'm right" discussion; but where I would disagree with Marion is that I believe we should go beyond the logical conceptual metaphysical arguments about possibility and impossibility to another notion of the possible. This other notion does not derive from metaphysical hairsplitting but is derived from the imaginative resources and semantic energies of the scriptures, from the words themselves, in Greek and Hebrew—*asher eyeh hasher, dunamis*—the Vulgate's *potentia*, Nicholas of Cusa's Latin *possest*, and so on. They are there in the scriptures, not invented out of some kind of abstract, inhuman, otherworldly language. I prefer drawing the notion of God as possibilizing, enabling, empowering from such testimonial and narrative accounts. We know that Etty Hillesum used it in a very strong sense in her own testimony to the God of the possible in *An Interrupted Life*[1] ("You cannot be God unless we help you to be God," etc). And we find this in many authors and poets also, many of whom I quote in my lecture here yesterday (chap. 3)—Hopkins, Musil, Rilke, Emily Dickinson. I personally find these poetical and confessional testimonies of the divine possible to be more helpful than purely logical concepts, which often tend to take the life-blood out of the "possible." That may be confirming David's point rather than defending Jean-Luc.

On the question of the impossibility of forgiveness, I totally agree with David. I think that, if anything, the forgiveness of God should be something that enables us to forgive rather than something that teaches us its impossibility. I have to say that the overemphasis on the impossible in Jean-Luc's essay—but also in Derrida's language—is a problem for me. I think we know we can find a possible at the other end of the impossible. But to put the impossible in capital letters is, to me, a certain disabling of human action and of the need to return from text and thought and reflection to action. That is a hermeneutic bridge that I would want to see reestablished between some of these discourses on the impossible—relating to the "divine," the "infinite" and the "other"—on the one hand, and our daily actions, on the other. There I prefer David Wood's ladder and *Jacob's ladder*—footbridges between the self and the other, traversals between immanence and transcendence. I find the discourse on the impossible sometimes paralyzing and disabling in that regard.

One final comment and then I'll pass on the question, if I may, to Jack Caputo, about the overemphasis on the impossible. Can God love if God doesn't have a body? Well I would argue, God does have a body and I think this is what several speakers were saying—Sallie McFague and Catherine Keller, as I understood them. God always needs more of a body, more incarnation, and God cannot have it without us: We are God's body. What is the evidence for that, you might ask? Well the first evidence I would cite is the fact that people give cups of cold water to people everyday. If we are to believe the gospels, that means that God is present and embodied in the giver and the receiver of that cup of cold water. But secondly—on a slightly more festive note, a more erotic note—it's there in the Song of Songs. I'm convinced by the Song of Songs that God is a pretty hot lover. And the Song of Songs was not confined to Solomon and the Shulamite woman. It is being sung every day.

Catherine Keller: These are very possibilizing responses, making it possible at least for me to understand my own reaction, my own frustration, with Marion's essay. David Wood's argument from yesterday morning especially helped me. He said that transcendence appears when we construct a bounded space. Yesterday, we were thinking of that bounded space in terms of a particular construction of a stagnant or self-enclosed immanence. But it also seems that possibility is functioning this way in this paradigm, so that impossibility is appearing when we construct a bounded possibility. Impossibility—when I hear it proclaimed by Derrida and the other Jack [Caputo]—does seem to me to work as the kind of heuristic hyperbole that opens up the boundaries of the possible. But I have the sense with Jean-Luc Marion—perhaps because he's coming too close to my own field—that here impossibility is being turned into a Christian doctrine, and then it's functioning somewhat in the way that transcendence functions when it morphs from movement into state. Richard made a point earlier today about the problem of this love of impossibility in which omnipotence is sneaking in through the back door. I think this is very perceptive. This is a violative love. I don't know what exactly your phrase was, something like . . .

Kearney: . . . ravishing.

Keller: A ravishing love, right. Christian love gets very dangerous when it's yoked with omnipotence. St. Bernard, the great love-mystic, is also the one who with ravishing success called forth the devastating Second Crusade and never for a moment applied the question of Christian love to the Muslim other. So it's scary how the love-dogma can work like the wolf in lamb's clothing. The operative omnipotence, with its irresistible grace—the grace to which one cannot say no—has a strong tradition that I think you were trying to transverse.

Merold Westphal:[2] I'd like to pick up on David Wood's first objection to Marion, because I think it raises something that extends across quite a bit of the discourse. It seems to me that the two essays that present a transcendence in its strongest and most uncompromising sense were Marion's opening essay, and then Fergus Kerr's presentation of Barth—or at least reminder of a Barth—for whom transcendence is quite uncompromising.[3] Over and against that there were, at least as I heard them, four presenters who wanted to come down in a very important sense, and perhaps as a bottom line, on the question of love and who found it necessary to move away from that sort of transcendence in order to do so. I think we heard the most dramatic and uncompromising move away from that transcendence for the sake of love in Vattimo's essay (chap. 2), and in David Wood's comments just now. As I heard them, I think both Sallie McFague and Cal Schrag, in a less dramatic way, also wanted to move away from that uncompromising transcendence, for the sake of love. There is an irony here, of course, because the Catholic and Protestant traditions that come to voice in the work of Marion and Barth are traditions for which: first, God is love; second, God commends us to love and invites us to love; and, third, God enables us to love. I think these four essays, and perhaps some of the others as well, pose a very troubling, serious and important question about the relationship of transcendence to love and whether there are some tensions there that need to be thought through. Do contemporary readings misunderstand the tradition that thought that kind of transcendence was the appropriate ground of love? Did those traditions not think through carefully enough the implications of what they said out of one side of their mouth and what they said out of the other? It seems to me that these are the most central questions that have emerged from the discourse over these last few days.

Sallie McFague: I made a similar kind of analysis. I was making notes about ways in which the speakers were similar, and this is my sense of order: I like to make lists and be able to say how people are similar in spite of all the differences, all the various places that we started from and all the intricacies we went through to get somewhere. Starting with Marion on forgiveness (chap.

1); the multiplicities of transcendence and of human love from David (chap. 9); from Catherine, the courage for the flux (chap. 7); from Elisabeth, the God of justice and liberation (chap. 6); from Vattimo, the practice and charity (chap. 2). Jim talked about the field of force, the intermingling of the transcendent and the immanent (chap. 5). Richard talked about God as a possibility, not fruition—helping God to be God, as he put it (chap. 3). Fergus gave a wonderful reading of Barth (see n. 3, below). I have to lecture on Barth next week so I'm so grateful for this reading of Barth—of the Barthian transcendence as really an evocation and a prayer, a response to God's call. Cal spoke of transversality (chap. 11). Then I talked about the body of God (chap. 8). What are we all doing here it seems to me—I'm not trying to run us all together, the *différance* is so important—but it seems to me that we're moving away perhaps from ontological and metaphysical statements. But we're certainly moving toward the sense that really what it comes down to is how we are—that is, to modes of being in the world. In one form or another it comes down to action. This has not always been the case, I don't think, in Christian theology and in philosophy. Certainly in the earlier part of the nineteenth century and in the earlier twentieth century, the issues of faith and reason, of belief and revelation, were critical. Are they now as critical? Is our real question—the question that faces us about the state of our planet—something like the questions that faced the German Christians in the Nazi era? What does one have to do in the face of what we are facing? It is harder because it is not encapsulated in just one person, as it was in Hitler, or in one social philosophy. But it is, as I would put it, that the very way in which we are living, the mode of our living, is not appropriate to the situation that we are faced with—our planet's deterioration and its poverty. I could go on.

I was so happy to be invited to this conference when I got the invitation about a year ago. I had not, as I said, done a great deal of reading in this kind of thing. I had read quite a bit in deconstruction. I had read some Derrida. But the only theological connections that I had seen—the work of somebody like Mark Taylor, say—did not strike these kinds of notes. I found it more playful and interesting, but not really important for the kind of questions that I was interested in. Talking to Jack [Caputo] before the meeting, thanking him for inviting me, he said, "Well you know there is the one school of deconstruction that's interested in the death of God and then there's a school that's interested in the desire for God." That is what I found so welcoming about this. Although many people here would not use the word God, I see us as fellow travelers on the way that we need to go, a way to move the discussion right to this point, which is this: How are we going to be in the world? Who are we in the scheme of things? How are we going to respond? I just find this a great gift. So thanks.

Caputo: One theme that came up over these three days was the question of creation. I was not clear what James Mackey—so this would be a question for you—was making of the classical notion of *creatio ex nihilo* (chap. 5). This idea is in a certain sense definitive of the classical idea of transcendence. The world is utterly, completely and thoroughgoingly dependent upon the absolute omnipotence of God, the creator God, who creates out of nothing. Now, James Mackey was saying some very important things about the creative evolutionary rhythms of the earth, of the universe, and I wasn't sure whether he was suggesting something like what Catherine Keller has to say (chap. 7): Not *creatio ex nihilo* but *creatio ex profundis*, creation not from nothing but from the *tōhû wā bōhû*. Was he suggesting a departure from an orthodox, classical idea of creation *ex nihilo*? I am also interested in Mackey's reaction to Catherine Keller's essay.

James P. Mackey: I have a number of things to say about *creatio ex nihilo*. First of all it was common currency in the Middle-Platonic and Neoplatonic eras. As you know, when you get to Middle Platonism, Plato's texts are sacred texts. Plato himself is a *theios aner*, a divine man, and his texts have the force and power of sacred scriptures. People write commentaries on them in the same way as Christians later write commentaries on their sacred scriptures. So you find, if you actually track the commentaries—especially on the part of the *Timaeus*, where Plato talks about the *dēmiourgos*, the creation—you'll find the actual idea of creation out of nothing there.—You are looking at me skeptically.

Keller: At just what point the ex-nihilo argument emerges, I think, is an interesting question. You were locating it earlier with Porphyry?

Mackey: It's there from the Middle Platonism on.

Keller: Right. That's my point. I don't think we have a very serious argument. There is a Platonism that is the Platonism being reacted against by the church fathers, gradually and with more and more intensity, by the turn of the second century [AD]. But you have an original Christian Platonism in Justin, who is delighted to see the amazing convergence between Genesis 1 and the *Timaeus*. In fact, Justin makes a rather postcolonial, subversive case that Plato got his creation idea from Moses! But that is an early argument, very early—not an ex-nihilo argument at all, but a creation from the formless chaos. And that begins to shift. The argument I was deriving especially from Gerhard May's *Creatio ex nihilo*, is that it is not a shift that can be read out of 2 Maccabees or even Hellenized Judaism.[4]

Mackey: What kind of shift are you talking about? I'm just talking about the idea of *creatio ex nihilo*.

Keller: The way that idea came into Christian thought would be first of all through Basilides, who was a Gnostic, and also a Platonist. That is the argument that May made; and then you have Tatian . . .

Mackey: But I think that argument that May makes is wrong. The idea was there not just in Basilides; it was there in Neoplatonists themselves.

Keller: Basilides is writing in the early second century [AD].

Mackey: Yes, well it was there.

Keller: I'm just not sure *where* it's there before this period. It starts getting constructed as an orthodox doctrine, as far as I can tell, with Tatian and

Theophilus—but they're operating after Basilides is done. Anyway I don't think everything rests on exactly where or when this logic emerges. The point is that it's a logic that seems to crystallize in the formation of a strong sense of Christian orthodoxy; but there are ironies in that formation, and there is a lot of disputation, a lot of contestation among Christians, among Christian Platonists. There are wonderful arguments by Hermogenes, who was an anti-Gnostic Platonist, arguing against *creatio ex nihilo* because of the kind of amoral omnipotence that it implied. He was hereticated, shut down, especially by Tertullian. Very early on these sorts of questions were closed down—questions by which a logic of creation from the chaos or from the biblical *tōhû wā bōhû* could have been pursued. That's my argument in *Face of the Deep.*[5] The questions were there among a variety of Christian views, and they got silenced as the much more powerful dogma developed, one that only 150 years later is sealed by the power of Christian empire with Athanasius. That is just an historical account and we have some differences there, I guess. Exegetically, what your essay does is convergent, if not correspondent, with what I mean by the *creatio ex profundis*. You are making strong arguments for creation as formation, which is precisely the kind of argument that the Platonists, who like the idea of the *dēmiourgos* and the creation from a something-ness that was a no-thing-ness, were making.

Mackey: I do not take myself to be differing from you in what I said about *creatio ex nihilo* originating early enough for the Christians to borrow it—which it was, and which is what they did. Let me just say one thing about it. Quite frequently, when people see this phrase they take it to mean one and only one thing, and that's far from the case. For example, it is often taken that there's a clear contrast between creating the world out of nothing and creating it out of matter. But there is not, because matter itself, prime matter, is *to mē on*, that which doesn't exist because it cannot exist on its own. Only formed matter exists and is a finite thing. The form is the *finis* that shapes and forms it. So when you ask, Where does creation out of nothing come from? You have to take it into a context that you might otherwise not think of as *creatio ex nihilo* texts. Creation out of nothing is often taken to mean that there wasn't anything before this act of creation, but that is nonsensical. There is no before-the-act-of-creation; there's no time. We have a certain imagery of the light and darkness, whereby the darkness comes into being as it were when the light shines; and in the same way the nothingness and even the materiality of things—which is prime matter and itself *to mē on*, the no-thing—comes into existence with the act of creation of the thing. What you really have therefore in the mainstream of the Platonic tradition is a presentation of that case. I think, by the way, Barth is one of the few theologians who guessed at that with his concept of *das Nichtige*, which is something that is a byproduct of the creation of the thing. Now that is exactly what you get if you read the imagery properly—if you read the presentation of this idea of divine creation through the imagery of the abyss and all this other imagery that gets tied up in it, like the *tōhû wā bōhû*. They amount to the imaginative presentation of what this little word "nothing" as an abstract concept tries—and patently fails—to do on its own.

Keller: All of the complexity of the second verse of Genesis, that tripartite complexity of the *tōhû wā bōhû* (that is, the materiality that would become earth), and darkness over the *tᵉhôm*, and the spirit vibrating over the waters— that is a lot of something for a nothing. I think it is a powerful constructive theological move with rich historical resonances to interpret that something as no-thingness. In the apophatic tradition from Gregory of Nyssa on, there is the mysterious suggestion that God creates from nothing—from the no-thing that is God. I just do not think such a *nihil* should be confused with what Christian orthodoxy meant by nothingness, which was a very negatively charged and absolute nothingness—an emptiness opposed to the fullness of the divine Being. Thus Augustine's *Non de Deo, sed ex nihilo.* So to use the phrase *creatio ex nihilo,* in order to have harmony with orthodoxy, may be a productive strategy; but it is nonetheless helpful to parse the differences, to distinguish the authoritative ex-nihilo thinking that fortified and was fortified by the divine sublime of imperial power.

Caputo: I think maybe we can pursue this further later, if there are questions from the floor.

Mackey: But can I say one thing first? I thought that where I differed from you, Catherine, was in linking the idea of omnipotence to the *creatio ex nihilo* in its most clear-cut conceptual form.

Keller: It's the historical and orthodox linkage that I was tracking, and I think you could make another formal decoupling happen.

Mackey: But the, shall we say, objectionable understanding is only one of many ways in which you can understand omnipotence. Being capable of doing all that is done, or all that can be done, or all that will ever be done, or all that it is possible to do—there are many ways of saying that. Not all of them, in fact, not too many of them, yield this unwelcome concept of the omnipotence of God, which is more tied to two things, I would say, rather than to the actual usage of the term omnipotence itself. First, the unwelcome idea and image of divine omnipotence (arbitrary, autocratic and male) is tied to the imperial image, and that is the link that Whitehead *so perceptively* picked up; and, second, it is linked to a certain reading of the image of the word as the medium of creation where you take the word not to be an intelligible formulation, but you take it to be an expletive, a command . . .

Keller: . . . into being, as you put it earlier.

Mackey: Yes, but the point I am trying to make is this: If you take the idea and image of the divine word that is actually present in the Genesis story, it is an idea and image, not of an autocratic divine command, but rather of a word, a logos, a formula for forming things—out of something thought of or imag-ined as matter, but "prime matter," the no-thing that comes into existence only when forming makes things to appear—and for involving formed things in furthering the forms ("Let the earth bring forth").—Involving, eventually, formed things, like us, that can freely cooperate or not in what is now creation as a continuous activity of evolution. So it is not the doctrine of creation out of nothing as such—which is present in Greek philosophy in various forms, certainly from Plato onward, as Porphyry's commentary on the *Timaeus* suggests—that is responsible for images of divine and human autocracy; it is the doctrine of creation out of nothing mistakenly imagined and thought of as resulting from a raw and irresistible divine command.

Caputo: This linking of the idea of omnipotence with creation is actually the point I want to take up next. There was an interesting theme running through a number of the essays delimiting the idea of omnipotence, even beginning the first night with Marion. Marion criticized the idea of omnipotence as capricious, suggesting a God-can-do-anything arbitrariness. That, as I mentioned in my comments on the opening night, can end up with the position of someone like Peter Damian, who said God can simply change the past if God wants to change the past. Richard Kearney is also a critic of the idea of omnipotence in its classical form, where it means the power of God to do anything. It also comes up in David Wood's question about whether God can love, if one of the things we mean by loving is making yourself vulnerable—if to love someone is to put yourself at risk, to risk rejection and to suffer from the rejection. So there is a fair amount of theological reflection which goes in the direction of saying that God makes Godself vulnerable by loving, and that involves some kind of redescription of omnipotence. So one of the things our theme of "transcendence and beyond" has raised, is the question of "beyond omnipotence." I invite you to comment on that.

Westphal: I also heard that discourse coming up frequently—this rather allergic reaction to omnipotence portrayed as a kind of naked power. It seems to me that, within the biblical traditions at least, the mistake is separate the question of God's power from the question of God's love and to treat the attributes of God as if they operated independently of one another, as opposed to their being united with one another according to the classical doctrine of the simplicity of God. If the power of God is an expression of the love of God, then the worry about arbitrariness and the imperial business is not going to come up in the same sort of way. If what love means is vulnerability, then creation is already *kenōsis*, because in creating beings who are free God makes Godself vulnerable. Incarnation makes God vulnerable in a new way, but the act of creation is already that. I am reminded here of a passage from Kierkegaard's *Journals* where he says that the greatest manifestation of God's power is that God creates free beings who become agents independent of God, which is another way of talking about God making God's self vulnerable.

Kearney: Could I just add something briefly to that? You see I think the whole problem, Merold, is precisely the confusion of omnipotence and love. I would much prefer—if I had to choose between two evils—the concept of an omnipotent cause to an omnipotent love, because at least a cause is impersonal and mechanical and it does its work. But if you get into omnipotent love, that is a love that cannot really be vulnerable or fragile or amorous, except by some sleight of hand or confidence trick. It would be like saying, we'll go through the motions à la Hegel—the gestures of *kenōsis*, crucifixion and Golgotha, for example—but, deep down, it is really just all part of the "labor of the negative," and that dialectical moment will ultimately and necessarily be guaranteed reentry into the Absolute Spirit of a happy ending. That's the problem with equating omnipotence and love. It is not love. It is just a *pretense* at suffering and risking and sighing. It would be like Christ faking real suffering on the Cross. Or the Shulamite bride faking real jouissance. Cries without substance. On that score I entirely agree with David Wood, that such a God is incapable of love. But I do agree with you, Merold, when you say that divine creation and incarnation are instances of divine vulnerability. Yes—but that is precisely a renunciation of total omnipotence. Simply put, if God has the omni-power to save his son from torture, or all his other sons and daughters from famine, rape, torment, disease and genocide, and chooses not to do it— that is an omnipotent God to be sure, but not a loving God, not a good God. As Etty Hillesum put it in her concentration camp shortly before her death: God cannot prevent this evil, we must help God to be God by making divine love as present as possible even in these moments of hell . . . But that human responsibility for the incarnation of good and evil is precisely due to God's lack of omnipotence, his dependency on us to be given a body, to be enacted in each moment we choose to respond (or refuse to respond) to the divine call. Without us, the word of love and justice cannot be made flesh. As Mary of Nazareth reminds us, without the "yes" of her "amen," there is no incarnation—unless one believes in divine rape. Mary was free to say yes or no to God's love. And if she wasn't, then can we really call it love? I think not.

Westphal: That seems to me to underplay the notion of the suffering of God.

Kearney: Well that is precisely the issue. Is it real suffering or is it just going through the motions for the sake of the dialectic of omnipotence?

Keller: The suffering of God is a powerful symbol that began to arise especially in the twentieth century with [Abraham] Heschel and with [A. N.] Whitehead and eventually with [Jürgen] Moltmann. But it needs to be understood that traditionally it was heresy. God is not to suffer. It was the human not the divine "part" of Jesus that suffered on the cross. Patripassianism, the suffering of the father, was considered a heresy and for good onto-theological reasons. The idea of the unified divine attributes included the changeless, immutable eternity of God. Theologians recognized that this was in real tension with the popular desire for a loving God. So you have Anselm arguing himself into a corner, that God's compassion is only an *apparent* compassion. God cannot be really compassionate for us because that is a passion—which means being affected, being changed—but God is supposed to be the unmoved mover, the changeless one who controls the changing world. The unilateral *agapē* that is bundled into the unity of the attributes creates tremendous friction with the popular faith in a loving God whose vulnerability is something that we somehow call upon in our desire or God's desire of us. That love just does not quite hold up in the face of actual doctrinal omni-arguments.

Mackey: Sometimes we Christians theologians resent the fact that we have to admit that the theologians borrowed from the Greeks, including the *creatio ex nihilo* and most of their Trinitarian doctrine. I sometimes think they didn't borrow enough or they didn't learn their Greek theology sufficiently well when they were borrowing it. Take precisely this point of the immutable, unchangeable God that is completely exempt from suffering. If you read your Plotinus carefully, you'll find that in fact you don't get such an impassible God in Plotinus. He does clearly state that the One is always within—not just within your mind, but within the universe. He also clearly states that the universe was created by the One, came from the One, and that God insofar as she—he probably wouldn't say she—is within the universe that she has formed, suffers, is passible, by that very fact. Now the Christians who borrowed a lot of that stuff just didn't understand it in all its fullness. They were a bit thick actually.

Keller: And yet it would have resonated so much better with scripture.

Mackey: Of course it would. They learned poorly what they were trying to learn. Exactly the same thing happens in the case of the Trinity. They learned poorly in the case of the Trinity and they made a mess of it, which has never been cleared up to this day.

McFague: I wonder whether one of the difficulties in talking about the impassible God and the suffering of God is that we have tended to understand the suffering of God within an Anselmic substitutionary, sacrificial atonement theory, so that the suffering of God appears to be a one-time thing that happened for everyone once and for all. I find it much richer to understand the concept within the model of the body of God, which I've been doing. Here we can see the crucifixion or the cross not as a one-time event but as a mode of being-in-the-world which all of us are called to in some degree or another. It seems to me that we well-off North American folks have a particular burden in this regard. We are unwilling, it seems, to make any sacrifices—even a higher price at the gas pump—or to do something about the ways in which we have taken over more of the world's space than is our proper share. So I wonder about the whole business of suffering. Is God the one who must suffer, or is it us? Several people here have talked about God in a broadly process fashion, that is, God as dynamic, as changing, a suffering with those who suffer. Part of what I see as the suffering of God is not a one-time act which occurred, but a manner, a pattern of self-limitation, of suffering-with. I think theological anthropology is probably the most important doctrine of all—that is, who are we in the scheme of things? Where do we fit? Here I find the cosmic evolutionary story very helpful and very humbling. We are not the top of the mark by any means. We are a product of this incredible process which is magnificent and has resulted in us, but it should give us a different sense of our vocation. So I'm just wondering whether some of the difficulty with the impassible God and the suffering God has been that we put it in atonement theory, which is still with us in many ways and seems to weigh heavily in popular thinking. Understanding suffering within the model of the world as God's body is very different.

Keller: The Christological exception that proves the rule.

Westphal: When I was talking about the suffering of God I was thinking about Yahweh in the Old Testament agonizing over the unfaithfulness of Israel. I don't think it's a concept that can be or should be restricted to atonement theory.

Calvin O. Schrag: I would like to go back to the beginning—to Marion's essay, and to both Richard's and David's response. I take it that the answer to the question of the beyond of transcendence was, as I think Richard put it, moving to the possible beyond the impossibility of impossibility for God, some sort of a schematic structure like that. I would like to make two points: (1) I simply need some clarification on that. I guess I need to read the essay, but it's not clear to me what is going on in the first part where we have this play of the possible with the impossible. There seem to be at least three language games going on. That is, it could be an issue in logic, where you deal with contraries or contradictions; an issue in the language game of epistemology, where you deal with conflicting knowledge claims; or it could be a kind of play in the language game of metaphysics. It is not clear to me just what is going on there, but apparently we are to understand this as a kind of base for moving to the possible, but a possible that is beyond the possible and the impossible. That is the bugbear, isn't it? Richard Kearney moved out in an interesting way suggesting that the content of this new possible is found in scripture, in a move to narrative and poetics. I was wondering if Jack Caputo or Richard could flesh out a little bit what this is. How are we to find the content of this new possible beyond transcendence in the move to scripture?—not just any scripture, but a certain scripture? That's the first part. (2) Now would you also agree that whatever this new possible is, it ultimately involves a move from narrativity to action, from discourse to action? So it's not simply finding discourses of love in the scriptures, which are very powerful, or discourses of love in literature; but following Kierkegaard, in seeing the necessity of the discourse of love becoming works of love that flesh-out the possible. It's very simple, an elementary question: What can we pack into this possible that is beyond the impossible and the possible? I can play with logical quandaries and I can play with epistemological quandaries and with metaphysical quandaries and show that they don't do the job. But then how does this move to the "new possible," if you will, do the job?

Caputo: I'm going to let Richard answer that but before he does let me say a word, because I was the commentator on Marion's essay. What Marion does, in effect, is reorchestrate his general view of the saturated phenomenon[6] in the specific terms of the horizon of possibility and impossibility. The saturated phenomenon—that is the impossible. The uncontainable, the unphenomenalizable, the inconceivable, the incomprehensible icon of all icons is now the impossible. What is impossible for us is precisely what defines God, for whom nothing is impossible. That is the impossible is in this essay, which is for him the paradigmatic religious phenomenon. When we get to the impossible, we are really getting to God. Then he quotes Nicholas of Cusa at this point: You can tell you're in God-territory when you start hitting impossibles. That, we might say, is God's job description; that is what he does. That is the context in which Marion says that impossibility is impossible for God. There's nothing that's impossible for him. That is not only true of those people who want to overcome metaphysics—and here he makes a reference to Derrida—it's also true of Luke. Then he goes into the Annunciation and says that in that scriptural text (Luke 1:26–38), the impossible is one of the main ways in which God is described—with God nothing is impossible. That's what Richard, also, was doing this morning (chap. 3).

Kearney: I concur. I would say, in response to Calvin, that what you outlined is correct. The logical, epistemological, and ontological nit-picking present in the essay is arguably a necessary deconstructive work that has to be done to unpack and unravel the terms of the impossible. These terms actually have held huge sway over our thinking in western metaphysics and western thought, particularly as it relates to the question of omnipotence and the possibility of the impossible. I see all that as a necessary deconstructive detour. But I don't think we should rest there, with the impossible. That's why, following your map, I think we've got to come back to narratives—narratives that are not actually about a "new possible" at all. It is new for western metaphysics and modal logic, but it's actually the oldest thing in the world; and it's not just, in my view, confined to biblical scripture. I think it's probably in all the wisdom traditions. I don't know that, but that would be my wager if I had the competence to read them. I think it's also in secular literature. That's why in my essay I tried to cite some testimonial examples and literary passages from people who are perhaps not believers at all. But, to come back then to your final point, narrative and text are rooted in action and the ultimate power of the possible and the persuasive evidence for the possibility is found in action. It is what was impossible for Mary—I am not citing that as a single example but, let us say, for all the Marys of this world: What seems impossible can be made possible. For Gandhi what seemed impossible, defeating the British army, became possible; it was utterly impossible to set out without arms to resist or defeat the largest imperial army in the world, and he succeeded. Or for Martin Luther King, and we can all give other examples. That, it seems to me, is the evidence for the *possest*. It is there all around us but sometimes we don't have ears to hear and eyes to see. Philosophers sometimes need to let the fly out of the bottle, and one of the flies we had in the bottle was the metaphysics of omnipotence whose logos often got in the way of seeing divine possibility in the flesh.

Schrag: That's good. Why doesn't Marion say that?

Kearney: I don't know.

Schrag: What's interesting here is that we all seem to end up pretty much at the same place, but it does appear that it takes Marion a distressingly long time to get there.

Wood: I have a question for my co-panelists. I completely accept what Cal and then Richard are saying, and I appreciate the weight and significance of all their historical examples—of Gandhi and Martin Luther King and so on. And now I know how I can use the word, God. I can apply it to those situations, those countless cases in which it's vital for us to believe that something is possible that seems completely impossible. That is a kind of humanist insight. We can then add the idea of God as having a body or being a body, and we can go on to identify that body with the universe or the earth in its creative dynamic dimension. Now in neither of these scenarios—the one where we're thinking about human possibility and impossibility, and the other where we're thinking about a relation to a kind of cosmic, self-creating, dynamic, creative force—do we have a personal God. We don't have a relation to God as a person. I guess I want to know—I'm not going to ask for a show of hands—but are we all agreeing that we have abandoned and that we no longer need the idea of God as a person? It seems to me that this where we are moving. Or are some of us holding back a secret?

Westphal: I would just respond to that by saying that the deepest motivation of all of my comments is to try to keep open the space for a truly personal God. What seems to me most important is a God who can really be said to love. That's why at the outset I raised the question about the relationship between transcendence and love. I take that to be perhaps the most important question that has emerged from the conference because, for me at least, everything depends upon that.

Keller: I think a lot of us in this room are attracted to the apophatic tradition, and to Eckhart's distinction between the *Gottheit*—the impersonal depth or bottomlessness of the divine—and the personal God. Something like that distinction keeps working for me. That bottomlessness is not only an attractive and liberating kind of *infini*, an unfinished infinite, that continually empties out our preconceptions about God and the things that we make into gods; but it also allows interreligious connections, for instance, to sunyata or the Tao. This impersonal *Gottheit* or Godhead does a lot of theological work. But for me there is still a personal relation *to* it—the infinitely more than personal—and in that personal relation all that I am as person is brought to bear and is understood also to be part of the impersonal. In the panentheistic logic at play here, which is in a sense quite classical and orthodox, all things are in God and therefore these personal attributes are also.

Wood: The issue for me is whether you have a personal relation to this impersonal being, or whether this being is itself to be thought of as a person.

Keller: For me the apophasis will always wash out any literalism about a person-thing, a person-entity, and yet by the same token release the appropriateness of the personal metaphors whereby we invoke or call upon this wisdom in the universe. This wisdom that we sense is a resource for our all-too-human love, but that surely can't be identified with it.

Schrag: I am sympathetic with Merold's response to David on the lack of personality or personhood. But my problem now is: If you start using the grammar of a personal God, it has to be some kind of a being—maybe the highest being, but still a being. Doesn't this then catapult you right back into the metaphysics that we have overcome? That's why I want to agree with Catherine's approach here.

Fergus Kerr: God is not *a* person. You've got to get to the Trinity.

Schrag: Is God a being?

Kerr: No. I would say if you were to buy the Barthian story, which would actually be my story too, it's got to be a Trinitarian God; so you have three persons, and you would have a lot of trouble about working that out, as Barth had. "Persons" is perhaps a word that's so ruined you have got to say all that kind of stuff. But to the simple question, Is God *a* person? I would say no, and Barth would also say no.

Schrag: You'd say it's an event, right?

Kerr: I think the Trinity is an event, yes. If you are going to start talking about the Trinity, if that's the next move—which it would be for me as for Barth, maybe not for everybody here, but if you make that move—then you are going to talk about the dance of the Trinitarian triads and all of those sorts of things, and you will bring in things from the early scriptural texts as well then.

Kearney: But isn't this maybe a false question, an either/or? Do we have to choose between the impersonal and the personal God? There are aspects of God that our narrative and wisdom traditions tell us are personal, and aspects that are not personal. But I don't see why one should try to evacuate or mask one of the faces, one of the aspects of God, which is a personal aspect couched and qualified, as Fergus says, as the three persons of the Trinity. There is a certain transcendence of the Trinity, but there's also the idea of the three persons related to each other as the dance around, giving to each other . . .

Kerr: My problem is that if you talk about *a* person, then I think you're right with Calvin [Schrag]: If you can say "*a* person," then you've bought in *a* being.

Kearney: Yes, but the language of personal caring and loving captured in the Kardiotissa icons, or of one person ceding the place to another in the dance of Trinitarian perichoresis, does matter to believers. I think it makes a difference whether we speak of God and narrate God and relate to God as if God were personal and interpersonal (though not necessarily one single person). It matters. It is a hermeneutic wager of course—a matter of interpretation, imagination, faith. But that is all we have to respond to the call of love coming from the divine. And it makes a huge difference to most people's way of thinking about God.

Kerr: But not *a* person. Because then I think you really are buying strongly into what Calvin is saying—which a lot of people do, or maybe want to.

Kearney: Agreed. But let's not get too hung up on a numbers game here. It's all hermeneutics. Even the mathematics of divine personality and impersonality is ultimately a matter of our finite, limited human interpretations. The ultimate truth of divinity remains, as Catherine says, apophatically beyond our certain grasp.

McFague: I'd like to get into this too and to approach it from another way, that is, in terms of demythologizing. I think a lot of us—I certainly did—grew up with a notion of God as the being in the sky. One's childhood sense of God as a great being, probably masculine, with a beard or whatever, is very hard to get away from. The hymns of the church of the nineteenth century often support this kind of thinking—deism, the sense of a super-being, and so forth. It's so hard to change one's sensibility in this regard. I find that my own spiritual journey, such as it has been, has been helped enormously here by reading the mystics. They are the most personal writers you can find. They will use language that none of us probably dare use of God in terms of eroticism, maternity, and nature. It is very rich, very personal, very intimate. But at the same time what I got from them was not a sense of God as a being, but for the first time in my life I began to realize what the third person of the trinity was all about. That is, not the "Holy Ghost" that I'd been brought up to believe in by my Episcopal church, but the Spirit that moves in all things. This is not anthropocentric because all living things are moved by breath, by spirit, by life. I began to investigate this and I saw that the depths and richness of it opened up the little square box where I had placed this "being up there." I find, and there are others who seem to agree, that personal language and transcendence are not antithetical. As I said, I am taking now the example of the mystics, whom I see as examples of a mature spirituality, where you find both of these together rather than separate. I just add another little footnote before I stop, which is that I hope all of you get a chance to read Dorothee Sölle's last book— she died a few years ago—called *The Silent Cry: Mysticism and Resistance.*[7] In that book she connects very deeply, interestingly and helpfully, the most profound kind of spirituality and mysticism with social action, with resistance. We've been talking here about how we get to the deed, so I'm so glad that she did that work before she died.

Kearney: Sallie, could I ask you a question relating to what you just said, which I very much concur with, but also relating to what you were saying yesterday about the body? We discussed omnipotence and transcendence, but the body seemed to be a very important motif coming through yesterday (chap. 8). I think I agree with almost everything you said in the essay, but there was one quotation that I found difficult and I stumbled a bit over it. It was the quotation from Simone Weil, "look but don't eat," now interpreted as look but don't devour. I have no problem with that but, given Simone Weil's history and personal suffering . . .

McFague: I know where you are going.

Kearney: . . . in terms of anorexia? And given our culture, which is one of excess and bulimia but also of anorexia, doesn't this raise a question? The body of God is a body of suffering and the examples we all gave, myself included, today have been ones of risk and rejection and betrayal and crucifixion and suffering. Even the theo-passianism you evoked, the passion of the body of God, was again in terms of suffering. But isn't there another aspect of divinity which is less about crucifixion than about eros, less about Jeremiah than Isaiah, less about bondage and death and more about the Song of Songs and fecundation and jouissance and nativity? Why not take our tune from the Psalmist's invitation to "taste the goodness of the lord"? From the idioms of imbibing, tasting and flourishing that are also present in the scriptures, making up a theology of feasting rather than one of famine or famishment? Sometimes in Levinas—I referred to this earlier today—the examples of passion and embodiment are those of persecution and hostageship. Given the history of the twentieth century, I understand Levinas's emphasis. But there are other moments in history which call out for celebration and hope and an affirmation of life. Maybe we might recall here the anecdote related by Umberto Eco, about Thomas Aquinas being so large that they had to cut a hole in the table in his Dominican friary so he could sit down! I'm not just trying to defend holy fat men here, so let me add to my list my own compatriot, St. Brigid of Kildare, who said you should never fast on an empty stomach and was known to eat four partridges in one bite before she set out to meditate in the morning. And then there was Hildegard of Bingen who celebrated the divine flourishing in all living things—*viriditas*. And Teresa of Avila who spoke of her relationship with God as with a secret lover in a "wine cellar" of divine intoxication and jouissance. (She was a ravenous lover, too, so much so that her confessor, St. John of the Cross, used to give her the smallest Eucharistic host he could find, when administering Holy Communion, so as to not encourage her insatiable appetite!) Interesting how many women come to mind—and body—here. All good disciples of the Shulamite bride in the Song of Songs, no doubt. Indeed, I think we could even include the very reverend/irreverend Molly Bloom on this list of divine lovers, with her famous "yes I will Yes" in the last lines of *Ulysses*, prefaced by her memory of the Eucharistic kiss with Leopold on Howth Head, where they exchange seed-cake from mouth to mouth. "Kiss me with the kisses of your mouth!" She is saying, echoing the opening cry of the Shulamite woman (Song of Songs 1:2). "What else were we given all those desires for?" Molly asks, conjoining Greek love of earthly immanence and Jewish love of divine transcendence: "Greekjew is jewgreek. Extremes meet. Woman's reason." All of these voices are part of the ongoing canticle of divine enfleshment (*ensarkōsis*, is what the Scotists called it, right down to Joyce and Gerard Manly Hopkins). The notion that the sacred is calling us in each moment of creation, desiring us to experience "epiphany" in every living person and thing. What I am really trying to suggest with these examples is that there is an important eschatology of the feast that needs to counterbalance the emphasis on God's body as persecuted and famished. The sacrificial lamb was also a fatted lamb, let us not forget.

McFague: I agree with almost all of what you have said. The first part of my essay was about praise and it was about how wonderful it is just to be here on earth. It was a celebration and I was calling to account some deconstructionists who, I thought, had a too minimalist sense of the fertility of the land, the beauty of the world, the magnificence of this body of God, which we have been given as our home. So the first part of the essay—which is the part I like the best, of course—sings the praises of how great it is to be here. But the second part must also be paid attention to. I mean life on earth isn't great for a lot of people; in fact, it's not great for most people. It's great for us in this room, for the most part. We have our individual personal tragedies and so forth, but we are very comfortable on the whole. I would like to add a comment about Simone Weil and the problem of anorexia. Several people have asked me about it, and I think it's a very legitimate question. I won't go into all the details of it here but I will simply say that, as I understand it, she was limiting her intake of food so that it would be no greater than what those on the most stringent rations during the Second World War were getting. This was not, therefore, principally a matter of concern with body-image, but it was certainly an asceticism and a fasting in order to limit herself. I couldn't agree with you more about the final goal of all this. In my book I used the parable of the feast as the symbol of the kingdom, that everybody's invited, as several of you have said, without any exclusion. How can we not at least direct our lives in such a way that we live more closely to that ideal—even if we can't bring it about— than to the market capitalist ideal that we are living? At that point I bracket the whole issue of body-type and anorexia in our culture, which is large, I agree. I see myself—as is true of most of us—as principally cannibalistic consumers who aren't inviting other people to the feast, but are taking much more than our share. That's what I found interesting about Simone Weil. Saints are seldom balanced. I mean she was a crazy lady. I read her quite a bit this summer, particularly the notebooks, and I found myself just shaking my head time and again. This woman is crazy. But she forced me to see things that I hadn't seen with that kind clarity anywhere else. I think that's what these unbalanced people do. If she were to qualify things sensibly the way the rest of us do, then I would feel off the hook. But she doesn't let you off the hook. So I really agree with what you said. I think there are two sensibilities: The praise, the compassion, the celebration, the magnificence—the sacramental, Catholic sensibility—which I think we all need; it is balanced by what David Tracy, who also deals with this dialectic, calls the Protestant, prophetic sensibility, which sees that things are also bad! I mean it's not just a Yes, but there's also a No out there, and for most people it is No.

Caputo: Well I think that is a fitting note on which to bring to a conclusion what has been something of a feast for all of us. I want to thank, first of all, the speakers for venturing out into the elements and getting here this weekend; and to thank them for their marvelous essays, as well as for this exciting discussion this afternoon. I want also to thank all of you in the audience for your support. When we walked in here Thursday evening we didn't know what to expect. Finding a room full of people who were determined to be here no matter what was tremendously gratifying to those of us who tried to put this event together. With that I say thank you, Godspeed, and have a safe trip home.

NOTES

1. Etty Hillesum, *An Interrupted Life* (New York: Henry Holt, 1996).

2. Merold Westphal, who read and commented on Gianni Vattimo's essay in his absence, kindly agreed to participate in this roundtable. The paper presented at the conference and referred to in the roundtable was entitled "The Age of Interpretation," and was subsequently published in Richard Rorty and Gianni Vattimo, *The Future of Religion*, ed. Santiago Zabala (New York: Columbia University Press, 2005), pp. 43–54. The essay by Vattimo we present (chap. 2, above) was written especially for the present volume.

3. The essay by Fergus Kerr ("Revisiting Karl Barth: Christianity after the Demise of the Subject," unpublished), who also participated in the conference, is not included in this collection.

4. Gerhard May, *Creatio ex nihilo: The Doctrine of "Creation Out of Nothing" in Early Christian Thought*, trans. A. S. Worrall (Edinburgh: T & T Clark, 1994).

5. Catherine Keller, *Face of the Deep: A Theology of Becoming* (London: Routledge, 2003).

6. See, e.g., Jean-Luc Marion, *In Excess: Studies of Saturated Phenomena*, trans. Robyn Horner and Vincent Berraud (New York: Fordham University Press, 2002).

7. Dorothee Sölle, *The Silent Cry: Mysticism and Resistance*, trans. Barbara Rumscheidt and Martin Rumscheidt (Minneapolis: Fortress, 2001).

CONTRIBUTORS

John D. Caputo is the Thomas J. Watson Professor of Religion and Humanities at Syracuse University. He is also David R. Cook Professor Emeritus of Philosophy at Villanova University, where he taught until 2004. His newest books are *The Weakness of God: A Theology of the Event* and *Philosophy and Theology*. He is editor (with Michael J. Scanlon) of *Augustine and Postmodernism: Confessions and Circumfession*.

Richard Kearney, the Charles B. Seelig Chair of Philosophy at Boston College, is author of more than twenty books on European philosophy, two novels, and a volume of poetry. His most recent work in philosophy comprises a trilogy entitled *Philosophy at the Limit*. The three volumes are *On Stories, The God Who May Be: A Hermeneutics of Religion* and *Strangers, Gods and Monsters: Ideas of Otherness*.

Catherine Keller, Professor of Constructive Theology at Drew University, is author of *God and Power: Counter-Apocalyptic Journeys, The Face of the Deep: A Theology of Becoming, Apocalypse Now and Then: A Feminist Guide to the End of the World* and *From a Broken Web: Separation, Sexism and Self*.

James P. Mackey is Professor Emeritus of the University of Edinburgh, where he was the Thomas Chalmers Chair of Theology, and Visiting Professor at Trinity College, University of Dublin. His works have been translated into five European languages, and include *Jesus the Man and the Myth: A Contemporary Christology, The Religious Imagination* (with John McIntyre), *Power and Christian Ethics* and *The Critique of Theological Reason*.

Jean-Luc Marion, Université Paris/Sorbonne and the University of Chicago, has had a major impact in the English-speaking philosophical world with his work in translation, which began with the appearance of *God Without Being: Hors-Texte*. His works also include *Being Given: Toward a Phenomenology of Givenness, In Excess: Studies of Saturated Phenomena* and *Reduction and Givenness: Investigations of Husserl, Heidegger, and Phenomenology*.

Sallie McFague is Carpenter Professor of Theology Emerita, Vanderbilt University, and Distinguished Theologian in Residence at the Vancouver School of Theology, Vancouver, British Columbia. She is author of *Models of God: Theology for an Ecological, Nuclear Age, The Body of God: An Ecological Theology* and *Life Abundant: Rethinking Theology and Economy for a Planet in Peril,* as well as other works in religious language, ecology, and theology.

Michael J. Scanlon, O.S.A., holds the Josephine C. Connelly Endowed Chair in Theology at Villanova University. He is a past president of the Catholic Theological Society of America, and has published and taught in the areas of Christian anthropology and eschatology, the doctrine of the Trinity, religious language, and the thought of St. Augustine.

Calvin O. Schrag is the George Ade Distinguished Professor of Philosophy Emeritus at Purdue University. He is the founding editor of *Continental Philosophy Review,* and is author of nine books, including *God as Otherwise Than Being: Toward a Semantics of the Gift* and *Convergence Amidst Difference: Philosophical Conversations Across National Boundaries.*

Elisabeth Schüssler Fiorenza, Krister Stendahl Professor at Harvard University Divinity School, is an internationally known scholar in biblical interpretation who has done pioneering research in feminist theology, rhetoric and hermeneutics. Her work has been translated into a dozen languages and has been acclaimed for its path-breaking scholarship. Her most recent book is *Open House of Wisdom,* which is available only in Japanese.

Gianni Vattimo, Professor of Philosophy at the University of Turin, is a former member of the European Parliament and arguably Italy's most widely known philosopher. His works in English include *The Future of Religion* (with Richard Rorty), *Nihilism and Emancipation, After Christianity, Belief, Beyond Interpretation, The Transparent Society* and *The End of Modernity.*

David Wood is Professor of Philosophy at Vanderbilt University where he co-directs a Research Seminar on Eco-Spirituality and American Culture for the Center for the Study of Religion and Culture. His many books include *The Deconstruction of Time, Thinking After Heidegger, The Step Back: Ethics and Politics after Deconstruction,* and *Time After Time.*

INDEX

Index

Index

Index